Unless

You bless me

A story about a cosmic dancer and his God

As told by Christopher Smith to the author

Jos Boelryk

Order this book online at www.UnlessYoublessme.ca and www.trafford.com
or email orders@trafford.com

Most Trafford titles are also available at major online book retailers.

Author Credits: See credentials in statemenmt above.ous

Printed in the United States of America.

ISBN: 978-1-4907-1212-3 (sc)
ISBN: 978-1-4907-1214-7 (hc)
ISBN: 978-1-4907-1213-0 (e)

Library of Congress Control Number: 2013914648

Trafford rev. 09/17/2013

 www.trafford.com

North America & international
toll-free: 1 888 232 4444 (USA & Canada)
fax: 812 355 4082

INTRODUCTION

ONCE upon a time, in a free and glorious land named Canada—a name derived from the Iroquois word "Kanata", meaning community—there lived a twenty-six year young aspiring particle physicist named Armand. He believed in himself. He also believed in uncompromising, mind-boggling science. And, although he had great imagination, he knew how to separate fantasy from facts.

The passions of his life were sunshine and the blue, wide open sky of his homeland.

Looking up and through that blue sky—when it wasn't overcast, that is—into a universe bursting with facts and mysteries, he knew the undeniables. He knew that he and the land he stood on were circling around the axis of mother earth at a speed of about one thousand one hundred and eighty kilometres per hour (733 mph). He also knew that he, his homeland, and the earth were revolving around the sun, as a team, at a clip of about one hundred and seven thousand kilometres per hour (66,660 mph). But all that was snail stuff compared to the speed with which he, his homeland, his earth, a handful of other planets, their common sun and a hundred billion other suns, were smoking around the center of their own private galaxy at seven hundred and eighty thousand kilometres per hour (484,683 mph). And, because I am afraid that some readers might suffer from motion sickness, I hardly dare to mention the speed at which the distance between his galaxy and some of the other billion galaxies in his cosmos was increasing. Eight million and eight hundred thousand kilometres per hour (5.5 million mph) makes *me* dizzy just writing about it.

Anyway, one dark and gloomy night, while tossing and turning in a hotel bed, in distant downtown Tel Aviv, our young physicist made a deal. Out of pure self-interest, he made a deal with a possible higher power. Just for once, he overlooked the fact that, even though he loved making up stories himself, he had no use for religious nonsense.

The higher power kept her, his or its end of the bargain. But our physicist did not.

Time progressed. Life went on.

Meanwhile, probably because the higher power felt cheated, she, he or it patiently waited for the right moment in space/time to re-engage our physicist. That moment came on the day our cocky hero threw a ball into the higher power's heavenly court. Lucky for him, the higher power loved playing ball. So that ball kept going back and forth and their game seemed endless. But it wasn't.

At age 84, retired and an amputee, loser or winner, our physicist was taken out of the game. Lucky for me, just before his time on earth was up he shared with me the play by play game strategies he had used.

I, being a retiree ten years his younger, who had already concluded in my teens that religion could be no more than old fashioned hog wash, eagerly criticized his style and every one of his moves.

It was a good thing that I, during all my criticizing, was unaware of those undeniables. Rocketing at thousands of clicks in one direction while flying in another direction at hundreds of thousands of clicks and motoring in yet another direction at millions of clicks: that's a lot of clicks. Especially, when all this clicking happens, while I am spinning around on our merry-go-round planet trying to relax in the café at our retirement complex and drink my ginger tea. For, if those speeds are real, I must be breaking cosmic speed limits everywhere.

But then, how on earth am I supposed to know my cosmic limits?

CONTENTS

1

THE DEAL

"AUBURN CURLY HAIR, A white frilly blouse, soft turquoise green skirt—tight around the hips and flaring at the thighs—high heels, walking slowly like a fearless deer, she was stunning." Armand put his hot chocolate on the laminate top of the small, round, bistro table in a corner of the café, eager to get into his story. While moving a chair to make room for his scooter, I listened to his words. At age 26, he had made a deal with a possible God to get this knock-out of a woman for a wife. That morning, some sixty years later, he wanted me to hear how this possible God had obliged while he, Armand, had given up on his part of the bargain.

The café was part of the retirement complex we both lived in. Two sides of the café had floor-to-ceiling windows that drew in the ever-changing sky and a forested area with walking trails. The third wall had three French street-café pictures. The fourth held the order window. A blackboard beside that window listed the menu. Among other items, it included, 'salmon sandwitch.' When we drew the serving girl's attention to the error, she chuckled, "It helped sell salmon."

She was right. We ordered salmon too. As a rule, I have meat.

While waiting for our order, Armand continued his tale.

"My eyes caught sight of her as I looked out on the street through the display window from inside a small butcher shop in downtown Tel Aviv. My parents were born and raised there. On my twenty-sixth birthday, my dad treated me to a ten-day trip to show me my roots. On day six, we walked through his former neighbourhood. It was partially clouded when we stepped into the butcher shop that he remembered from his childhood. It turned out, the former owner's son had taken over, and dad knew him. As they talked, I saw the sun come out. Lover of sunshine that I am, I wanted to seize the opportunity, step outside, and enjoy it while my dad visited."

Lover of sunshine was right. When I first met Armand, a week earlier, it had been his strange ideas about sunlight that intrigued me.

It all started in our building elevator. No; not with Armand and his princess, but with Armand and me. Coming down in the elevator from my third floor apartment last Thursday morning and stopping on the second floor, he had skilfully manoeuvred his electric scooter beside me. Trying to sound amicable—a real challenge for me because I am not a sociable person—I had asked, "And where is your hot-rod taking you this morning?"

Seeing a new face every time I step out of our apartment is a pain. But I try. Everybody wants to know where you come from, why you moved here, how old you are, and if you play bridge. So, I tell them. I lived in Toronto, moved here because I like Nimidimin (a name derived from the Ojibway word for 'dancing together'), I'm 74, and most definitely do not play cards. That usually ends the conversation.

"It's taking me to the parking lot to practice for the Invalids Indy," he had replied as our eyes met. His were blue. I thought I saw mischief in them, so I quickly replied, "Hmm, as far as I can remember, there's no such announcement on the bulletin board."

"Insurance regulations. Last year one of the guys tipped his scooter and cracked his artificial hip. Anyway, this year I'll be the winner."

After leaving the elevator, we both headed for the exit. I had to walk fast to keep up with him. Speeding over the rust-coloured tiles of the spacious lobby, which smelled of pine cleaning agent, he kept talking. At the door, he conjured up a pointed stick. With the blunt end, he pushed the automatic door button. Then, waving it like a billy club, he gleefully exclaimed, "Yes, sir, I'll beat them all.

You see, electric scooters lose their zip when the batteries drain. But mine will stay fully charged throughout the race. I'll have it hooked up to a small combustion engine that runs on vapour from fermenting corn, stashed in a small cylinder on my back."

I realized he was pulling my leg.

"You're new here," he added. "I saw you move in."

Yes, we had sold our bungalow with the big yard and settled for an apartment with a small balcony. Tired of cutting grass, raking leaves, trimming trees, cleaning eaves troughs, and shovelling snow, I was happy we made the move. Except for the social business.

Ten yards from the front door, he parked his scooter in the sun, next to a bench and said, "I'm Armand Huete."

"Chris Smith," I replied, shaking his wrinkled hand while hesitating. Was I going to sit down on the bench? "My wife's name is Jane."

"My wife's name is Sonnetta. She passed away four years ago."

And it was this Sonnetta—apparently a pearl of great price—that he was talking about in the café that day.

"While turning to get out of that Tel Aviv butcher shop," he continued, "I saw Miss Gorgeous walk by. I sped up to get a better look at her and tripped over the threshold. Literally falling out of the door, I landed on the sidewalk and at her feet. Startled, she stopped, bent over, and asked if I was okay. Feeling like a total idiot, I got to my feet and our eyes met. Hers were azure-green and deep. Amazingly deep. It seemed as if, for a split second, I looked through two small windows into another universe. She smiled, hesitated, and said; 'I'm glad you're all-right.' Then, as she went her way, she hesitated again. And from a fair distance, before she was taken up in the crowd, she even quickly looked back and I was sure I saw her smile at me once more.

"I wanted to run after her.

"'Let's go son,' my dad said standing behind me. 'We still have to visit cousin Moshe at the other end of town.'

"I was at a loss. It was like a bad dream. I felt I'd met my long-lost best friend only to lose her again. I wanted to explain the situation to my dad but couldn't find the right words quickly enough. By the time I was able to say what I wanted to say, we had already covered five blocks and I realized, I simply had to accept the fact. She was lost forever."

Two salmon sandwiches were set before us. Armand folded his hands and, while I was already chewing my first bite, he silently said grace and quietly began to eat. It suited me fine. When I struggle with food, I'm not much of a talker myself. As far as I'm concerned, it's a perfect time to reassess whatever situation I find myself in. So, this future wife he was talking about had passed away four years ago. That's what I remembered from our first encounter when I stood beside his scooter after meeting in our elevator. At that time, he had made himself comfortable outside facing the sun. With eyes closed, his beige cap slightly pulled down to shade his eyes, his hands comfortably resting in the pockets of his red and blue tweed jacket, he had asked, "How would you like to fire the starting gun this Saturday? Last year's shooter won't do it. He got hit with a cane. One of the drivers forgot his hearing aid, missed the big bang, and got mad. What do you say? You'll get to meet some real nice people that way."

It had been obvious. He was playing a game and I kind of liked that. So I sat down on the sun-warmed bench and, for a while, did not respond. While looking away from him, I figured out a way to play along.

"Why not first show me your driving skills by doing a practice lap?" I finally said.

"No problem, but first I have to warm up."

He didn't open his eyes and didn't move. After a short silence, I asked,

"Is this how you warm up?"

"Yes, this is how I warm up for everything in life. I line myself up with the sun and allow the seven spirits of the living God to embrace and encourage me. But tell me: you like this retirement community? What about the things people talk about? Health problems, Medical system, Stock exchange. I'm hungry for idea exchange. Yes: idea exchange!"

And that's when he got my back up. "Don't expect much from me, mister," I had shot back. "If you can cleverly change the topic from hot rods, painted senior's grey, to rainbow-coloured hot gods, you lose me. I'm an atheist, or agnostic, or whatever. The God-business does *not* interest me."

"Great! Non-believers are more fun to mentally skirmish with than burdened believers. By the way, I'm a particle-physicist."

"I was a cheater-chaser for Revenue Canada."

"A big-wig tax collector? That job is in the Christian Holy Book!"

"So you are a Christian?"

"What if I quote Buddhism's Eightfold path, or the closing lines from Hindu's Bhagavad Gita?"

"Quote what you want. Whether you make it up, quote out of context, or give me the real McCoy, I won't know the difference. All I know is how my holy stepfather, minister of some Christian Church, used *his* Holy Book like a sledgehammer. Driving his personal convictions, interpretations, and opinions into every mind he encountered, including mine, he never let up. 'This is how it is, brother. Here's the verse to prove me right. WHAM! You shouldn't do that, brother. Here's the verse that backs me up. WHAM!' I hated the man and I hated his religion."

I should have told him last Thursday how religion disgusts me. For that's the truth. It was a bit of a miracle that I, Chris Smith, was sitting in that café, socializing with this man and listening to his life's story. He pushed his empty plate aside and continued to tell what happened after his new found heart throb had vanished in the crowd.

"Through the rest of that day, and the next, I became increasingly angry with myself. How could I have been so foolish to let her disappear? Later, with only two days left of our stay, I asked my dad if he'd mind if I spend the day on my own, hanging out downtown, just to get the feel of it. I took a book. I parked myself on a bench from which I could see a large part of the butcher shop's street. I looked a lot and read very little, hoping, against all odds, to see her walk by again.

"The book was a collection of World War II short stories. I had started it in the plane. I was finishing the tale of a soldier who had participated in Canada's worst military disaster, the Dieppe raid of August 19, 1942.

"He went ashore, saw his buddies killed like flies, and fell on his knees. Crying out to God as a Christian, he promised, 'God, if you save me from this hell, I'll devote the rest of my life telling the world about you!' He was shot in the arm, taken prisoner and, after he had been set free from the concentration camp in 1945, became a missionary. The story didn't do much for me. I wanted to see my girl. Sure, I felt bad for all that senseless killing, but the concept of God meant nothing to me. My Jewish parents were not practicing their faith. They never even talked about it.

"Late that afternoon, I went back into the butcher shop. I tried to be casual about inquiring if they, by chance, knew this beautiful young woman that came by once in a while.

"'All Tel Aviv women are beautiful,' the butcher laughed, as he recognized me. 'You and your dad should move back. He and I would get along great. And I'm sure you will find yourself a Tel-Avivian gem.'

"He was no help.

"That night, tossing and turning in my hotel bed, the eyes of the girl and the soldier's deal with God kept churning in my mind. 'No way,' I said to myself, 'I can't become a Christian missionary. I'm in love with physics. Two more years and I'll be able to devote myself to the exciting string theory every physicist is working on. Maybe I'll be able to truly make that theory tie everything together; from black holes to the smallest subatomic particle. Maybe I'll even be the physicist who finds that elusive particle, that boson which gives mass to everything.' By the way, Chris, I'm talking about the god-particle. It's in the news these days. It got its name, inadvertently, somewhere around 1993. Anyway, that sleepless night, I concluded, what's the use? Imagine this possible God makes deals and I get the girl of my dreams. Then we'll have to live in a mud hut in some third world backwoods village to preach whatever. Forget that.

"So, I pondered. What aspect of my life was I willing to sacrifice to have her as my wife? Many physicists do not believe in a God. They figure sooner or later every secret of the cosmos will be understood. For me to try and find proof for the reality of a God, while doing scientific studies, would be nuts. 'Unless,' and I softly said this under my breath, Unless you, possible God, favour me with another face-to-face encounter with my dream girl before we leave. And, in the recesses of my mind, that's the deal I struck.

"Next morning, my dad thought I was crazy. He was right. To take public transit, instead of a taxi to get to the airport, was nuts. But how else was I to meet my girl again? From the moment we left our hotel until we ultimately lined up to board the plane, my eyes were everywhere. Finally, it was all over. We stepped into the entrance of the curvy walkway that ends up at the plane door. 'You lose,' I said under my breath to the possible God. 'You just lost a physicist willing to plead your cause.'

"We came around the bend and, standing face to face with the two stewardesses welcoming us on board, I grabbed my dad's arm. 'This can't be,' I mumbled. 'Unbelievable!'

I stepped into the plane, tripped again, and fell into the arms of stewardess number two. She steadied me and heaven opened up. She held on to my arm longer than necessary. It was HER!

Thursday, November 15, 2011

2

ENCOUNTERS

"Last week you told me how you hated your stepfather and his religion," Armand said after lunch as he aimed his scooter for the sunny outdoors with me walking beside him. "What happened to your real dad?"

"He was flash-fried by my stepfather's loving God! But why don't you tell me how you two love birds made out on that plane?"

Even though I felt more at ease, I wasn't ready to bare my hurts.

Once outside, we again headed for the bench in the sun. While he parked his scooter identical to the position he had parked it the Thursday before, my eyes focused on his trouser legs, empty from the knees down. Taken in with his soldier-like posture despite this handicap, his kind facial expression, his old, worldly cap and the calm he emanated, I felt relaxed enough to sit down on the bench beside him like I had done the week before.

11

Next to the bench was one of the many flowerbeds protruding from the small concrete patios of the ground floor residences. Some primroses, low to the ground, still showed colour. Everything else looked dead. In one of the bushes, a yellow, plastic, discount-store shopping bag fluttered intermittently in the breeze. Behind us, white spindled iron balcony railings shone brightly in the low November sun. And, as I looked at the three-story, reddish-brown brick building with small crow step gables breaking up the roof line, it suddenly sank in. This now was home.

Nimidimin, Ontario, Canada, located on the sandy shore of Lake Ayowebiwin—Cree for 'day of rest'—was far enough from the Big Smoke to have us miss out on its pollution and close enough to enjoy its culture and night-life. Although, come to think of it, we haven't taken in much of either since we moved. We seem to be more relaxed here.

"At first," Armand started, "my dad was tickled pink with the special attention we received on that flight. Then we learned she was a Muslim girl.

"'What's the big deal? You're not practicing your faith.' I said to him. 'Maybe we're lucky and she isn't practicing her faith either.'

"'Yes,' he confided, 'your mother and I are Jews by birth. But we have never been enthusiastic about it. Being chosen by Yahweh only to get persecuted by those who aren't chosen does not appeal to us.'

"'So, Muslims don't seem to get persecuted."

"'I know, I know! Still, son, think of a possible wedding. Your mother and I will never defile ourselves by entering a mosque. And I'm sure no Muslim in his right mind will want to be seen entering a synagogue.'

"Problems or no problems, I thought. Whether we have to marry, just the two of us, on a beach in the Bahamas or in the middle of the Amazon jungle, I don't care. Every time she came close, walking by to serve other passengers or stopping to ask if we needed anything, it was as if we became one. It had nothing to do with sexuality. It seemed as if a glow enveloped us both whenever she came near. I knew about butterflies in the stomach, of tingling hands and feet, of buzzing ears and heaven knows what else a person can feel when in love. This was different. It couldn't be verbalized.

"To my unspeakable joy, with the last drink she served before landing, she slipped me the flap of a discarded cigarette pack. It had a phone number and address. Remember, back then, smoking on planes was allowed and email, Facebook and Twitter did not exist.

"'Wow,' I said out loud to my dad. Imagine; she lives in Toronto too."

"After we'd left the plane, I turned for one more look at her. For the third time I tripped, really hurt my knee, and limped for weeks. How sweet a limp it was! Luckily she was too busy with other passengers to notice.

"We dated, got engaged and married. In the euphoria of it all, I forgot about my deal with God. He didn't remind me until about five years later, early in the morning, in the parking lot of the Mount Palermo Observatory, just before I was about to step into my car, ready to go home. An astrophysicist friend had shared some of his viewing time with me. But that's for another day."

"A lucky stroke, that's what I'd call it. You realize, deal or no deal with a possible God, she would have been a stewardess on that plane anyway."

"Maybe yes, maybe no. How sure can we be that a possible God didn't arrange the flight she was on, knowing ahead of time the deal I would be making with him? After all, a chance meeting like ours is part of the mechanics, part of the actions that make our quantum cosmos tick."

"Are you pulling my leg again? What does the quantum business have to do with a chance meeting with a good-looking woman?"

"You tell me. A quantum is a specific amount of energy required for a particular change at the atomic level. In the sub-atomic realm quarks team up with quarks to form protons and neutrons. Protons and neutrons team up to form nuclei. Nuclei team up with electrons to form atoms. This seemingly random teaming up of related and unrelated entities results in specific outcomes. And I believe that, in the spiritual dimension of purpose, every human encounter has a specific outcome as well."

"Hmmm, you're losing me. Spiritual dimension of purpose, what on earth do you mean by that?"

"No, no, friend, it's your turn now. What happened to your real dad?"

"Okay, okay. He was a bush pilot. One evening—I was twelve—he drove home over a country road. At the intersection ahead of him, a negligent gravel truck driver, by forgetting to close his truck's back gate, had dumped a layer of gravel. Just before my dad got there, a speeding pick-up truck passed him. Its driver jumped the brakes at the stop sign. The loose gravel made him slip, slide, and spin off the road into a hydro pole. The pole cracked, the live-wire snapped and recoiled into my dad's open car window on the passenger side. He was killed instantly and cremated on the spot. And that, according to my stepfather, was all part and parcel of the good and perfect will of the God *he* believed in. He also made it clear, indirectly of course, how my dad had been destined to become everlasting charcoal in the pits of hell anyway because he'd never asked some Jesus to be his saviour."

Armand allowed me my space. He didn't say a word.

"So my mom fell apart. She struggled for about a year before taking counselling. The minister of the church, to which she had taken my sister and me once in a while when dad was still alive, received her with open arms. Literally. He left his wife and moved in with my mother."

"Did your mom love him?"

"After my dad's horrible death, she never was the same. Filled with fear, she behaved like a caged rodent. She'd lost her pillar of strength. My dad had unshakable self-confidence. This preacher must have given my mom new security in the way he spouted his knowledge about God and a supposed life hereafter."

As I spoke the last words, I realized I had just bared some deep buried hurt to this stranger. Slowly I stood up and added, "I guess, that's life. Anyway, Armand, thanks for lunch. But I just remembered I promised my Jane to pick up some veggies at the supermarket."

He opened his eyes, turned to me and again tried to look into mine. "Thank you for lending me your ear. Maybe this time when you grocery shop, you could bring yourself home something special."

"Like what?"

Armand patted the spot where I had been sitting. "Five more minutes," he gently commanded. "Get used to being retired and tell me . . . when you look up into a clear night sky and see the billions of stars, do you believe there is a power at work out there that's greater than you?"

"I guess so!" I hesitantly answered.

"That power, whatever it is, has been named Great Spirit, White Spirit, Holy Spirit, Allah, Brahma, Yahweh,

God, Supreme Intelligence, Dumb Power, and more. You may not agree with any other human being on this planet about what attributes and characteristics this power has. Yet, you believe it's there. And if there is a mysterious unknown power at work out there, it also is at work in you and me. You and I are just as much a part of this incomprehensible cosmos as the stars you gaze at. You may think I'm losing it when I say I am basking in the loving warmth of the seven spirits of God and, who knows, maybe I am. But the fact is, the sun sends out a wide range of electromagnetic waves. Bundled up in those waves is the light that shines on me, you, and everything else. And, bundled up in that light are the waves our eyes translate into seven distinct colours. They're the colours red, orange, yellow, green, blue, indigo and violet. Those seven visible colours, hidden within that white light, are part and parcel of what gives life and energy to everything.

"Now tell me, what do you think? Would this higher power exist outside of this life-giving light, or would it exist within it? And that's the question you may want to ponder while you're walking through the fruit and vegetable isle at the grocery store. White light will be shining on everything. The red peppers will be absorbing most parts of the white light and mainly reflect the red. The lettuce will also absorb most parts of the white light but mainly reflect the green. Every piece of fruit and every vegetable receives the same white light with all colours bundled up within it. Yet each will absorb and reflect only certain colours according to its own unique individual atomic structure. And, the light that gives life and colour to a stray strawberry you may pop in your mouth is the same light that gives colour to a galaxy that's a billion light years away. Why couldn't there be a connection between these seven colours that are contained in white light and a prophetic statement about the seven spirits of God?"

After staring at him for a few minutes, I replied, "Remember I told you I don't care? I once asked my dad if he believed in a God. 'Son,' he answered, 'people with bigger brains than yours or mine have tried to figure out the God-question. If there is a God, he would want me to become like him, a little god. If there is no God, I must become a little god unto myself. In both cases, I should try to be compassionate, considerate, and creative.' And that," I said while standing up for the second time, "is all I need as a focus for *my* life. And what is it that you want me to bring home from the supermarket?"

"Before I tell you, how about first untangling that yellow plastic bag?"

"Why? That's a maintenance job. Or, is the bag yours?"

"No, it's not. But I believe cleaning up litter is everybody's job."

His remark irritated me. The last thing I needed at this stage in my life was a sermon. So, in order to make my farewell as uncomplicated as possible, I stepped up to the bush, unhooked the bag and held it up.

"Now what?"

He smiled. "You can give it to me and I'll drive over to the litter bin. Or, you can walk to it and drop it in yourself."

My irritation increased. I was in no mood to go out of my way to dispose of this litter which I had picked up against my will. While crumpling the bag, ready to stuff it into my jacket pocket, I stepped back on the sidewalk. Gently, he reached out and took the bag from me. "And for the bringing home question," he said, "bring home some personal excitement about the miracle of colour in the fruit and vegetable section."

I grunted, said good-bye and left in a huff. As I walked to the underground parking garage, I remembered his fun story of how he met his wife. Nothing at all like the way I met my Jane. I could still see her walking into the hardware store where I worked after I'd left home. With her hair up in a knot, dark blue blouse, plain grey skirt, and flat shoes, I thought she was a school teacher. She wasn't. She was a sales clerk in a shoe store down the street. The flat shoes were to prevent her from having backaches after being on her feet all day.

Having said goodbye to mom and sis one morning when my Holy-roller stepdad was away, I had found a small, dark, depressing but cheap basement apartment. I was studying nights and weekends to get my accounting papers. I loved numbers. They were what they were. No doubts, no questions. Jane fitted right in with them. Her yes was yes. Her no was no. But before we teamed up, we needed another chance encounter. "Mr. Armand," I sighed out loud when I stepped into my car, "I don't envy you or your present day stumpy legs, but I sure envy your colourful past.'

*   *   *

Standing in the middle of the veggie section, I had to agree, reluctantly of course, the symphony of colours was amazing.

However, while picking up what I needed, it occurred to me that the light wasn't coming from the sun. It came from fluorescent tubes. God's seven spirits were looking down from the tubes. How ridiculous can you get?

Outside, as I packed the groceries into the trunk, I noticed how brilliantly blue the sky was. If there are seven colours hidden in the white light coming from the sun, why would the sky be blue?

Physicist Armand should know.

3

BLUE

SITTING NEXT TO THE bench again, upright like an army general inspecting the troops, eyes closed facing the sun, it seemed he hadn't moved. Yet, it had been several weeks since our second encounter. Rain had kept him indoors and, when the sun was out, I had other obligations. Even though I really didn't want any more God-talk, I had gone for a walk, hoping to find him soaking up sunshine. I was curious about the blue sky question. Seeing him sit there reminded me of my dad's love for life and when I tapped him on the shoulder, he surprised me. He opened his arms to hug me. Half—heartedly, I let him. He embraced me as if I was a prodigal returning home.

"It's too bad you're allergic to religion," he replied when I asked about the blue of the sky. "You see, there are two explanations. The one is religious. The other scientific. Personally I prefer the religious one. Besides, I believe it's good to get different perspectives on a subject. So, if I have your permission, I'll give you the religious explanation first."

"Okay, let's be up front. Are you trying to convert me to something?"

"Listen, dear friend," he replied without moving. "If you want to pick my brains, it is your job to sort through the pickings."

"Alright," I grunted after a short silence. "Give me the pickings."

"Of course, you know how the first two human beings, Adam and Eve, lived in a paradise where everything was peaches and cream. In those days the sky was a warm, homey orange; Adam's favourite colour."

"I've never heard that before."

"It's evident. Orange is the only colour Adam honoured by naming an item after it. Ask for a red, a yellow, a green, a blue, an indigo or a violet in any fruit and vegetable place and they'll stare at you. Ask for 'an orange' and everybody knows. Anyway, don't interrupt when I'm having good ideas. As I said, the sky was orange.

"Then Adam and Eve messed up. God showed them the gate and posted an angel with a flaming sword to prevent them from sneaking back in. What did Adam do? He sat down on the grass outside the paradise walls, picked up his new guitar, and sang the blues."

"New guitar?" I interrupted, despite his request not to.

"His good-boy reward! You see, Satan was very pleased with Adam's stellar performance. As the world's first free-will-disobedient bad boy, Adam had given mankind a perfect start. He deserved a present. Satan knew Adam liked to make up songs. He'd often heard him serenade Eve with, 'Don't sit under the apple tree with anybody else but me.' And, snakey Satan was sure that, if he could get Adam to write lots of lyrics, he could easily tempt him to change every 'don't' lyric God had taught him into a 'do.'"

Such imagination, I thought. Nothing like that ever came out of my holy stepfather's mouth.

"As I was saying, Adam sang the blues."

Then, to my great surprise, right there on the sidewalk, sitting on his scooter, oblivious to passersby, Armand, in a beautiful tenor voice, began to sing,

"*Blue Monday how I hate Blue Monday,*

"By the way," he interrupted himself while turning to me, "I'm sure you know the lyrics of this fifties song. Theologians have used it to prove that the Adam-Eve fig leaf affair took place early Monday morning. This means Satan must have swooned Eve when she was on a solitary Sunday afternoon walk, while Adam had his snooze. But I question that. Adam never worked a stitch in his life. Why would he waste a precious Sunday afternoon napping? Anyway, he's got a job now. He has to start earning his keep by the sweat of his brow."

Then, raising his voice again, Armand continued with the song. He sang about slaving all day Monday, having it tough on Tuesday and being beat on Wednesday. On Thursday, when Eve happens to call, tell her I'm out because I'll be a basket case. But, thank heavens, on Friday I get paid. The song closed with, 'Cause Monday is a mess, Blue Monday.'

"When God heard Adam crying the blues," Armand continued, "God said to himself, 'Now here is an excellent idea! From this day forward, I'll make the sky blue. That way, all Adam's descendants will be reminded every day how blue their forefather was after he disobeyed me.'

"Some scholars believe Adam was blue because he'd committed a sin.

"Others believe Adam was blue because God wouldn't let them back in.

"Personally I believe Adam was blue because he saw a struggle with God he'd never win.

"What do *you* think?" Armand unexpectedly asked, flashing a big smile while looking me straight in the eyes again.

I hesitated. Yes, I caught on. But I needed a few seconds to make sure I was in rhythm. Then, smiling back, I answered,

"I believe Adam was blue because he'd screwed up for his kin."

"There!" Armand laughed out loud. "You did it. You did it."

"Did what?"

"You exchanged an idea with me. Now you deserve the scientific explanation.

"As the seven colours bundled up in the white light stream from the sun into our atmosphere, they get scattered differently by the zillion air molecules and dust particles. The colours with the longest wavelengths—red, orange and yellow—get scattered less than the ones with the shorter wavelengths. Green, blue, indigo and violet all have shorter wavelengths but blue greatly dominates the others in its abundance. And that's why the sky looks blue."

Clouds were drifting in from the west intermittently hiding the sun. Armand remained silent after his explanation. He didn't react to the sun's occasional disappearance. I sensed he was waiting for me to give direction to our conversation. Because I had been forced often enough to listen to my stepfather, I knew Armand's rendition of the Adam and Eve tale was not in the Bible. I also knew science had all the proof it needed to show the Bible's creation story was plain crapology.

A few weeks ago this man had taken me for a ride with his imaginary Invalids Indy. Today he had spun me a sob story about Adam's blues. The question now was, how seriously would I take his idea of those seven colours in white light manifesting the seven spirits of a supposed God?

"As you know, Armand, red peppers are red under fluorescent light as well. Are you telling me those seven godly spirits shine forth from neon tubes too? I'm sorry, but I think you need a reality check."

"Look at it this way," he replied with animation. "The sun's white light, seven colours and all, shines upon the Great Lakes. Its heat evaporates the water to form clouds. Clouds drift inland and pour down rain. Rain gathers in the Niagara River. The water in the river flows out to the ocean while turning the turbines that generate the electricity needed for those fluorescent lights to glow. Tell me: ultimately, what makes the red pepper red? And, ultimately, what makes anything on our earth have colour, or have life?"

"Alright," I grumbled, "the sun's white light. But it's too farfetched for me to think the seven spirits of a possible God are in some way manifesting themselves in the colours I see."

"Does it make more sense to believe God, known as Allah to Muslims, is as close as your jugular vein—a large vein on either side of your neck? In that case, God would be frighteningly close to every grape you swallow. Or does it make more sense to believe God, known as Yahweh to the Jews, hems you in behind and before? In that case, he would be right next to that large piece of broccoli you're sneaking out the backdoor with the garbage because you never developed a taste for it. Or does it make more sense to believe, as physicists do, that the power which generated the Big Bang is still present in every atom in the cosmos. That, my friend, puts the presence of 'the higher power' in every atom of every morsel of food you chew on."

"Frankly, Armand, I don't get it. You, an intelligent man, a physicist at that, seem pretty strung out on this God-business. Yet you know as well as I do, people have tried since the dawn of history to figure God out. All they've come up with is a thousand different ideas and consequently just as many holy wars. Talking about holy wars. What about the big lie in the Christian holy book about the sun stopping in the middle of the sky? You know that story. It tries to tell us how God made the sun stand still for a whole day while his favourite fighter men creamed another tribe. If an all-knowing God inspired the writer of that story, he certainly failed physics."

"Imagine, yes, imagine with farfetched imagining you were that writer. Living in that day and age, you were the most brilliant physicist around. You knew for a fact that the earth was flat and the sun and stars circled around it. What would you have done if the all-knowing God had inspired you to write down the ridiculous statement of an earth that stopped turning?"

I remained quiet. Armand continued.

"A colleague of mine once said to a Hindu priest, 'if you wish to understand God, you must learn calculus. That's the language he speaks.'

"True, calculus may be the language God speaks to physicists and mathematicians. But to a farmer, a priest, you, me and every other human being, he speaks in the language used in the listener's culture."

"Tell me, Chris. Knowing the reality of the solar system, when was the last time you told someone about this beautiful 'earth-rise' you enjoyed?"

I didn't answer. His earlier remark about the power of the Big Bang still being present in every atom had brought back two memories simultaneously. A good one and a bad one. In the good one, I was about eight. My dad, my sister, and I were walking in a wildlife preservation area close to our home. It was spring. Dad drew our attention to the green buds on the trees, the birds flying back and forth building their nests, the holes of the rabbits, the tadpoles scooting through the water in the swamp, and he told us this beautiful story of how everything in nature is connected. 'A long, long time ago there was lifeless dust. Over many thousands of years, the dust came to life and the life within it expanded and evolved into cells. Some of these living cells began clinging together and became little creatures like the tadpoles. The little creatures grew and grew and became like fish. The fish ventured onto land and developed lungs so they could breathe the air. Some also developed wings to become birds. Others developed legs to become land creatures. Over time, the land creatures evolved and, through a long chain of changes, became human beings like you, and sis, and me.'

When he was finished, sis and I started to run and jump to touch branches hanging over the path. She always mimicked me when I was having fun. She knelt beside me and, like me, scooped up handfuls of dust. We both laughed, shouted, and flung the dirt high in the air, letting it rain down on us. The story had excited me. It made me feel like I was part of everything alive around me. My dad chased us. We hid behind trees. I remember being so very happy, sensing the bond I felt with dad, sis, mom, with the trees and all those different shades of vibrant green surrounding us.

In the bad memory I was fourteen. My stepfather, standing on the dais in front of his wall-to-wall carpeted church, was shouting, 'God said, let there be light: and there was light.' 'BINGO,' my scornful mind had added. Even now, as I think of it, the scorn is just as heavy. Imagine, in *his* creation story, God says six times, 'Let there be.' And six times, 'BINGO,' there it is. It's like a big-box-store executive planning six new franchises. Instead of calling a construction company, he calls in a magician. 'Let there be! And then there is.' How can anyone feel connected to that?

I looked at Armand. Trying to sound casual, I said; "So, even though you weren't raised in the God-business, you made a deal with him. You got what you wanted and now feel obliged to pull him into every conversation. I mean, you're a physicist with brains. Instead of talking God every time we meet, why not give me some interesting titbits about the sub-atomic world? I've read that people who think they understand it; probably don't get it."

"Terrific," Armand enthusiastically replied. "You're opening up! But I need to tell you, the sub-atomic realm is about as unreal to human understanding as true religion. The so called sub-atomic particles have turned out to be no particles at all. They may be no more than certain characteristics, or properties, as physicists call them, working together in relationships that produce the illusion of particles. Everything we humans call real is made of things that actually can not be regarded as real. The core of existence may very well turn out to be relationships between properties like charge, mass, velocity, etc. But, Chris, what makes you think that you, a true to life boxer, will get it?"

"Boxer? What do you mean by that?"

Showing his broad, mischievous smile, Armand turned his scooter key and said, "How about we meet next Thursday again? If it's sunny, we meet here. If it's cloudy: inside. Eleven a.m. sharp. Deal?"

Still uneasy about committing myself to planned-socializing, I hesitantly grumbled to his back, "We'll see."

4

BOXES

"WHAT ON EARTH ARE you doing?" I huffed when I finally caught up with Armand. Circling the apartment complex on his scooter, he was picking up litter. Using the pointed end of the stick he wielded to push the button of the automatic door on our first encounter, he speared candy wrappers, empty water bottles and paper cups, putting them in a plastic bag hanging off his steering bar.

"I thought, when cloudy, we'd meet in the coffee shop?" I added.

"Yes, eleven sharp. I waited till 11.10." He switched off his scooter.

"I didn't know this was a business meeting. We're retired you know."

"Retired or not, punctuality knows no age! Anyway, I'm making good use of my time by picking up my quota."

"Quota? You have a job here?"

"No, I'm self-employed. I used to pick up litter here and there, till one day I walked on a beach strewn with it. Realizing the impossibility of picking up all that litter, I thought of how the number seven in God's vocabulary expresses completeness and wholeness. Seven days of the week. Seven visible colours of light. Seven main continents. Seven this, and seven that. So, to give expression to my desire to rid our world of litter, picking up seven pieces a day seemed a God-given solution. If everyone who loves our earth and loves it clean would do the same, litter would be gone. What's your solution? Would you give a tax break to those who put litter in its place, or the death penalty to first time offenders?"

His silly question increased my irritation. I also remembered the yellow plastic bag he made me untangle the first time we met.

"Whatever! I don't see it as my job to clean up after ignorant people."

"Suppose you have a mentally challenged brother living with you. No matter how many times you tell him to pick up after himself, he simply doesn't get the idea of picking up after oneself. Do you let the house become a mess? Or do you clean up after him in the hope that some day he'll catch on? This world is our living room, isn't it? True, we have a lot of mentally and spiritually challenged siblings living with us. But didn't your dad suggest we should try to live like compassionate little gods?"

"Alright, alright! But man, you waste no time dragging your God-business into every conversation. Let's go inside and change the subject. You promised to talk about the quantum business to me. And, by the way, while you picked up that junk, did I see your lips move? Did you, under your breath, maybe, mumble, 'ignorant bastards'?"

"No, I whispered a magic formula. I'll teach it to you when you're ready. Right now you couldn't possibly pronounce it."

He switched on his scooter again, turned effortlessly around on the narrow sidewalk, headed for the main entrance in the direction of the coffee shop and, with me walking beside him, he said, "First I'd like to explain your 'boxer' title."

When we were seated with a hot chocolate for him and ginger tea for me, I waited. Still annoyed and unsure about how to relate to his calm self-confidence, I focused on my cup. Unperturbed by my irritation, he explained, "A convict sentenced for life is a lifer. A person who thinks is a thinker. Someone who sentences himself for life to live and think in a box, I call a 'boxer'. Boxed in, such a person also throws defending blows towards anyone infringing on his or her boxed space. Could you be living and thinking in a ten-sided box?"

His question sounded accusing. Through it, I heard my stepfather say, 'brother, your thinking is wrong.' I half waited for the 'WHAM'—the scripture verse to back him up. Instead, there was a smiling Armand. And his smile bothered me. I didn't like the idea of someone trying to pick me apart while grinning. If I lived and thought in a box; so be it. I was who I was. Why would I tolerate him prying into my private affairs, into my . . .

While avoiding his eyes, I looked at him. His easy-going demeanour gave him an air of transparency. Could it be, he really cared?

"So, you call it a box eh? A ten-sided box? Doesn't top, bottom, front, back, left, and right, make six?"

"True. But add the space/time dimension, which tells us your box is here and now, and you already have eight sides. Add to that the two parameters of the most important dimension of all, the spiritual dimension of purpose, and you have ten. After all, why would there be a box, if it didn't have a purpose? What do you think?"

"I never think about such business. Besides, I've never heard of a spiritual dimension of purpose. That must be *your* idea. Tell me about it."

"I will. But first, consider the possibility that you're going through life, walking upright, boxed in by the following burdens. The board hanging over your head could be the hatred you have for your stepfather and his religion? The plank underneath your feet could be your sense of being betrayed by your mother? The right side board could be your disgust with a God who allowed your dad to die? And the left side board could be solid with the restrictions you've set your own mind since the day that happened. The board behind you could be the crowd you have chosen to walk with in life. And the board in front of you, the door that keeps you locked up, could be made out of solid fear?"

I shook my head. He had the last board wrong for sure. What on earth did I need to be afraid of? And about the other boards . . . , I had dealt with all those issues by simply stuffing them. He was the one who kept stirring up the stepfather, God and religion crap every time we met.

"As I see it, Chris, most people purposely nail up a box around themselves for protection. And they lock the door, made of fear, quickly and tight every time someone tries to touch any of the other boards. That's where the spiritual dimension of purpose clearly shows. It is measured by the two parameters called intents and consequences. Intents reach for us humans into our past, and consequences extend for us into our future. This is because the bodies we live in exist in the dimension of space/time. Few people have the courage to deal with wrong past intents. Fewer still dare to consider the possibility that they are living through some of the consequences of those wrong intents.

For a long time neither of us spoke.

In the silence, I remembered how I had planned to put rat poison in my stepfather's mashed potatoes. I had also planned to drain the brake fluid of his car so he would, hopefully, slide through a red light and have a big truck 'whamenize' him out of my life. I wanted to kill. Maybe I just wanted him out of my life. I never did any of these things, because I feared being found out. I feared having to spend my life in jail. He can't mean that kind of fear. That fear saved me from disaster. So what other fear can I possibly have? And why, for heaven's sake, am I always stuck for answers to these indirect attacks people like this Armand, and my stepfather, make against me? I know! It's because they're always pulling God into the ring. Whatever discussion, argument, or debate they get into, they know that, without their God, they'll get clobbered. And, God-business is not my bag. I'm a numbers man. Ten sides to a box? Sure, if you draw spiritual speculations into an equation, you can make it prove pretty well anything. While twirling my empty cup, I finally said, "it's amazing how you can make God show up in every beverage break we have. You're quite the preacher."

"Quite the dancer."

"Dancer? Dancer without legs?"

"Legs or no legs, the cosmic dance is for everyone. In our world of light every human being should be desiring to take part in the exhilarating dance in our cosmos. But those who want to learn the steps must first muster the courage to open up their door of fear. It's the hardest step of all. Most people fear having to admit to themselves, and to others, that, at times, their thinking is restricted or wrong. So,"—he looked me straight in the eyes again—"if you do see some truth in the box idea, how about sticking at least one ear out of that door of fear when you hear the God word."

"Not likely, my friend. As a matter of fact, I'm thinking of putting an end to our verbal skirmishes. Remember I told you I have no religion? And, frankly, at my age, I'm not interested in getting one."

"Could it be, Chris," Armand pensively replied, "that, in fact, you have the same religion as your stepfather?"

"What?"

"Could it be you're both members of the Church of the blessed locked-up-boxed-ins? The board above your stepfather's head may have differed from yours. His could have been inferiority. His desperate need to be right might explain his constant quoting of God's Word. But the door of his box, the one he faced day after day, was the same as yours: fear!

"Chris, Chris, don't get uptight." His tone had changed. His voice now reminded me of my dad speaking to me after I'd done something wrong, saying, 'son, I do not like what you did, but I'll always love you.'

"Chris, consider the possibility that almost every human being belongs to that church. Whether atheist, agnostic, Humanist, Jew, Hindu, Muslim, Christian, scientist, leader or follower of any kind, most are determined to stay secure in the box they have constructed around themselves. Fear, I believe, is the door of everybody's box. Few people, whether in authority or not, dare to dance the cosmic dance. Scientists are no exception. Many of them are scared to look at facts of spiritual experiences. Similarly, many preachers are scared to look at facts produced by science. They all prefer to stay secure in their own restricted thinking. And yet, there's such beautiful music in science and in spirituality, in art and technology, in commerce and recreation. To hear how others experience life is like listening to different melodies. To apologize to others for the fear that kept us from joining the dance much earlier, is like singing a love song to them. We could all be dancing on a global dance floor engraved with the words, 'enrich me. Enrich me! Enrich me!'"

Enrich me? Enrich me? What nonsense! My stepfather's religion certainly never enriched *me*. On the contrary. And could it be that Mr. Could-it-be, sitting across from me, dreamed up this spiritual dimension of purpose simply to have a trump card whenever he talks religion?

"And, Chris, I believe this spiritual dimension of purpose envelops and permeates the entire cosmos. Out of it, anything and anyone can materialize anytime, anywhere."

While I tried to figure out a non-confrontational way of ending the conversation, he kept talking. He explained how physicists accepted the existence of extra dimensions in the subatomic realm. They do so because of the positive results they give when incorporated into their quantum calculations. Good, I thought; now, at least, we're into the quantum business again. No such luck. Right away, he tied it to his spiritual dimension. The reality of this dimension could be proven, according to him, by simply incorporating it into our understandings of unexplainable phenomena of past, present and future. I didn't buy that. If that were true, physics would have accepted its existence long ago. So I nailed him on it.

"What, if I may ask, do your peers think of your spiritual dimension?"

"'Old geezer,' they replied when I introduced the suggestion. They rubbed in the fact that they were physicists, not theologians. Besides, two of my closest partners could not shake the memory of what I had shared ten years earlier. At that time, I had a spiritual dimension experience myself."

I sensed his eagerness to share that experience. But, I had enough God-talk. Spiritual speculation just wasn't my cup of tea. I considered it useless.

When I didn't react, he carefully asked, "How about meeting again next week, same place, same time? I enjoy your company."

I hesitated. Keeping my eyes on the cup in my hands, with his scooter engine humming right beside me, I thoughtfully replied, "I don't know, Armand. Suppose you're right. Suppose there is a purpose to everything.

And even if you can call this a spiritual dimension, mine definitely wasn't spiritual. Mine was mental. Early in my teens I made up my mind. Never again would I get involved with anything smelling of God or religion. I had learned to hate both with a passion. Then, at age 74, you come along. Don't get me wrong. You're okay. But is religion such a big deal to you that we need to talk about it every time we meet?"

"Chris, it's not religion that's the big deal. It's the fact that you, like so many people, have your mind dictate religion or no-religion to your heart. This weighs you down. Instead, if you would let your heart, or your soul/self as I call it, sing spirituality to your mind, you could be mounting upon wings like an eagle."

"Let my heart sing *spirituality* to my mind? You must be joking. If my heart does anything, it's more like spitting criticism, ridicule and bitterness."

"Chris, every human heart holds a spiritual spark. All it needs is for someone, or something, to fan it into a flame."

5

CHRISTMAS

Pensively observing the fluffy snowflakes lazily drifting down to the parking lot pavement, I was weighing my options. Would I meet with Armand again tomorrow to continue our get-togethers, or would I phone to say I have other interests. I love the quiet I experience when I sit in my high-back chair, facing the window. It effectively separates me from whatever is going on behind me. Whether I read, day-dream, or nap, the chair's back looks the same. Jane has a problem with that. She likes to know what I'm doing. Giving me my space, that morning, to solve my yes-no, Armand dilemma, she was in her den with a soap opera. One thing was sure: if we were to meet, it wouldn't be outside. There was more snow in the forecast. No surprise. Only five more days to Christmas.

Was I going to let myself, in a sub-atomic-particle roundabout way, get sucked deeper into the religion-business, or would I draw the line? Jane was no help. She wasn't sure whether to encourage or dismiss my contact with Mr. Armand. True, she was curious when I shared our first conversation. Interrogating me, like a criminal on a hot seat, she kept asking questions. 'What did he say then? What did you answer? What else did he tell you? Etc. etc.' When I told her about his Adam and Eve nonsense, she thought it funny and asked if I could record our conversations. So, if we do meet again, that's what will happen. Then, at least, I don't need to try and remember his every word. What I'm not crazy about though, is Jane's suggestion to ask him for dinner some night during the holidays. Knowing her, her remark, 'I'll straighten him out on his religion-stuff,' worried me.

But, did I want this man's acquaintance? If he would stick to scientific subjects, I'd have no problem with him. It was his going back and forth, between what's interesting and what's not, that irked me. But then, what else would I be doing tomorrow? I hate shopping. What if I would just keep giving him a hard time for a while? Who knows, maybe Jane and I together could wreck some havoc in his spiritual fairy land.

*   *   *

Thursday, December. 20, 2011

Overnight, five centimeters of snow had fallen on everything including the bench. This time, wearing a light brown, down jacket, and his cap of course, Armand insisted we sit outside under the cloudless, blue, winter sky. With a woolen, plaid blanket draped over his lap and stumps, he was visibly enjoying the crisp, fresh air. Sitting on that part of the backrest I had cleaned and with my feet on the seat, I had already expressed my difficulty in grasping the existence of his so-called spiritual dimension of purpose.

"Imagine," he eagerly started. "The atmospheric pressure on Jupiter is heavy enough to push everything and everybody flat down to the ground. There are only two dimensions, length and width. The Jupiterian town we're observing is Squaronia. Its inhabitants are called Squares. A misnomer, really, because since the dawn of their history, they have evolved into triangles, rectangles, circles and all sorts of other shapes. But, whatever their shape, everybody is flatter than a pancake. Squares play on flat pianos, eat flat bread and drink flat beer. Their beer can't perk them up, because 'up' is not in their vocabulary. Squares don't mind. They're never burdened down anyway. 'Down' is not in their vocabulary either. They're flat, they think flat and only know flat.

"One day, a boy named Stein Ein was born into their midst. As he matured, he spent much time in deep meditation. One day, while meditating, he experienced the sensation of entering into what seemed to be another dimension. Back flat on Jupiter, he tried to share this experience with fellow Squares. Most made fun of him.

They called him 'Stein the tripper.' Some, however, started meditating, according to his guidelines. Lo and behold, more Squares experienced the same phenomenon. Then Stein had a brainwave. He figured; if width is measured in left and right, and depth in forward and backward, then, this new dimension has to have two opposite directions as well. He called them 'up' and 'down.' A few thought he was a genius. But, most squares thought, he was a flat nut. They flatly refused to accept the existence of another dimension. They were having the same problems you have, Chris. With their flat eyes, they couldn't see it. They all thought, if it couldn't be proven flat out, it couldn't be true."

"Funny," I replied, trying to project a flat voice. "What I hear you say is, any drug addict, coming out of an overdose and reporting a spaced-out experience, should be taken seriously!"

"Chris, I am talking about people who, through quiet meditation, experience their connection with the eternal. Physicists only look for truth in the physical realm. For them, the great adjustment in the last fifty years has been, to accept facts at the subatomic level without physical proof. Only by incorporating their theories into their calculations, can an approximate certainty be obtained. But, let's change the subject. Tomorrow my son-in-law is picking me up. I'm leaving for Detroit to spend the Christmas holidays with his family. I'll be back early January."

"I bet; you'll have some great idea exchanges with your family."

"Yes, I'm looking forward to it. My daughter will share about the work she's doing as a volunteer in her Presbyterian Church. My son-in-law, a VIP at GM, will talk about cars and profits. My oldest grandson will share about the books he's read, challenging his parents' faith. My granddaughter will talk about everything imaginable in no specific order. And my youngest grandson will never leave my side. Like a well-trained nurse, he'll look after my every need. He and I will laugh a lot, talk about life, school, pain, fun, the future and the past. He is sixteen. His name is Josh. He wants to be a physician; wants to heal everybody. And, among the guests, there will invariably be a few who, after some wine, will open the door of their box a little."

"Presbyterians drink wine?"

"Sorry, I never checked that out. All I know is that the Jesus my daughter believes in helped the guests at a wedding party he attended to forget their daily cares by changing water into wine. And, few Christians on the globe question that miracle.

"In any case, I love the fellowship, the atmosphere, the decorations, the gift-giving and the laughter. I love it all. What about *your* Christmas?"

"Nothing special. I don't like celebrations. My memories are in the way. When I think of Christmas, I remember this perfectly decorated church, packed with people. After lots of hullabaloo, great choir, wonderful singing, and excellent preaching, people would stand in line to shake their holy, perfect pastor's hand. Then, back home, we'd have Christmas brunch. Holy moly, mom, my sister, and I, would quietly sit there—mom, worn out from two weeks of decorating, helping at the church, sending Christmas cards, buying gifts, making presents, preparing meals, and heaven knows what.

"Then Mister Holy had the gall to say, 'isn't it sad. We, in the church, do everything to perfection. Yet, your mom can't even make sure we, at least, have some special Christmas napkins. She seems to have a hard time comprehending Jesus' command: 'Be thee perfect as thy heavenly Father is perfect!'

"I would hold on tight to my chair in order not to jump, grab the bastard by the throat, and scream, 'she bought the friggin napkins, you creep. They fell out the shopping bag in the snow. Some idiot drove over the package before she noticed. Don't you see everything else she's done?' Oh, how I then wished to strangle the man and to strangle his perfect God."

"Jolly old St. Nick must have been the perfect antidote for you," Armand remarked with a smile.

"You wish. In our home Santa was a misspelling of Satan. If Mr. Misfit would have had his way, every member of his congregation even humming 'Rudolf the red-nosed reindeer' would have been excommunicated. No, I've decided long ago, Santa Claus is good for kids. The other meaning of Christmas is good for the gullible and for hypocrites. Besides, my friend Jerry told me how this whole Christmas thing is one big farce. It's from pagan origin. Ages before Jesus was born, December 25th was already a party-day in ancient Babylon. They celebrated the birth of the son of Isis, the goddess of nature. And, all over Europe, pagans were having their big winter solstice extravaganzas around that date as well. All it took was some smart pope to tie the whole party scene together. By cleverly declaring December 25th as the birthday of the son of *his* God, he tried to con all party animals around the globe into his Christianity. No, I'm no fool. Jane and I will have friends over for dinner and just sit around and shoot the breeze. Good company, gourmet food, classical music, and a few glasses of wine; nothing too special. Christmas will be like any other weekend when we have visitors."

"What about your sister?"

"She's a Moonie in California. And Jane's relatives live in England. We don't have kids. By the way, we thought of inviting you for a meal on one of the holidays. But, as you just told me, you won't be around. Do you have more family besides your daughter in Detroit?"

"Yes, a son, his wife and two grandsons, in Halifax. Another daughter, who is still single, works as a volunteer in Nicaragua. They won't be there.

"Thanks for the dinner invitation. Although, by what I hear, I won't be missing much. Your way of sailing through the season sounds depressing.

"But, you're one hundred percent right about the date and origin of celebrating Christmas. Indeed, it took a brilliant pope who practiced what he preached. Pope Julius I looked at all mankind in 350 CE and saw everybody as his neighbour. 'Let's hold hands and celebrate together,' he said. 'Some of you celebrate the mystery of nature. Others celebrate the mystery of sunlight. We Christians celebrate the mystery of the birth of the creator of nature who came to bring the light of life. Let's find out how we can enrich each other.' He must have been divinely inspired. Any other religious bellyaching to try and rob me of my Christmas joy?"

I didn't answer. An uncomfortable silence followed. Finally he asked, "Are you upset because the higher power, if it exists, and if it is capable of loving, loves pagans too? Did you know, the word pagan used to refer to people who didn't believe in the God of the Jews, the Muslims, or the Christians? Of course, Hindus, Buddhists, and many others took offense to that. But, judging by what you've shared so far, Chris, you would make an excellent pagan. Chris, Chris; aren't you missing out on life? I cherish the warmth of celebrating the birthday of this remarkable Jesus, regardless of what anyone thinks of Him. He has influenced history more than any other person. I also cherish the laughter, the joy, and the gift-giving that has become part of His birthday party through the imaginary Santa Claus."

Again, I had no answer. My holy step-father never called me a pagan. He just called me a sinner. And he wouldn't let up reminding me of the terrible hereafter awaiting me if I didn't repent. I wondered if Armand was, in a round-about way, trying to get me ready for *his* understanding of the repentance business. I didn't like being called a pagan though. It sounded crude. Atheist sounded intellectual.

"I'll miss our clutches," Armand added after a short pause. "I enjoy sharing ideas with you. You listen, ask questions, and bite back."

"But my bites lack teeth. Religion is not my thing."

"An embittered non-believer is enough opposition for me. As I said, I'll miss our run-ins this Christmas."

Then, while making a gesture with his right hand as if directing a choir, he pointed with his left hand to the blue sky. I was proud of myself. I caught on. Simultaneously, we began to sing the song everyone knows.

It's about having a blue, blue Christmas without you. It sings of being blue while thinking about you. And when we sang the lines about decorations in red and green that mean nothing without the presence of some loved one, an elderly couple approached.

Armand took off his cap, flipped it over and, as they passed, held it in front of them like a street musician asking for money. They completely ignored both his cap and our singing, not even giving us a smile. But we sang the whole song. He knew the words better than I did. Then Armand pulled out a mouth organ and played the tune again. Jazzing it up with clever improvisations, stuffing the melody with joy, he reminded me of my high-school years when I had played sax. I could imagine Armand dancing. No, if he had legs, he'd most likely be swinging.

"Now those two dead-beats certainly acted as if they're living in a box," I said, referring to the spoilsport couple, when he finished.

"Maybe they came home from a funeral, burying a friend" he reprimanded. "Or, maybe they came home from their doctor who told them bad news. Or, both have hearing aids with dead batteries. Anyway: here!" He handed me an envelope. "Forty-three years ago, I wrote this letter to a supposed God. At that time, I too was a stranger to the cosmic dance. When bored these holidays, read about *my* frustrations with the God-business."

6

SEARCH

It wasn't until mid-week between Christmas and the New Year that I, bored indeed, picked up Armand's letter. Jane had stuck it in the basket on the gas fireplace mantle with the few Christmas cards we had received. When I brought it in last Thursday, she started to read it, but didn't get very far. 'Her mind wasn't with it,' she said. Too busy fancying-up the apartment, and finding the right spot for a small, artificial holiday tree we had bought, she moved around like a losing tennis player. After I had told her about Armand's understanding of the word 'pagan,' she had insisted on something Christmassy close to the window. She wanted people walking by to clearly see we weren't pagans. The tree was the easy part. With decorations already attached, I simply pulled it out of the box, plugged it in and, 'Happy Holidays.' Looking at the silly artificial thing, I remembered how my dad, sis, and I, used to cut our own. Walking back and forth through the Christmas tree farm, comparing dozens of them, sis always wanted to take a scrawny one. She would feel sorry for it. But we knew; mom wouldn't like it. Once home, we would have lots of fun decorating the outdoorsy-smelling evergreen with cut-outs, pine cones we painted, cookies we baked, candies we had saved in the weeks before, and lots of tinsel.

Then dad died. The first two Christmases mom took us to the farm and let us choose a tree. We wanted the memory but we weren't enthused about decorating. The first year mom did most of it. The second year, sis did it all. I couldn't be bothered. After that, it was Christmas with the intruder. No pagan customs for him. Christmas tree! Don't ever use that word again!

Since I married, I often thought of going just once, simply out of spite, to cut my own tree. But Jane doesn't want the mess. Besides, whether fake or real, Jerry and Sylvia would laugh at the thing no matter what. Jerry . . . now there's a pagan, if there ever was one.

I opened Armand's letter.

April 26, 1970
Possible God,

Eighteen years ago, we made a deal. I have searched high and low but found no scientific evidence of your existence. Whatever possible attributes and/ or characteristics people have dreamed up for and/or about you seem to be fantasies. Together with Sonnetta, I have checked out as many religious persuasions and denominations, as we had stamina for.

A year and a half ago, we started attending as large a variety of places of worship as were listed in the phone book. We prepared ourselves by reading about the origin and beliefs of the persuasion we would visit. To find out, first hand, how different believers perceive their God, we then listened and observed. Realizing we could never judge any religion by simply reading about it and attending one of their services, we focused on, hopefully, witnessing your possible power to manifest itself somewhere.

Today, Saturday, is the Jewish Sabbath. This morning we entered a synagogue with high expectations. Jewish scripture assures, 'Yahweh is enthroned upon the praises of his people.' We had hoped to spend considerable time worshipping, and thus experience your presence. Three songs, sung with the same lack of enthusiasm we found in many other places of worship, was all we got. Yes, there were prayers. They read scripture. They had a cantor with a beautiful voice. The Rabbi gave a reasonable sermon. And yes, the people were friendly; eager to make us feel at home. The greeter at the door was like a brother. He lent me a yarmulke and, when I confided we weren't Jews, he told us to simply imitate the crowd. 'Stand when they stand. Sit when they sit. And no-one will know,' he said.

Friday a week ago, I was in a large, older home, dedicated as a mosque. Sonnetta stayed home. She didn't like being separated from me. If you're for real, God, you know, of course, Muslim men and women worship apart. Because I am not a Muslim, I had to sit on the floor in a marked off area with some teenage boys. Even though they were disturbingly irreverent, this was good. I wasn't keen on prostrating in the direction of the Masjid al-Haram, the great mosque in Mecca wherein the Ka'ba is enshrined. It wouldn't be right for me to bow to an Allah I don't believe in.

And, I was very happy to find my new shoes back again in the pile at the door where I had to leave them on entering.

My visit to the mosque and our visit to the synagogue were the last on our agenda. We wanted to come into these places of worship, which are part of our heritage, well-equipped with many other experiences.

We have joined a Sikh's meeting in a high school auditorium. With them, we sat down afterwards, on the floor, to share their communal meal.

Our intent was to visit a variety of Muslim, Jewish, Buddhist, and Hindu sects, just as we have visited most Christian denominations. But, we're tired of it all. We're getting nowhere. Mega-confusion is all we see. We're throwing in the towel. The first reason is you, God. The second is mankind.

Mankind has created a religious chaos. Every major religion is divided into sects, denominations, or schools, or whatever they're called. Yet, they all proclaim a desire for unity.

Islam, judging by superficial research, has some thirty different branches. Yet, their Holy Book, the Quran, specifically warns; 'As for those who divide their religion and break up into sects, thou hast no part in them in the least: their affair is with God.'

Jews pray, 'Shema Israel, the Lord your God is one.' Yet, their disagreements are numerous.

Most baffling, though, is Christianity. Their messenger, Jesus, has left a trail of thousands upon thousands of different denominations, groups, and schisms. Yet, he fervently prayed, 'May they all be one, as you Father are in me, and I am in you.'

What are Sonnetta and I to make of the back biting amongst all those sects and denominations? A Baptist minister makes a snide remark regarding the Roman Catholic Church. A Catholic priest warns against Protestantism. And, what's the difference between a Presbyterian, Baptist, or United Church? Yes, the Presbyterian minister wears a black robe, the Baptist minister a business suit, and the United Church minister, whose service *we* attended, wore a dress. I liked her. She was a real ham. I still remember two of her jokes. I forgot her message though.

After leading their congregation in prayer, most ministers would sit back when their robed choirs performed. Then they would lay it on the line—their line—when they preached. But, most preachers didn't leave much room for you, possible God, to do *your* thing. No time for silent reflection, or quiet meditation, in which you would have a chance to manifest yourself.

It was people in action all the time. A pastor prays or preaches, a choir sings, a congregation prays, or mumbles, or sings, or attempts to sing.

From the closed-door fraternity religions we learned that they, of course, stand above all that. However, their secret get-togethers were taboo to us. 'We do not throw pearls before the swine,' the smiling bouncer at the door of one place said. What we heard him say was, 'We believe we've got the pearls, stranger. As long as you don't sign up with us, you're pork.'

This didn't bother us. We're convinced that you, possible God, if you do exist, will make your truth freely and easily accessible to all who search for it. Although, come to think of it. Why then aren't you revealing it to us?

Actually, Sonnetta and I have concluded that you are the first and main reason for our frustration. Are we the only two people catching on? According to us, you're the author of an insurmountable contradiction, in almost all belief systems.

In almost all Holy Books you, through its writers, speak of your love, your compassion, and your unfathomable mercy. Yet, in the same Holy Books, we read about your anger, your wrath, and your absolute judgment.

Are you going to be full of judgment against our sincere, honest, and compassionate parents because they don't belong to any religious group? And, will you be full of mercy towards liars, pretenders, and hypocrites, just because they do? Or will you be full of mercy towards our parents and, full of judgment against the phonies, even though they wear a religious sticker?

How can we win? If we become Muslims, we're doomed according to the rabbis. If we return to my Jewish faith, we're doomed according to the imams. And, if we become Christians, we're doomed according to both.

True, most spiritual leaders are friendly, accommodating, and eager to witness for their understanding of any possible truth. Few, however, have any sympathy for our dilemma. All we need, according to most of them, is to see things their way and our search will be over. But, judging by what we have seen and heard so far, we have drawn our own conclusion. As far as we are concerned, there are only two distinct religions. And, these two have been with mankind from the beginning.

Religion one is the religion of the water creature complacently content within its own dark ten square meters of ocean floor. This is the religion of all those who, within every faith, are content. Born, bribed, conned, or freely having chosen to enter into it, they do not believe in mankind's great potential. They do not see it. They do not ask questions. This religion, according to all religious leaders, is the ideal one. This religion, any leader can handle. Their God, in whatever form he, she, or it is, is safely contained in a box—their box. The excitement in this religion is the nitpicking over meanings behind written words.

Religion two is the religion of the water creature that looks up, hungrily searching for better and more all the time. While bottom feeding on the ocean floor, it responds to the living fire that burns inside. It desires to rise to its potential. It struggles onto land and, it never stops struggling. It believes—no, it knows—that some day it will mount on wings like an eagle. This is the religion of those who, within every faith, are not satisfied with pet answers, status quo mediocrity, or run-of-the-mill guidance. They too are born, conned, bribed, or have freely chosen to enter into it. But, in whatever faith they have landed, they rock the boat. They do not doubt mankind's potential. They do not always see it, but they believe in it. That's why they want to be sure that what they believe is truth; not a lie. That's why they never stop asking penetrating questions. They know, deep within, universal and eternal truth does not come through the mind, but through the heart. They know this truth will set them free. This religion, most religious leaders find hard to accept. The God of this religion does not fit in a box, no matter how big they make it. The excitement of this religion is the search for truth, and the interaction with *all* who are eagerly searching.

And, possible God, just to let you know, Sonnetta and I are religion two people. We want to know truth. But, so far, it has eluded us.

One more issue. The synagogue we entered yesterday was to be our last visit to a place of worship, unless . . . you'd show up in some small way. Were you talking to me through that rabbi? Through his sermon about a certain Jacob, you made me wonder. If you are for real, you know how one night this Jacob, son of Isaac and grandson of Abraham, struggled with an angel, or a man, who could not overpower him, smote his thigh and said,

"Let me go, for it is daybreak."

*But Jacob replied, "I will not let you go **unless you bless me**."*

My kind of guy, that Jacob. He makes deals with higher powers too.

The angel asked him, "What is your name?"

"Jacob," he answered.

Then the angel said, "Your name will no longer be <u>Jacob</u> (meaning 'he who grabs the heel'), *but <u>Israel</u>* (meaning 'he who struggles with God'*) because you have struggled with God and with men and have overcome."*

Were you, possible God, through this story giving me a message? Were you telling me that I, like every other human being who struggles with the concept of God and with God-concepts forced upon them by other humans, can emerge with a blessing just like this Jacob?

But I feel I've struggled enough. I cannot simply let go of scientific facts and human understandings, unless You, possible God, bless me with deeper insights. Therefore, if there is such a thing as 'Your Heavenly Court,' that's where the ball is. Amen.

Armand Huete

P.S. I will now burn this letter (I've made a copy) and will let it rise to you in smoke.

Armand's burn and smoke reminded me of a fire and brimstone sermon of my holy stepfather. I was seventeen; ready to move out. He claimed the thigh was the seat of reproductive power. The smiting of Jacob's thigh symbolized the smiting of Jacob's descendant, Jesus. And, by the smiting of Jesus, only God's elect became justified. He then rubbed it in good—people like my dad and I were, most definitely, not part of the elect. I clearly remember. Because, when he finished, my mom's elbow poked me hard. She'd overheard me mumble, 'There, dad Smith and son. You can stick that in your pipe and smoke it.'

I liked Armand's last line. Possible God, if there's such a thing as Your Heavenly Court; that's where the ball is.

7

DUALITY

"AND, WHAT DID GOD do with the ball?" I asked, as I handed Armand back the letter relating his religion struggle. Curious to find out how he had gotten back on his God-track, I had arrived five minutes early. Why was I curious? I don't know. My holidays had been boring, as usual. Maybe I was looking for new input.

Sitting again in our retirement community's coffee shop, he was all smiles. And I, being totally focused on finding out about his possible God's next move, didn't even think of asking him about his Christmas. Graciously accommodating me, making no attempt to change the subject, he happily replied. "God threw the ball back one night while I was having a warm bath. Relaxing, aching all over from helping a friend cut firewood, I was hit with, what I thought was, an amazing understanding.

"But, before I can share it, you need more enlightenment on the sub-atomic realm. You need to know that, for the sake of human understanding, a beam of sunlight is considered to be like a beam of shrapnel, and the shrapnel consists of 'photons.' At present we believe the photon to be the smallest parcel in which light travels. The strangeness of a photon is that it can be observed as both a particle and a wave. Stranger still, these two contradictory characteristics can never be observed simultaneously. If I'm intent on measuring the particle nature of a photon and set up instrumentation accordingly, it will behave like a particle. If I set up conditions to measure its wave nature, it'll behave like a wave. But, it's not the photon that changes its character. The photon is one and the same. It is I, who interpret the photon's behaviour in terms of what I understand about our microscopic world. The consequence is; whoever observes the photon compels it to manifest itself in one way or the other. And this, according to everyday thinking, does not make sense.

"My great thought in the bathtub was; could the weird laws of the subatomic realm help us to understand the laws of the spiritual realm. For example; could the dual characteristics of the smallest part of a beam of light help me understand the duality of God? After all, the Hindu Christ, known as Krishna, calls himself the light-giver. Jesus calls himself the light of the world. Judaism talks about Yahweh being the light of life. And all the information that astronomers have about the universe has been revealed to them in and through light. So, if the photon leaves it up to me to decide which characteristic it will manifest, could it be that a possible God does the same? Could it be that I, through my intent, determine which one of His two natures God will manifest to me? If I, through thoughts, words, and deeds, express my belief in mercy, he will show me *His* mercy. If I express through thoughts, words, and deeds, that I believe in merciless judgment, he, will judge me accordingly.

"That night in the tub, a possible God's complementary duality suddenly made a lot of sense. Light has no meaning without darkness. Positive has no meaning without negative. Mercy has no meaning without judgment. And, this understanding fully incorporates our human, free will."

"Man, oh man, every time we meet, you get me in over my ears. I know, this time it's my own fault. Asking what happened to the ball was my mistake. Anyway, let's change the subject. How about giving me an update on what, I assume, was a very joyful Christmas in Detroit?"

"It was wonderful, just wonderful," he eagerly replied. "We attended a beautiful Christmas Eve celebration in my daughter's Presbyterian Church. You should have been there, Chris. The pastor made it crystal clear in his sermon: Christmas never really happens, unless it happens in our hearts. Afterwards, we went home to an incredible spread of breads, sweet breads, cake, and what-have-you. Christmas day, we exchanged gifts, sang songs, played board games, quipped, teased, laughed, and made music. Josh and I play by ear. He plays piano, I play clarinet. It's amazing how alike we both think and feel. And Rachel, my granddaughter, showed off her boyfriend, Jason. He's in robotics; an interesting chap.

"Now listen to this.

"When sitting together, Jason told us that the company he works for has a contract with a conglomerate that's building a new theme park in Florida. 'Peace on earth' they'll call it. His company is designing and building a mechanical leopard. It will be randomly chasing a mechanical deer across a certain sized savannah. After three minutes of chasing, the leopard stops in his tracks. The deer, slightly ahead, supposedly senses this, stops and turns its head. After a few moments of hesitation, it slowly walks back to the leopard. Then, the two rub noses and lie down together for three minutes.

"'How corny can you get?' Rob, my grandson, shouted when he heard the story.

"'That,' Rachel remarked, 'relates to a Bible promise which says that the leopard will lie down with the kid.'

"'No kidding!' Rob laughed. 'Imagine a leopard chasing a geeky, running baby goat. Remember, guys, when papa took us to that goat and sheep farm? We killed ourselves laughing, trying to imitate running like goats, sheep, lambs and kids.' While Rob said this, Rachel was already doing her 'running goat' act. Sandra, right away tried to outdo her daughter. And, of course, we were all laughing at their antics. The more we laughed, the crazier they got."

Armand kept relating their togetherness like the narrator of an e-book. Yes, I felt honoured to be let in on such a very personal family happening. At the same time, I couldn't help growing more and more envious of the intimate joy the story emanated.

"'Imagine,' Rob then remarked, 'imagine how slow a leopard has to go to stay behind a baby goat for three minutes.' While saying this, he was already crawling on the floor, imitating a real slow leopard. Suddenly he jumped, grabbed Rachel, and shouted, 'this is what the leopard will do.' He wrestled her to the ground and, between pretend bites, grumbled, 'Well, Mr. Robotics, how do you deal with this?'

"'I'll have a leopard tamer pop out of the ground right here.' Josh shouted, as he jumped right in front of Rob, flicking a tea towel he had quickly grabbed from the kitchen. 'Quit chewing my kid sister, ferocious beast!'

"Rob, playing along, drew back. Pleadingly, he growled, 'but, I kid you not, Mr. Tamer, I haven't eaten meat for weeks.' Rob is such a comedian," Armand interjected. "In high-school, he once played the chimney sweep in Mary Poppins. Man, was he good! Anyway, here was Rob, growling like a leopard on the floor. And Josh, the tamer, knowing Rob's love of ketchup, tells him, 'I'll get you a big juicy goat-chop drenched in ketchup, if you first do some impossible tricks.'"

Was I ever glad I had my recorder running. I would never have been able to relate this story in all its details to Jane and give it the gusto Armand gave it. Going like a luge racer, he couldn't be stopped. He was reliving the whole episode, not missing a detail, and enjoying it again as much.

"After a few ridiculous acts, Jason—new to this family-clowning—got up. Apparently not shy, he stepped to the middle of the room and said, 'I bet you, Mr. Tamer, you can't make your leopard do this trick.' And, to everybody's amazement, Jason started walking on his hands around the living room. Well, then . . . it was free for all. Everybody tried to outdo the others in imitating Jason. It was a riot. I slipped out of my wheelchair to the ground to have more room to laugh and to be right there with them. Instantly, they all ganged up on me. 'Yeah, Papa,' Josh shouted. 'We'll teach you how to walk on your hands. Then, you can play soccer with us again, like you used to.'

"Oh, Chris, these family times are like captured sunshine to me."

"Yes, sounds wonderful," I mumbled.

"What about *your* Christmas?"

"Oh . . . the usual. Reading your story is the only thing worth mentioning. It surprised me though. How come you'd never been in either a mosque or a synagogue until some seven years after your wedding? Where on earth did you get married?"

"On a cruise ship in the South Pacific, underneath the diamond ring of a total solar eclipse," Armand replied matter-of-factly.

"Where?"

"Yes, trying to accommodate our parents became too much hassle. So, we booked this cruise designed to be at the perfect place, at the perfect time, to witness a total eclipse. The captain had authority to tie knots, and that's what he did for us. On the upper deck, in the middle of the ocean, we both said 'yes.' We did it, just before the sun eclipsed. It is then, when the moon blocks the rest of the sun, that the still visible light creates a ring-like appearance. Wherever that light passes through mountains and valleys on the moon's surface, it seems to create a sparkling diamond. Bailey's beads, they're called. That was our diamond ring. What about *your* wedding?"

"Under artificial light, in a stale, municipal, justice of the peace office, together with ten other couples," I replied, not even trying to hide my envy.

"Maybe, that's the price you paid for having no religion."

"Hear who's talking. There was no religion on your boat either. Yet, your wedding was an unforgettable experience. If you had married in a synagogue or a mosque, you wouldn't have had the sun draw a diamond ring around the moon for you."

"What do you mean; no religion on my boat? I was convinced, I had the only true religion man can have. I worshipped the unspeakable grandeur of the cosmos. And, the cosmos responded to my love for it, by having two celestial bodies present us our ring."

In the silence that followed, it flashed through my mind how my Moonie sis' marriage had been blessed by religion, sun, and moon as well. She, with four thousand other love-starved believers—try fit them in a stale municipal office—was married on July 1st, 1982, in Madison Square Garden, by Mr. Sun Myung Moon. Sis was forty nine and hadn't met her partner until the wedding day. She didn't even know if he spoke English. But, she was lucky. He knew enough to say, he'd try hard to make the marriage work. Messiah Moon had assured everybody, 'it's done this way, so you'll base your relationship on inner values.' He also told them, 'You should all be ecstatic. Your match is made in heaven.' That's how sis at her wedding got religion, sun, moon and Myung—as a bonus.

"You know, Armand, I have a hard time hiding my envy over your diamond ring wedding."

"Cheer up. You still have your wife. Mine is gone."

"What happened?"

"AML. Acute Myelogenous Leukemia. It's when the bone marrow doesn't produce enough good white blood cells to strengthen the immune system. They tried to get her a bone marrow transplant, but weren't able to find a suitable donor in time."

"It must have been hard for you, without legs, to look after her."

"No, then I still had them. I lost them a year after she died. One late afternoon, driving to a friend who lived out of town, I had a pity party about being alone. At a stop sign, I looked to the left. All appeared clear. But the tears in my eyes, and the setting sun, impaired my vision. They cut me out of the wreckage and amputated both legs at the knees in the hospital. The other driver wasn't hurt. I still feel sorry for him."

"What?" I interjected. "You lost both legs, he's got nothing, and you feel sorry for *him*? What nonsense is that?"

Armand looked me in the eyes again. "The young man just got his driver's license. It was my fault. Instead of moping over my loss, I could have been thankful for the wonderful married years I did have."

"Let's get back to your search-story, Armand. Tell me, what good did all this searching do for you? I've never given religion a second thought, and yet, you and I, we end up on the same page. Religion makes no sense."

"True. But, while your story finished on that page, mine only started. Possible God, by making me understand his duality, had thrown back the ball. Next for me was to find an acceptable understanding of why there is mega religious confusion in our world. But, we've talked enough. When do I get to meet your bride?"

"She suggested you come with us next Monday to the Boat Show in Toronto.* A son of a good friend has designed a sailing dinghy. He is bringing it to the show. We'd like to see it and encourage him. What do you say?"

"Sounds great! Is it possible to leave after nine thirty? I'd like to first have breakfast at my father's house."

"Your father? He's still alive? That's incredible. You're 84, aren't you? I'd like to meet *him*. Where does he live and, how do you get there?

"A friend picks me up. And yes, someday, I'd like *you* to meet him too."

"By the way, Armand, about you meeting my bride, you better be prepared. I told her about your religion tick. According to my Jane, religion spells . . . 'horse-feathers.'"

---

* The name Toronto is derived from the Mohawk tkaronto, meaning 'where trees—wooden stakes to catch fish—stand in the water.'

JANE

"W ELL, SO YOU'RE A Presbyterian," Jane remarked, leaning forward from her back seat, smiling amicably while launching her attack. After having exchanged the usual pleasantries while helping Armand to get comfortable in the passenger seat, she could hardly wait till we started driving on our way to the Toronto boat show.

"What gave you that idea?" Armand replied without turning.

"Well, Chris told me you went to a Presbyterian Church at Christmas."

"Would going to Johnny's Fish and Chips for Christmas lunch make me a Johnny, or a fish, or chips?" he chuckled.

"Well, no, I guess not. So, what are you?"

"Why are you so eager to put me in a box and label it?"

"Well, it's not that. I'm just trying to get the religious ball rolling. Chris told me, you like talking religion. So, why beat around the bush? Go for it. As long as you know, it's all horse-feathers to me. But before you start, you talked to Chris about some weird double stuff. I don't get it. Chris said you were having a bath and suddenly you understood something. It had to do with futons, or pontoons, or whatever you call them.

"Photons: think of *photo*graphy. A photograph is made when the photons that make up a light beam hit a subject, and reflect from that subject into the lens of a camera. Entering into the camera through the lens, these photons then create the reflection of that subject, either on some photographic paper, or on a digital receiver. And, you are right, their behaviour is weird. Their dual nature has thrown physicists for a loop."

Taking a Toonie (Cdn $ 2.00 coin) out of his pocket, Armand continued.

"Imagine, Jane, a colony of fleas are living on this Toonie. They congregate on whatever side is up. When tail is up, they instinctively venture out to bite. When head is up, they're prompted to venture out to kiss. And, because it's impossible to have a coin lie with both sides up, it's impossible to observe them simultaneously as biters, and as kissers. By flipping the coin, I decide what behaviour I want them to display. And so it is with photons, and with all subatomic particles. By setting up certain measuring equipment, the person observing them decides which side of their dual nature these photons will display. And, in a way, I believe this is how it is with humans. The difference is. Fleas depend on me flipping the coin. Humans flip their own. Each morning, when I step out of bed, I decide whether I will be a biter or a kisser. And the higher power which has brought me forth will, I believe, act towards me accordingly. If I readily judge people, which I compare with biting, he'll judge me. If I practice compassion and mercy, he'll do the same to me. Does this make it understandable?"

"Well, kind of. I always need time to digest stuff. Still, it's weird. But then, all God-stuff is weird. On the one hand, these television-preachers claim their God loves everybody. On the other hand, they warn he'll get you good if you don't obey a pile of rules."

"It is confusing. I agree."

The silence that followed was comfortable. We were thinking.

Jane was doing a fine job needling Armand. She actually surprised me. She even seemed to enjoy this religious nit-picking.

"Well," she ventured after a while. "This is how you see the God-thing. Tell me if I'm wrong. If I were to believe in a God, I flip my own coin. I decide by the way I live, whether I make him judge me or love me."

"You got it, Jane," Armand laughed. "You're not slow. Although, the great thing about God is, even while he judges you, he still loves you."

"Well, I still don't believe there is a God. If there was; someone, somewhere, would have proven it. And, since no one ever has, I say there ain't. I don't understand why smart scientists can't get together with religious big-wigs, and settle this thing. If scientists can prove the universe doesn't need a God, let them do it. And, if those religious guys can prove the universe does need a God, what are they waiting for? Why can't science and religion hash it out together and give us common folks an answer? You're a scientist. You believe in a God? How does that work?"

"I'm sure, Chris told you about the deal I made with God early in my life. My science background was part of that deal. Without it, I would have never been able to see the beauty of complementary duality. It still amazes me how this understanding has given me so many answers. The argument about creation versus evolution no longer exists. Creation is realized through evolution. Together, they're the two sides of the same coin, named 'bringing forth.' It's too bad, scientists remain focused on the evolutionary process that has, and still is, taking place. Religious leaders, on the other hand, seem to be locked in on the creative and sustaining power that also has been, and still is, at work. I'm convinced that the branch of science called physics and the foundation of pure religion known as spirituality need each other to find absolute answers. I even dare say: any universal truth needs to hold within that truth two absolute, complementary opposites. Sorry, I'm getting carried away here."

"Well," Jane thoughtfully replied. "It sounds like you've thought about this stuff a lot. We figured; if smart people can't answer this God question, who are we to try? But, I'm just thinking. If what you believe is true, it proves again there is no God. If there was, he would've made all this stuff clear through one of those supposed prophets. As Jerry, our friend, says, 'religion must be a sham. How can preachers preach the universe was made in seven days, while the guys from National Geographic have proof it took billions of years?' By the way, how do they prove that?"

"The 13.8 billion year age of the universe can be calculated by studying the light coming in from the so called microwave background. But it is too involved to dig into that now. Let me guarantee you, Jane, it's foolproof. And, about the seven day creation story, imagine being the wife of Moses."

"Moses? Who is he?"

"Sorry, I thought you knew."

"I don't. No religion in my home. My mom had a notion of going to church, but dad threw a fit every time she hinted at it. For the sake of peace, she just left the whole religion bit alone. So, who's this Moses guy I'm supposed to be married to?"

"He was the leader of a tribe of nomads called the Israelites who lived around 3500 years ago. By the way, did you read my religion search story?"

"Well, kind of. It was over my head. But, I think, I got the drift of it."

"Do you remember the last part wherein a man, named Jacob, struggles with an angel, and has his name changed into Israel?"

"Yes, the guy who ended up with a bum hip."

"Right. His descendants, the Israelites, settled in Egypt under a pharaoh who appreciated their presence. However, the next pharaoh did not. Scared of their increasing numbers, he made them into slaves. It was Moses who led the Israelites out of that slavery into a land promised to them by God. And it is generally assumed it was Moses who wrote the creation story. He is a great prophet to Muslims, Jews, and Christians. So, now you know who Moses is. Let's get back to imagining you're Mrs. Moses.

"Moses and you are leading this multitude of people through the desert. One night, after milking the goats, you step into your camel hide tent. You see your VIP husband lying prostrate on the floor. He's crying out, 'God, I know you're there. You've talked to me before. You must talk to me again. These people you gave me to lead keep pestering me. "Moses," they say, "you can talk with God like a man talks with his friend. Ask him how this flat earth we're living on came to be? And how did all those stars get stuck high above our heads? And, who made us?" What do I tell them?'

"Now, imagine God talks back." Lowering his voice, and in a theatrical manner, Armand then said, 'Relax, Moses, relax. I will tell you what to say to my people. However, you must first choose from the following three options: I can speak to them in parables. That way it will make sense to you, to them and to many generations to come. Or, I can be slightly more to the point. In that case, Moses, my friend, it will have to include some calculus. This will be sky high over everybody's head. Or I can speak absolute truth. In that case, neither you, nor any of them, nor the most brilliant physicist for some thirty-five hundred years, will fully understand what I'm talking about.'"

Then, while looking directly at Jane, and changing his voice back to the one he had used for Moses, Armand pleaded, "Wild honey, help me. Tell me, please, what do I answer God?"

"Well . . . ," Jane hesitated. Suddenly, speaking sternly, she replied, "tell God we're up to our ears in chores. We need to sleep on this."

We burst out laughing. Jane had played her part.

Too bad, I had to spoil the fun.

"You two have to quit," I said. "It's too tempting for me to listen in. We're getting close to Toronto. I have to mind this crazy traffic. Jane, why not share a bit more about yourself? I've heard it all before."

"Great idea," Armand affirmed.

"Well . . . where do I start? My Dad was a war veteran, decorated for bravery. After the war, he became an alcoholic. Mom, his high school sweetheart, figured that when they married, she could get him off the bottle. No such luck. He got worse. He never wanted to talk about what he'd seen or gone through. He became more and more abusive. So, at sixteen, I left home. When I left, mom said, 'It's good for you to go. I can't. Your dad's life was ruined while trying to do *his* part to bring peace to others. I vowed to sacrifice *my* life, to bring whatever peace I can give to him.' She stayed with him till the end. A big heart she had."

"Jane's like her mother," I interjected.

"You stay out of it," Jane admonished. "Mind the traffic.

"Well anyway, from sixteen till about twenty, I lived with my dad's mother. Then, after I went to live on my own, I met Chris."

As she said it, I drifted into memories of my own. I met Jane for the second time as she was standing at the exit of the movie theatre where we, unknown to one another, had been watching a new release, *The Old Man and the Sea*. It was end April, '58. I know. Some people in the lobby were cracking the worn-out joke about it raining cats and Russian dogs. The Russians had launched Sputnik 2 in November the year before. On board had been the first living creature to go into space, a dog named Laika. That

April, the Sputnik, dog and all, had fallen from the sky, and incinerated.

'My goodness, it's pouring,' Jane had said, as we recognized each other from the hardware store. Lucky me, I had my umbrella. With my trench coat with many pockets, and a floppy hat—the kind Chicago gangsters wore in the movies—I thought I looked cool. I asked if she had far to go. It was only to the bus stop. It happened to be the same stop I was heading for. So, I offered my umbrella's protection. In the bus, while trying to figure each other out, we only talked about the acting and the plot of the movie. She had read the book. I hadn't. It was about an old man who had been fishing for years, but lately had no luck. The townspeople believed he was under a curse. One day, he headed out to sea again and caught the big fish which, he believed, had been his personal adversary all his life. While dragging it home, overjoyed because he could now show everybody he wasn't crazy, the fish got eaten up by a school of little fish which, of course, spoiled his day.

I intentionally overshot my stop, in order to help her stay dry walking home from hers. She told me, she appreciated that. She even suggested we go together to see the next movie advertised in the preview. She was direct. No head games. When I found out later she was eager to cuddle, cooked like my mother, had no religion, was always upbeat, had an apartment facing south with big windows and enough room for two, how could I resist?

"Well," I heard Jane say, "my Grandma talked religion only once, and scared the living daylight out of me. 'Mind poison,' she called it. 'If there was a God and he was such a lover,' she said, 'he would have arranged things better for our family.' Then, to make sure I'd never get involved, she told me this religious horror story in all its gory details."

I couldn't believe my ears. She had never mentioned that last part to me.

"All my life I've been trying to clear my mind of that sickening story. I've always wished to meet someone who could honestly tell me if religious people really do such ghastly things."

After a brief silence, she softly added, "When I read how you tried to figure out if God was real, I got curious. I thought, maybe, I'd like to hear more. You seem to know religious stuff. Maybe, you even know the story."

She had never asked, if I knew it. I probably don't. But, that's beside the point. Imagine. We meet after watching an old man hooked on the sea and here she was sharing her secrets with an old man hooked on the cosmos.

"No," Jane finally sighed. "It'll ruin our day. This is not the time to open up my can of worms."

9

BEGGARS

"T ALKING ABOUT WORMS," ARMAND animatedly started, as he aimed his scooter for the boat show entrance at the far end of the parking lot. Walking beside him, we perked our ears.

"Hear this. Josh, my grandson, and I planned a fishing day trip. He was about eleven. Neither of us had ever fished. Standing in the bait shop, beside the wooden box with rich black soil and hundreds of worms crawling around in it, Josh said, 'Papa, you'll put the worms on my hook, won't you?'

"'No, no, Josh,' I replied. 'I don't like those squirmy, slimy fellows any more than you do. If we both want to learn how to fish, we both have to get used to baiting our hook. You still want to go?' Hesitantly, he agreed. 'I'll just close my eyes when I do it,' he said.

"We bought a big container with three dozen worms. Inexperienced as we were, I thought, we might waste some.

At the bait lady's advice, we secretly put the container in the fridge, to keep the worms fresh. 'Your daughter may not like the idea,' she had warned.

"Next morning, six a.m., Josh and I get ready. We'd prepared breakfast to take, so we wouldn't wake anyone.

"'You get the worms,' I said to Josh, 'I'll get the rods.'

"Josh opened the fridge and immediately closed it again. 'Oh, no,' he exclaimed way too loud, covering his mouth instantly. 'They're all over!'

"'Just grab them, and stick them back in the container,' I replied, thinking he was kidding me. We often do that to one another.

"'No, Papa, it's true. They're all over.'

"I couldn't believe my eyes. The lid had come off, and all thirty six worms were on the loose. They were on the apple juice bottle, the butter container, in the left-over lasagna. You name it, and there was a worm on, or in it. It was a nightmare. But, knowing Josh and myself, I knew what would be next. I quickly pushed him out the side door. Sure enough, we both burst out laughing. 'Papa, what'll we do?' he asked between hiccups. 'Josh,' I replied, 'you and I will have to catch thirty-six, long, slimy, slippery worms.'

"Reluctantly at first, but quickly forgetting about the slippery slime, we grabbed them one by one. We were even getting happy to pick the next one and the next one, and put them back in the container. But, in between, each time when laughter bubbled up within us, we quickly slipped outside.

"When almost done, Josh said, 'Papa we should have counted them. If we miss one, and mom finds it, she'll die.' So, Josh got a sauce pan, dumped the container, mud and all, and counted. 'Thirty-five,' he said, 'we're missing one.' After a long search, we finally found the lost sheep, so to speak. He, she, or it, had been hiding, in the crisper, inside a head of Boston lettuce. We cleaned the fridge, threw out a lot, and put what was still good back in. When almost done, Josh tapped my arm. 'Papa,' he said, 'I just remembered. I ripped one in half when I pried it off mom's liquid vitamin container. We're still one short.' Out came the stuff again. Now we were racing against the clock. Paul, my son-in-law, gets up at seven. We were lucky. As soon as Josh stuck his head back in the fridge, he spotted the straggler hiding under the plastic cap of the fridge light. We made it out the door in the nick of time.

"We never caught any fish that day. We made too much of a racket, killing ourselves laughing, imagining, and acting out how each member of the family would have reacted if they had been first to open that fridge."

Speaking more to himself than to us, he added, "How I love that boy." Turning to us, he said, "You know; talking with Josh about God, or anything spiritual, is as comfortable as talking about the weather. Too bad we live so far apart."

*   *   *

After we had worked our way through the entrance and through half the show to get to our friend's son's new sailboat, I remembered Armand's last remark about Josh. Sure enough! Here he was again, talking sailing as easily as he talked his God-business. It turned out he had done a good bit of sailing in small racing dinghies himself. But, as was to be expected, he couldn't leave God out of the dialogue. 'Yes,' he said to the young man who had created the dinghy from scratch, 'when God stirs up an idea in your mind, it's very exciting when you can touch its final form.'

We wished the young man luck, said good-bye, and started strolling past the rows of people eager to get a glimpse of the interior of the big expensive yachts. They lined up in the isles, and on the make-shift wooden stairs leading up to roomy platforms. High above the hustle and bustle of the show, these platforms surrounded the hulls of 32 to 52 foot mega boats. Those lining up wished to step on, look into, and dream of one day winning a big lottery. Only then could they afford to splurge, and buy one of these rich people's toys. True, there was a lot of beauty on display here, beauty created through the clever craftsmanship of the hands of man. But Jane and I had never been lucky at any lottery, not even one single door prize anywhere, so why bother dreaming? Besides, Armand couldn't go up those stairs anyway. Add to that;

I hate line-ups. They remind me of a humiliating line-up dad, sis and I were in one time. It was for a ride on 'The Flying Dutchman,' a fall fair attraction that looked like a miracle to me. Anticipating being strapped in with my dad, the pilot, and then flying at the end of one of those long, colourfully-lit, steel arms, in all kinds of crazy patterns through the air, I was so excited that I wet my pants. Comfortingly warm when it happened but 'ugh' after that. When we stepped off, sis noticed my wet seat. She didn't believe my explanation. Dad did. I never heard the end of her pestering me about being a wimp. She hadn't been scared at all.

"Well," said Jane, walking in a motherly way ahead of Armand to clear the way for his scooter, "you'd never get me in one of those sailing things even if you paid me." Jane never learned to swim.

Quickly discovering that more boats, and endless boat paraphernalia, did not intrigue us, I suggested we leave the show and spend some time downtown. The weather was perfect. Blue sky. Minus three. And I knew, people would be skating on the city hall rink. I also wanted Armand to see the area I'd walked during lunch hour while working for Revenue Canada.

I parked on a back lot. The van was too high for the underground garage. And believe this; as soon as we stepped into the city hall square a wino accosted us. With filthy clothes, and the breath of an ape on a garlic diet, he stuck an empty coffee cup under Armand's nose and begged, 'Please, sir, some change for coffee?' I'd forgotten these guys were a permanent part of the downtown scene.

Armand stopped his scooter, smiled at the bum and—I couldn't believe my eyes—he pulled a five from his jacket pocket, asked the scum's name, shook his hand, and handed it to him. 'God bless you, my friend,' Armand said. The sponge grinned from ear to ear. Almost tripping over himself and thanking Armand, he mumbled, 'God bless you too, sir.' And if that wasn't enough to get my blood pressure up, Jane, right there beside Armand, shook the creep's hand as well. No sooner had he left than I blew my top.

"What do you think the two of you are doing? Giving this beggar money is like throwing it in the gutter. He's not buying coffee. He's saving up for his next bottle or his next fix. Your five bucks will go to some dope dealer who will hand it to his supplier and, ultimately, that money will end up in the hands of a motorcycle gang or the mafia. That's who you're supporting by handing these losers change. Can't you see how this whole homeless beggar scene is a lost cause? You're propagating it."

Armand smiled. Jane just stood there. Taken aback by my frontal attack, they patiently waited for more. When I remained quiet, Armand slowly said, "You have a valid point there, Chris. It's good to hear how you experience this. These panhandlers do seem to get your blood pressure up pretty good. Are you interested in hearing how Jane experiences them?"

I didn't answer. I sat down on a bench—steaming.

"Okay, Mr. Flea," Jane said with a smile, "is this kissin' or bitin' time?"

Slightly defused by her silly question, I replied, "My Toonie is on its edge." Armand laughed. Jane's smile grew wider.

"All right," I added. "I'll quit biting. But I'm far from kissing."

Happy about the good turn in the conversation, they moved closer.

"Jane," Armand then asked, "what were *you* thinking when you shook the man's hand?"

"Well, jeepers, I didn't know it was such a big deal with Chris. I just felt for the guy. He looked so hopeless. I've always wanted to reach out a bit to underdogs, but I'm uncomfortable doing it. You made it easy. I knew the guy wasn't into coffee." She hesitated. Then, softly, she added, "If it hadn't been for my mom, my dad could have ended up here."

Jane sat down next to me. Turning to Armand, she asked, "What makes it so easy for you?"

For a minute or so Armand didn't answer. Then he explained, "When I hear the laughter of skaters in bright sunshine, under a blue sky, I feel joy bubbling up inside of me. If I could, I'd join them. It's as if there's a fountain of joy waiting, deep inside of me, eager to spring up. Then: when confronted with pain and hurt—clearly visible in these destitute men—the fountain changes. Joy becomes compassion. And this compassion seems to be channelled through me. It makes me want to get up and hug them. I feel I want to hold them and tell them they're loved. I want to take them home, give them a shower, feed them, and do what I can to change them into new men. When I see these men, I'm reminded of a line in one of the holy books. It goes something like this, 'Oh, how I long to gather you, as a hen gathers her chicks under her wings.'

The silence that followed was uncomfortable. Jane fidgeted. I looked at the skaters, thinking 'how can I win?' Hardly a minute into our stroll and we're back into the religion business. We should've stayed at the show.

Finally, Armand turned to me. "When I had legs, Chris, I would take them to a fast food place and pay for a meal. Now, I give them five bucks. That's my hug. They decide what to buy. If it's a burger: great. If it's booze: you are right, I'm supporting, through them, the same network you buy your wine from. If it's dope: I'm supporting, through them, some gang or the Mafia. It's a catch twenty-two situation. I want to love and help. But, by doing so, I help the crooks. It's like wanting to live frugally by shopping at a deep discount superstore. You save money by handing operating cash to unscrupulous child-labor exploiters.

"Now . . . about your concern of us spending all afternoon talking to these, what you call, losers, lighten up. To express my desire to clean up litter, I pick up seven pieces. Today, if you let me, to express my desire to rid the world of suffering, I'd like to reach out to seven of these men. But, only if they approach *me*. Jane and I have loved one. Six more to go."

"Well," said Jane, eager to lighten the mood. "Let's continue our walk. For the next six guys, Chris, you do the touristy thing. Look up at those umpteen-storied, fancy-coloured, glass, bank towers and pretend you don't know us. Armand hands out his fives. And I'll just be me."

"Jane, you're priceless," Armand chuckled. "You just expressed one of the many complementary dualities contained in the word 'man.' He celebrates his greatness by strutting in and out of his luxuriously-furnished ivory towers on the one hand. On the other hand, he suffers his nothingness by crawling like a worm into his bedbug-infested sleeping bag on top of a subway air vent."

"And what's so wonderful about that?" I said, trying to show good will on the one hand, while on the other hand venting my irritation.

"If man didn't have to deal with misery, he'd be proud, conceited, and believing he built the universe. By building impressive structures, we can give form to our dreams during life on earth. This makes us *co-cre*
the universe. But, in order to become *co-owners*

cosmos for eternity, we need to learn how to give form to compassion. And I believe that only compassion can make us move up on the evolutionary ladder."

"Moving up on the evolutionary ladder, eh," I half sneered. It seemed, no matter what I said, he had an answer. I didn't like how he was robbing me, right in front of my wife, of my cherished know-it-all status.

"So what, great teacher, if I may ask, do we call the next rung up?"

While trying to look me in the eyes again, he returned the question. "Didn't your dad suggest we should all try to become like little gods?"

It was one thing for this man to stir up, now and then, a desirable memory connected with my dad. It was another thing for him to assume, he and my dad were of the same mind. In all our conversations, my dad had used the word God only once. Mr. Armand, on the contrary, couldn't get through any conversation without peppering it with that word.

"Well, let's quit the bickering," Jane refereed. "Why can't we do as I said? Just for a little while, Chris sees the sights, Armand lets his fountain bubble and I'll simply enjoy whatever."

They went ahead of me, stopped at the skating rink and watched. Seeing Jane stand next to Armand, I noticed how happy she looked.

10

STORIES

"WELL, BIG BEARD," JANE asked, once we were safely out of city traffic on our way home from Toronto. "While you were listening, during dinner, to our camel-driver boasting about his tax collecting skills, I was hashing things over." Leaning forward from here backseat, eager to re-start the game, she tried to get Armand back into his part.

"Beautiful, my desert flower," Armand instantly replied as he turned to face Jane. "Are we ready to give God an answer?"

"Yes. I was thinking, what's the use of God telling us the absolute truth, if even the most brilliant scientist 3500 years from now can't wrap his head around it? And to have God give us scientific stuff, with numbers and formulas way over our heads—especially mine—is useless as well. We have no choice. We have to settle for parables. But . . . ," she assertively added, "you must tell God; we have to write, 'It's only a parable,' right at the top of the story."

"Brilliant idea: prickly cactus. But, how do you think proud Joshua and his fighter buddies will react to that? You think they'll like the idea of God talking to them in parables because he judges them too dumb to understand the truth?'"

"Just a second," I interrupted. "You're having fun acting out this Moses—business. But Moses, probably, never even lived. I once read a big spread in some weekly. It said; there is no evidence the exodus of the Israelites out of Egypt, as recorded in the Bible, really happened. It even said: no evidence can be found that this king David, of whom the Bible talks a lot, was much more than some minor chieftain. And, if this king David's son, Solomon, ever built majestic buildings, he must have built them with disappearing stone. What do you say to that?"

"I read the article too. It was written by a 'revisionist academic'. This is a person who believes, he, or she, has enough academic, or scientific proof to revise, change, or alter, the understanding of whatever body of information he, or she, is dealing with. In the case of the Bible, such a person is called a 'minimalist'. Minimalists try to minimize the value of whatever is written in the Bible. Consequently,

, regards every word in the Bible as coming ith of God is known as a 'maximalist'. Sitting se two camps are you, and me, and everybody else who's trying to figure out what either camp dreams up, assumes, or speculates on. Even they, themselves, are often hard pressed to draw clear lines between their own clever academics, the realities they assume, and truth. And I, like most people, don't have the time or the money to do my own research. So, instead of getting hung up on the details of these stories, I focus on the lessons they contain!

"Let's go back to Mrs. Moses."

"No," Jane replied. "Before I get into my role again, I'd like to know: did you ever do crazy stuff like this with your wife? I mean, did you two sit down for supper and act out people you met?"

"As a matter of fact," Armand replied laughing, "she taught me. Being a stewardess, she had to deal with all kinds of people and she would make me double over with her stories. Imagine, an old man coming from the Yukon speaking Inuktitut. He's never been on a plane, and his son, now living in Europe, has sent him the ticket to come visit him. The man just can't fathom the fact that, even though he's sweating profusely from the ridiculously high temperature in the cabin, this seemingly intelligent stewardess is unable to open a window. Sonnetta would get up from the table and show me how she tried to explain this to the man without speaking a word. Then, a few weeks later, I would casually ask her to open a window and she'd catch on right away. Next thing you know, we'd have a whale of a time replaying, and exaggerating, her

Yukon man experience. She almost always had a story. And if she didn't, she'd act out the antics of a squirrel who, in front of her car, tried to cross the street while she was driving home."

"Well, okay. So, I'm Mrs. Moses. What was my problem again?"

"If we say to proud Joshua and his fighter buddies that God talks to them in parables, they'll get their backs up. Telling them it's because they're not smart enough will irk them to no end."

"Well, yes. That may be a problem. How about we give them time to digest the story and then tell them it's a parable?"

Speaking with his Moses voice, Armand replied, "I knew it, woman, you'd give me good advice." Changing back again to his own voice, he added, "Jane; that was a clever suggestion. God did just that. Some five hundred years later, he prompted King David, whom Chris just mentioned, to write down this sentence: 'God opens his mouth in parables.' And the Holy Book of Islam also states: 'God disdains not to use the similitude of things, lowest as well as highest.'"

"Still," I said, "this does not explain why they can't find any good evidence for big Moses."

"Maybe there never was a big Moses leading some 600,000 men, plus women and children, with great ado and in broad daylight, out of the main gate of Egypt. Maybe there only was a nervous Israelite grandfather. Following a voice he heard within his heart, he simply snuck himself and his fifteen children and their families out the back door in the dark of night. Fed up with slave life, they got away. In order not to get caught, they crawled around the desert using moonlight to find their way. They reached the Red, or Reed, Sea and crossed it when the winds were favorable. Then, constantly trusting his inner voice, this small-time leader ultimately brought everybody to a good place. And, throughout the ordeal, they kept up their spirits by continually expanding on grandpa's escape story.

"Suppose Josh and I had bought only half a dozen worms. It would've been plenty. We ripped them in four anyway. But, six worms on the loose in a fridge don't make a good gross-me-out tale. If Josh were to share this boyhood experience to his children, he would want to make it more exciting. To stay honest, he could say, 'all the worms out of the container escaped.' His son, telling it to his children, could then easily expand it by saying, 'it was a big container with a lot of worms.'

"For earlier civilizations, it was not uncommon to expand on stories, in order to make them more entertaining. At times they would beef them up, to make sure the lessons they contained would never be forgotten. With no televisions, radios, computers, books, or magazines, story making and telling, was done to educate. The story was the parcel in which wisdom was wrapped. In the books of Moses, it may not be about the stories. It may be about the lessons."

"Name me one," I said.

"Always double check the lid on your worm container," Armand replied deadpan.

"You know what I mean, smart guy."

"I do. But for me to share all the lessons and messages contained in the books of Moses would take a car session from here to Florida and back. However, are you aware there still is one big, juicy, worm on the loose right here with us?"

"What do you mean?"

"Remember, Jane, how you asked on the way down, why smart scientists and religious big-wigs can't sit down and hash out the yes-God-no-God question?

"I believe the problem is that human beings have different mindsets. Some have analytical minds, others mystical minds, and still others have creative minds. Scientists have analytical minds. They want to know how things work. In trying to discover this, they focus on the pieces.

"Mystics, the people who search for the riches of the spiritual realm, have mystical minds. I'm not talking about religious leaders. They may excel in leading while not being spiritual at all. And mystics, as a rule, are poor leaders. But, mystics try to see the interconnectedness of things. They focus on the whole.

"These two mindsets find it hard to see eye to eye. Yet, I believe that if they accepted the reality of complementary duality, seeing eye to eye would be a lot easier for them."

"What do you think, Jane," Armand concluded while pretending to hold a big worm close to her face. "Can I toss the creeper?"

"Well, I guess so."

"CHRIS, BIG WHEEL AT THREE O'CLOCK!" Armand suddenly shouted. While pretending to throw a make-believe worm out of the real car window, his eyes had caught the wheel.

Sure enough, one of the wheels of the thirty-two wheeler, slightly ahead, had come off. Rolling on the highway shoulder, at a speed identical to ours, it looked as though it had a killer mind of its own. The three lane highway sloped down. We were in the middle lane. The wheel picked up speed and then, on a diagonal track, entered lane one. The driver in that lane saw the wheel. He slowed down, gave it lots of room. It continued across his lane, picked up more speed, and entered ours. I switched on my four-ways and carefully slowed down more, because there were other cars behind me. The wheel, now safely ahead, was heading for lane three. Rolling faster than the speed limit, it began to wobble. I opened my window. Wildly waving my arm up and down, I tried to warn the car coming up behind me in that lane. The driver, of the black jaguar that I saw in my rearview mirror, paid no heed. He couldn't see the wheel.

We were in his line of sight. When he passed and saw the wheel, it was too late. It hit his shiny Jag on the right front fender. Thrown off by the sudden jolt, his car swerved. The driver regained control, but he had to keep going with the damaged fender. He also had cars behind him, all ignoring the speed limit. Lucky for him, the driver behind him saw what was happening. He slowed down. However, because of the nudge, the wheel was back in our lane. It began to tilt more. Thank goodness. The tilt, and the fact that the highway was now slightly sloping up, made it wobble back into lane three and head for the center rail. There, bouncing wildly, it finally plunked down. Nobody spoke. After a while, Armand said, "Sorry, about the three o'clock. It came automatically. I've done some flying."

"Thanks for the three o'clock," I responded, still wiping sweat from my forehead. "I understood. I've watched war movies."

"Well," Jane sighed. "How close were we to total and complete disaster? I don't even want to try to imagine how this could have ended. Thank God we're still alive and, better still, unhurt."

"Yes, indeed," Armand replied, "let's give thanks." He folded his hands, closed his eyes, and was absorbed in prayer.

'How absolutely, completely and totally ridiculous,' I thought, hardly able to hold my tongue. But, I restrained myself till he was finished.

"Listen, Armand," I instantly fired. "Let's get real. You thank this possible God. You believe he's involved in everything that happens. You believe his almighty hand made this truck wheel get off the road safely so nobody would get hurt. So why didn't he nudge that wheel into the ditch right away? I mean, why all this drama if nothing was going to happen anyway? In short, what are you thanking him for? Why didn't he make that wheel fall off at a truck stop? And, while I'm at it, if he is such a nice God, why does he allow highway carnages to happen in so many other places?"

"Excellent questions, all of them," Armand replied. "But . . . ,"

"Wait, please!" Jane almost cried. "Don't get into your heavy stuff again as if nothing happened. I'm still shaking. How can you two just ignore the whole affair and, right away get into your highfalutin arguments, as if you're sitting in the coffee shop and simply dropped a spoon?"

"Jane is right," Armand sympathized, "This was a close call."

It's amazing how women hang on to traumas even if they're past. Sure, my heart beat went up. But it all worked out. It's over and done with. It's history. Why dwell on it. I've been in close calls before. They're part of living in the fast lane. All you have to do is watch the news. If you let it get to you, you'll never drive again.

"I agree, Jane," Armand continued. "If you let your mind go, it can paint disturbing pictures. It's a good thing we're close to home. If you like, we can hash this scary happening over at our next coffee shop meet. It would be interesting to see if we could find some meaning, some purpose, in it all."

"You must be kidding," I said, shaking my head, as I parked the van at the main entrance of our complex. "Don't tell me you believe there's a purpose in a stray truck wheel scaring the living daylight out of people."

"Yes, I believe that."

"You, guys. Don't start again. I've had my fill for today. But I'd love to join your next Thursday's meet. If you let me, that is."

"Great actresses are hard to find," Armand chuckled. "You work it out with your hubby. My vote is YES."

11

PURPOSE

"LISTEN, ARMAND. YOU WON'T believe this. The other night, out of the blue, while watching T.V., Jane asked, 'in what holy book does God talk about chicken wings?'"

He laughed heartily.

"It wasn't funny," I protested. "Imagine, in the middle of a rerun of an exciting play-off game, she comes up with a crazy question like that."

Her interruption still annoyed me. That's why, after we'd picked up our drinks at the counter and settled in our favourite corner of the coffee shop, I just had to get it out of my system. It was a good thing we didn't want lunch because even though there wasn't any typo on the coffee shop blackboard, there wasn't much on it, period. Mushroom soup, most likely from cans, and grilled cheese sandwiches spelled correctly. The girl in charge was sick. Her replacement had only limited cooking skills.

Two elderly ladies—Armand knew them, Jane and I did not—were having coffee and talking a mile a minute. I heard words like 'cheap' and 'half price'.

"What did you tell her, Chris?"

"I told her, you never said anything about chicken wings. When seeing those losers, you said; 'you felt like a hen wanting to gather her chicks under her wings.' Anyway, Jane kept bugging me. To settle the issue, I checked the internet. First I went to a Quran concordance. It gave five results. None came close. Then I went to the Christian Bible concordance. I knew it includes Jewish scriptures as well. And there it was, in one of the Christian gospels. But, you know, Armand? You're messing up our lives. Jane and I must have talked religion for more than half an hour after that. We even got into a spat.

"So here's my beef. Jane and I were happy campers. No religion. No God. No hang-ups. We lived life as it came and we made the best of it. Then you come along. Yet, the last thing I want is to end up sitting on some cold mosque or temple floor, or hang in a synagogue, church, or kingdom-hall pew.

"Truthfully, Armand, I'm afraid you're slowly leading us to a place where we do not want to go. Being all over the map with your religious understandings, you could lead us anywhere. One day, out of the blue, you may say, 'got ya' and turn us into Hare Krishnas. You've thought about religion a lot. We've never given it a second thought. Anyone who talks religion with more knowledge than we have can convince us, and especially Jane, of anything. So, I've made up my mind. Unless you're up front about the church, or temple, or whatever you go to, I'm finished talking religion."

"So, you're blackmailing me," he laughed boisterously. "Loosen up. Live in the sunshine. I'm not leading you anywhere. You ask questions, I answer with my personal understandings. I'm having a great time. At last someone's listening to me: first you, Chris, and now Jane. If all three of us are not having a good time, I'm quitting too.

"Oh, you two," he said in a softer tone. "I feel like holding you both in a bear hug. Unwind. Sharing about God and his possible ways should be joy. It should be an occasion for laughter and surprise. Excitement, amazement, and an anticipation of gaining new insights should stimulate our minds."

"Well, Armand, I think Chris is right. You're getting us all entangled in your religious web, and we don't have a clue where we'll end up."

"You know, Jane, when Sonnetta would look as burdened as you do right now, I would take her hand and lead her to our big kitchen. There I would sing and dance with her. Armand turned to the two elderly ladies and asked, "Margaret, Joan, you don't mind if I make some happy noise, do you?"

"Not a bit, Armand," Margaret answered. "We'll love it. Go for it."

And, with his contagious tenor voice, Armand sang, *"You are my sunshine, my only sunshine.* It's a song that sings about someone making you happy when skies are grey. It sings about how much you love that person and it begs him or her to, please, not to take that sunshine away.

When finished, he pulled out his harmonica and, just as when he had jazzed up 'Blue Christmas', he now jazzed up this old Dixieland favorite. Even the girl from the kitchen came out, pulled up a chair, and sat down next to us tapping her feet.

"So, where were we?" he said with a big grin as he put the mouth organ away. "Oh yea, Chris doesn't want to end up sitting on a bare floor, or in a hard pew, in some temple, mosque, synagogue, church, or kingdom-hall. He doesn't want to be listening to a preacher stuffed with knowledge but lacking wisdom. Well, as far as my religion is concerned, I'll tell you what the sticker on my forehead says.

"'Physicist; thirsty for Truth.' I'm like a dry and weary land wherein there is no water. Or, as I like to think of it: 'deep calling to deep.'"

"Well, never mind, Armand, what church do you go to?"

"Intriguing, isn't it?" Armand replied, laughing again. "Tell me, when you open up an interesting book, do you read the last page first? Relax. I'm trying to make my religious struggle story more interesting by having you, in some small way, live through it with me. Just say 'enough,' if you don't want to hear anymore. Or, simply start talking about the weather, ailments, other people, or bargains. In that case, I won't have much to contribute."

Silence. It seemed, though, as if Margaret and Joan were talking extra loud sharing their bargain hunter victories.

"About me going to a church," Armand added after a while, "I'm comfortable in any place of worship. Wherever people gather to learn more about their own spirituality, or to simply pay tribute to their God, I am at ease. As long as the preacher is short, to the point, and speaks compassion, consideration, and tolerance. For no matter what faith community I attend, the temple wherein the real tribute to God is paid is my body. And the real learning, if there is any, takes place in my heart.

"Well . . . ," Jane slowly ventured, "who can disagree with that?"

"Every religious leader and every scientist can. If they believe they have the corner on truth, their box is full. In that case they'll disagree."

"Well . . . , my brain is full too. And you haven't even told us anything about this spiritual purpose stuff. You haven't even given us your idea about the possible purpose of this big wheel rolling on the loose on the highway? And, why do accidents happen that kill and maim people?"

"Jane, the answers are simple, and at the same time incomprehensibly complicated. They're all in the spiritual dimension of purpose."

"Well, that dimension stuff is way over my head. Chris told me about those flat guys on Jupiter who couldn't understand up and down. Still, I don't get it."

Jane was smart enough not to tell that she had replayed the recordings of our previous conversations over and over, trying to prepare herself for this morning's meet. I was glad Jane didn't get it either. Now I didn't have to ask for more explanations.

"Besides," Jane added. "If all this complicated talk is part of getting religion, I don't want it. Chris is right. Who needs it? You also told him we all live in a box. And, according to you, every box has a purpose. Do you think that I, at 73, feel like breaking my brains over that stuff?"

"Jane, I'm 84, and I find it exciting to challenge my mind with whatever question I encounter. It keeps dementia at bay. But, if you two don't think that way, what can I say?"

"Well, tell me, Armand. Do you never watch the news, or get to know some history. Jews crucified that good man, Jesus. Christians burn each other. Muslims murder people by the hundreds with their suicide bombers. What on earth is so interesting about religion?"

"Jane, I told Chris earlier, religion is like quantum mechanics. Many, who think they understand it, really don't get it. Muslims don't kill people by the hundreds. Jews didn't crucify Jesus. Christians don't burn each other. It's people who *claim* to belong to one of these religions, the zealots, fanatics, extremists, and manipulators who do such things. They know the fancy jargon associated with their faith. But their understanding of the love, the majesty, and the grandeur of the God they claim to believe in, is too little to fill a one-day pillbox."

"Well, if you'd only use simpler words. Take that dimension thing. How, for crying out loud, am I ever going to wrap my head around that?"

"Remember the Rubik's cube of long ago? One big cube made of many smaller cubes? Try to visualize these little cubes as bubbles. That's how I imagine the spiritual dimension that holds and permeates our physical cosmos. One whole, made up of innumerable smaller parts, forever divided into intertwining smaller ones. You, I; we all live in a bubble. And every small bubble exists inside increasingly larger bubbles, each with their own purpose, like families, cities, countries, and our world.

"So, whether you imagine yourself to be in a bubble or in a box, it doesn't matter. The idea is; we're all enclosed in a limited space. For some that space is larger than for others. And, because all the enclosures we live in are intertwined with all the other enclosures around us, whatever happens anywhere, and whatever anybody does, good or bad, has an effect on all the other boxes or bubbles."

"Well, there you have it. I can't see how what I do wrong will mess up the lives of people I don't even know."

"You know how weather forecasts can be off the mark? Every meteorologist knows forecasting can never be perfect. It's impossible to put everything that affects the weather into the computer. Theoretically, even the flap of a butterfly's wing can affect it. When I carry this reality over into the spiritual dimension of purpose, I can show how every thought, word, and action, no matter how insignificant, does affect larger events, and even the whole of mankind. Any seemingly insignificant intent generated in my mind will, in the dimension of purpose, play itself out to an unpredictable bigger consequence."

"Well, whatever. Why don't you tell us what sense you can make out of this dumb wheel that almost killed us."

"All right! Here she rolls from the shoulder onto the highway. The first person affected is the driver in lane one. I'm not God, so I don't know his heart, his mind, or his family life. I can only speculate on the purpose of the wheel for him. He sees it, gets a jolt, and realizes the danger. For a split second, he fears for his life. In a flash, he may realize how fragile life is and how suddenly it can end. Maybe, he's a small contractor, working seven days a week. The sudden confrontation with possible death may make him think, 'money isn't everything. I should spend more time with the kids.' In that way, if he changed his lifestyle, this wheel may have prevented his son from becoming a drug addict.

"For us, lane two people, only you and God know what went through your mind. My thought was, 'Armand, you blabber-mouth. Don't you know it's dangerous to distract a driver by playing with pretend worms?'

"Concerning the Jag driver, seeing the wheel aim for his shiny treasure may have made him realize how fragile his riches are. Let's hope, he got enough of a jolt to make him change his attitude towards worldly goods. That certainly could have a positive effect on his life, and on the lives of all that are dear to him. I believe everyone involved in a happening, good or bad, is, in some way, partly responsible for that happening. We all need lessons. And, for me, the level of awareness I have for these spiritual dimension lessons is intimately related to my level of humility."

Jane was picking thread-balls from her sweater. I played with my empty cup.

Finally I broke in, "You've got good imagination. Tell us, what purpose can you dream up for a tsunami killing 800,000 people?"

As if he hadn't heard me, Armand asked, "So, what do you think? Are you two planning to sit on a chair in this Kingdom coffee shop again next Thursday? Or is listening to this old man stuffed with ideas but lacking a theology degree too taxing?"

"Well, I'm willing to try another session," Jane replied, sounding greatly relieved—probably because Armand didn't hook in to my question—and with a laugh she added, "as long as you promise to sing us another song."

"Wow! We're into hymn singing now. You'd better check with your hubby. He seems reluctant."

"Are you planning to give me an answer to my question?"

Armand turned to give me his usual grin. "Chris, you know how I love making deals. If you come up with a sensible purpose for *manmade* disasters, like genocides that kill millions, their intents from the beginning, and their consequences to the very end, I'll share my understanding of the purpose for *natural* disasters."

Smiling broadly as he tooted away, he shouted over his shoulder, "Jane, I'm printing out a handclapping, foot-stomping, negro spiritual for next Thursday. I will only sing if you join in."

12

JOSH

"WELL, SOMETHING MUST BE wrong with Armand. He wouldn't be late without letting us know. You think we should go to his apartment and see?"

Punctual Armand was late for our Thursday morning meet. Jane and I had been on time. And now we worried. Jane spoke it. I pretended nothing was wrong. To hide my concern, I focused on trivial things. Why were the rusty-brown floor tiles six-inchers? Why didn't they use bigger ones? After all, people do spill their drinks in a café. Cleaning up from big tiles is easier than cleaning up from the grout between smaller tiles. And why were the iron bistro table legs painted dark green while the tops and the chair legs were black?

"Don't worry," I said. "He's just delayed. We'll give it another five."

Interesting! The dark mauve of the café walls was the same colour as the walls of the funeral home where a family friend had led us in a fare-well service for my dad. Strange! Here, the colour looked warm, peaceful, and relaxing. In the funeral home it had seemed forbidding and morbid.

Jane pointed at the clock, got up and then . . . there he was. He looked like . . . my goodness, he looked like . . .—words that I once heard in my step father's church popped into my mind—he looked like he had watched his own crucifixion. He bumped his scooter into a table, didn't say, 'I'm sorry I'm late,' didn't go to the order window, just parked in front of our table and looked at us. His eyes were red from crying. He wanted to speak but couldn't. He needed all his energy to fight back tears. Finally he whispered, "Josh and his best friend, David, died in a head-on collision last night on their way home from the cinema."

Jane jumped up, threw her arms around him and, not saying a word, held him. He responded eagerly and affectionately. Holding each other, they both cried. Who knows? If I had let myself go, I might have shed some tears as well. When they both regained composure, Jane sat down again.

Nobody spoke.

After a while, continually wiping his eyes, Armand added, "a drunk driver swerved into their lane."

Remembering his easy-going purpose explanation of our truck wheel encounter, the first thought coming into my mind was, 'so, mister, how do you fit that into your spiritual dimension of purpose?' An insensitive thought at this moment of devastation in the man's life, I know. But, that was my thought. Of course, I didn't speak it. Instead I said, "How awful. I hope they got the drunk. Better still, I hope he killed himself too."

"His truck was demolished. He suffered only minor injuries. Poor man! He won't be able to live with himself for the rest of his life."

"Poor man?" I softly hissed, barely able to suppress the anger instantly rising up within me. "You mean, the drunken bastard."

"Do you know why he was drunk?" Armand asked in a monotone voice, seemingly getting better control over his emotions.

"Do I want to know? Do I need to know? Isn't drunk driving enough of a stupidity regardless of any possible excuse? It's a criminal offense!"

"Remember the name you gave the elderly couple that wouldn't react to our antics when we sang Blue Christmas? You called them deadbeats. I later met the man. He apologized. The morning they passed us, they had learned that the wife had advanced ovarian cancer and only a short time to live."

"So, what are you saying?"

"Chris; who can judge? The morning of the accident, this so-called drunken bastard may have had his life ruined by a letter from Revenue Canada. A cheater chaser, in order to secure back taxes from many years, may have put a lien on his property, his assets, and his bank account. He could be a small businessman struggling to make ends meet. Maybe he hadn't declared his income for all those years—which, I agree, would be very wrong—and was caught at last."

"Ar . . . man . . . d," I said, pronouncing the name very slowly, trying hard to further suppress my increasing anger. "How can you think that way? Nothing can justify drunk driving. Not even such a letter. Besides, we all must pay taxes. The country couldn't function without a tax system."

"I agree." He paused. He had his answer ready. It was as if I saw it on his lips. But his emotions were in the way again. Some people behind us were laughing heartily about a loonie that had fallen on the floor, and was rolling away from them.

"Yes, Chris, the tax system distributes perfect justice. But it has no mercy."

Chewing nails by now, completely focused on my inner rage, I forgot about the bad news we were dealing with. Aggressively I replied, "Mercy, come on man. How can you try to justify this killer? Why should tax evaders be shown mercy? They use the highways, the medical system, federal and provincial parks. They expect full police and fire protection. Yet, they wilfully and intentionally close their minds to how these services came to be, and how they're maintained and financed."

He looked at me for a while. While blowing his nose long and slowly, he even tried looking me straight in the eyes. Then he said, "Chris, can you see any similarity between tax evaders and people who breathe air, drink water, eat food grown from the ground, soak up sunshine for life and health, and wilfully and intentionally close their mind to how these wonderful things came to be, and how they're maintained?"

Realizing what was happening, desperately trying to cool my boiling blood, I breathed deeply. Then, speaking somewhat slower and softer, I replied, "Armand, this is wrong. We have to change the subject. I know that you're hinting at me wilfully and intentionally closing my mind to a possible God to whom I need to pay tribute. But, you're getting under my skin. We're into a full blown argument while you are overwhelmed with grief. Let's focus on this painful news and on your sorrow, please."

It took a while before I managed to bring my voice back to normal and asked, "Being all by yourself, you must have an awful time trying to deal with this. How's your family coping? What can we do to help? It's such a senseless loss. How . . ." It seemed the question came out without me formulating it. Luckily the words sounded calm and friendly. "How can there possibly be a reasonable purpose for this?"

Armand did not respond. Staring at the floor, he was unsuccessfully fighting back more tears. Again Jane stood up. She leaned over to him and, once more, wrapped her arms gently around him, saying, "Well, well, Armand. Remember how you wanted to hug us last week because we were uptight about the religion stuff? Now I want to hug *you*. And not just hug you. I want to take away your pain, bring Josh back to life; undo the terrible thing that happened. But I can't. All I can do is tell you that we want to be there for you. Right now, allow me to comfort you."

Again he responded by tightly clasping her arms.

"Listen, Armand," I said, in order to let him know my hostility had ebbed, "I know you like honesty. Remember how you told us, during our Toronto visit, that compassion seemed to well up inside you when you saw those beggars. I couldn't relate to that. Now I can. When you just called that drunken killer 'the poor man', your unreasonable compassion triggered in me the same response as it did then. The same resentment, bordering on hatred, welled up within me. Your kind of compassion seems unworkable, ridiculous—even stupid. I just can't find the words to tell you how repugnant it appears to me. Yet my mind wants to override these feelings. I want to weigh your words, give them thought. But the resentment welling up is just too strong."

"Beautiful," Armand slowly replied while Jane let go of him. Regaining his composure, he even had sympathy in his voice when he added, "Thank you for this honest sharing, Chris. I'm not trying to justify Josh's killer. As I understand it, you and I are both experiencing how the spirit of mercy and the spirit of judgment are vying for our heart, mind, and soul. With our free will, we choose which one is allowed to reign in us. When I allow the spirit of mercy to express itself through me, I speak with care, compassion, and acceptance. When I allow the spirit of judgment to express itself through me, I voice anger, hatred, and resentment.

"But . . . , you're right. We should change the subject. I'm sick with grief. Paul is picking me up tomorrow. The funeral is on Monday. I want to get back to my apartment to get ready. I'll get in touch when I return."

"Wait Armand, wait," I pleaded. We're willing to drive you to Detroit. Aren't we Jane?"

Jane nodded.

"Call Paul. Tell him we'll bring you. We'll stay in a hotel. If it's okay with your family, we will be honoured to meet them and attend the funeral. After the funeral, you decide. You can drive back with us or, if you want to stay, Paul can drive you home later. What do you say?"

"That's too much to accept. But . . . , it would be a blessing for Paul."

"Here's my cell; call him right now."

"I'd rather call from my apartment because I will cry a lot."

"What time do you want to leave, Armand?"

"Nine-thirty would suit me best. You know why?"

"I do. You want to have breakfast at your father's house first. But wouldn't he want to come as well?"

"He will. He has his own ways."

"You're as evasive about your father as you are about your religion. Can't you tell us straight? What's the scoop with this mystery senior?"

"I will, in due time."

"Okay; I'll lay off. Do you need help packing?"

"No, my Personal Support Worker is coming back this afternoon. Thanks for doing this for me. It's an answer to prayer."

Armand backed away from the bistro table. He hesitated.

"We'll be spending much time together in the car," he thoughtfully said. "If God-talk makes you uneasy, you two lead the conversation. This last decade, the spiritual realm has become more real to me than the physical one. I cannot see anymore how anything can be fully understood without studying the interconnectedness and dependency of the two.

"And, Chris," he drew back to the table again. "About a possible purpose for the death of Josh and David, only God knows for sure. My speculation is this: The relationship of these two young men with the God they believed in was, at this moment in their lives, probably as intimate as it would ever be. Maybe God picked these two precious fruits, so to speak, when they were ripe. Both were going to university in the fall. In those surroundings, their pure faith would have been severely challenged. God, knowing past, present, and future, may have known it wouldn't have survived as pure. Maybe they were called home before any spiritual damage could be done. And the family? I know; Sandra will have a terrible time at first. Then she will hopefully take Jason, Rachel's boyfriend, under her wings. By showing him her faith, she may be able to lead him into a relationship with the higher power which he presently does not have. And Paul? Paul is going to church to please his wife. Sitting beside her, he probably still thinks cars and profits. I'm sure, one day he'll ask me how I cope with this terrible loss. At that time, my answers might help *him* to seek a real relationship with his maker. But my talk, about a personal relationship with a God you don't believe exists, must sound like Chinese. If you see life as a string of accidentals from beginning to end, my words probably sound ridiculous."

Struggling hard again with his emotions, Armand backed away more, and pointed his scooter to the exit. Looking at Jane, he mustered a smile and said, "Thanks for hugging me. Remember how, on our Toronto trip, you didn't want to open your can of worms? And remember the laughter of my fishing trip with Josh? Nothing would make Josh happier than to see the same joy he had, bubble up within *you*. Think about it. Maybe, while driving to Detroit, we could find a way of dealing with your worms."

With Armand gone, we lingered, not speaking a word, both absorbed in thoughts. I wanted to ask about her horror story, but didn't. She was grieving. I'm not much for grieving. The death and destruction we daily see on T.V. makes me think; join the club. Since my dad died, life hasn't brought *me* any joy. Hearing about misery simply affirms my outlook. Life is cruel. It has no meaning and it is hopeless for many. I looked at Jane. What if a drunk killed her while she was driving home from shopping? I stood up. She did too. As we headed out, she gently took my hand. Making sure she wouldn't notice; I swallowed the lump in my throat.

Then I had this strange thought. On a possible day of judgment, what would a possible God make the sky look like: cry-baby blue, homey orange or morbid mauve?

13

CHAOS

"WELL, IT'S ONLY ONE worm. But it's gruesome," Jane blurted, in response to Armand's query of, "Are you ready to open your can of worms?"

"And," she hastily added, "I don't think, any fancy excuse you can come up with is gonna do it for me. Claiming to be religious, and burning a young woman at the stake, that's like bringing hell to earth."

Thank God the heavy silence was broken. While driving from Nimidimin to the Highway that would take us to Detroit, it hadn't been easy to keep things light. At first, Armand had shared his telephone conversation with Paul, Sandra, Rachel, and Rob. Helping them deal with their pain, deep sorrow, and shock about losing precious Josh, had kept him on the phone for over two hours. In discussing the arrangements for the funeral, the decision had been made to have one service for both families. Sandra's church was big enough.

But, after this sharing, Armand had slipped into a quiet, meditative, mode. Even though he had suggested the night before to, maybe, open up Jane's can of worms, the right moment never seemed to come. The prospect of coughing up the horror story she had kept to herself all those years, had given Jane a bad night's sleep. 'Was I mad, about her not sharing it with me earlier in life,' she'd asked. Sure, I was ticked off, but curious at the same time. With Josh's death and Armand's sadness hanging over her head, however, I didn't want to rock the boat. So, when Armand finally half turned to Jane, sitting behind me in the back, and asked the long awaited question, I sighed with relief. But, he did not respond.

"Well, sorry, Armand, I thought you knew Joan's story," mustered Jane after a moment of silence.

"I do, Jane."

"*I* don't. Can one of you, please, fill *me* in?"

Jane, probably working through her lifelong, pent-up emotions, kept silent. I became impatient, opened my mouth again, and then Armand turned to face me and quietly started, "Joan of Arc was a young French girl; she was beautiful, and spiritual. She was able to silently speak with God and hear his response in her heart. According to the story, God told devout Joan to go and fight for her country. This was in the early fourteen hundreds, when France was occupied by the English. Brave Joan, obedient to God's prompting, commandeered the fighting men to great victories that freed her country. But, after all battles were won, the religious leaders arrested her. They put her in an iron cage; chained her by the neck, hands, and feet; made her stand trial and judged her a witch. After all, God doesn't talk to people. God had never talked to them, and they were the theologians and the leaders of the faith. If she claimed to have heard a supernatural voice, it must have been the devil. So, they burned Joan at the stake."

Amazing! Mr. Armand knows everything about the horrible things done, being done and, without a doubt, still to be done in the name of religion; yet he still thinks it's fascinating.

"Yes," Jane sighed with a shiver. "They burned her at the stake. Imagine being roasted alive. You stand there, tied up, unable to move. You hear flames crackling all around you. You inhale black, burning, smoke. You feel the excruciating pain of your feet getting scorched. You can't lift them. Then your legs. Your dress gets on fire. You scream, and you scream, and the people around you laugh and cheer. Horrible! My grandma kept filling in all sorts of gory details until I started yelling, begging her to stop. Then she warned me. Never, ever, get involved with religion, or you may get burned as well."

"Yes," Armand said reflectively. "It's sad but true. Throughout history, so-called religious people have been guilty of incomprehensible atrocities. In Joan's time the strings of politics and religion were mostly pulled by one and the same institution: the Church. And, as the saying goes, 'power corrupts, absolute power corrupts absolutely.'"

"Are you saying only Catholics burn people?" Jane asked, sounding almost relieved.

"No, I'm not saying that. Nobody knows all the evil that so-called religious people of all persuasions have done, are doing, and still will be doing to one another in the future. What we do know is that, because of religion, people have been hacked to death with axes, stabbed to death with knives, thrown from cliffs or high towers, and intentionally been trampled by angry mobs. But customs have changed. In this day and age, the religiously deranged seem to prefer suicide bombings, mass executions, or letting millions of people rot in refugee camps. Even today, everywhere in this world, hundreds of thousands of people are harassed, persecuted and killed because of their personal faith commitment. As I said before, many who claim to understand their faith are often glaringly ignorant about it.

"The only good thing about Joan's story is: twenty four years after her martyr's death, the Church owned up to its inexcusable mistake. They reversed Joan's verdict, and declared her a saint."

"Well . . . , how are we supposed to know; whether those religious guys are making mistakes or not? And, how're we supposed to know when they're speaking the truth or telling lies?"

"It's not easy. To develop a feel for that, a person needs to understand the difference between religion and spirituality. But, I think it's time for a breather. If you feel you've gotten rid of your ugly worm, we could be quiet for a while."

And so we were.

*   *   *

Feeling for Armand, and afraid he would slide back into sadness again, it was I who eventually broke the silence. "Remember, Armand, how you in your search story got hung up on two big questions? The one was about the two-faced character of God; his judgment and his mercy. You found an answer to that and labeled it 'complementary duality.' The other question was about the great confusion over our many thousands of different religions. Did you ever find an answer to that one?"

"I did. But, before you let me get carried away on the subject, I want you to know, my Off-button is sound sensitive. Simply say, 'STOP' if you want me to stop."

"Does the Go-button work the same?"

"Yes."

"Okay, GO," I replied while inconspicuously pressing to 'go' button on my recording device as well. I had hoped that, by asking a religion question, his mind would not focus on his loss of Josh.

No such luck.

"You know, while we were quiet, I remembered how, one day, Josh and I had been looking at pictures of the cosmos. The incredible images of star clusters, super nova, galaxies, nebulae, and all sorts of other wonders shown on their big plasma screen were overwhelming. When finished watching, Josh suggested we make some music, as we often did together. He sat down at the piano, was still for a few moments, then he played the hymn 'How Great Thou Art.'"

Softly but firmly Armand began to sing. Tears welled up in his eyes.

I'd heard the hymn in my stepfather's church. It's about God, and how great he is for making stars, and all other natural phenomena, like rolling thunder. Some women would use that song to show off their ability to reach the high note, optional at the end of the last refrain. Instead of gently touching on it, they would wail it.

Armand sang the first verse. I couldn't help but shake my head again. My mind couldn't fathom how this man, having lost his beloved grandson in a stupid, senseless accident, could declare God to be great. After he finished the first verse, he softly recited the refrain. Then he sang the second verse,

"When through the woods and forest glades I wonder,
I hear the birds sing sweetly in the trees,
when I look down from lofty mountain grandeur,
and hear the brook and feel the gentle breeze."

We waited. He didn't start the refrain. Instead he said, "Yes, Josh and I loved roaming the woods. He'd always be looking for a high tree to climb. Together we'd climb hills, throw sticks in fast running creeks to see whose stick was fastest. Yes. And then I lost my legs. Now I've lost Josh."

Armand and Josh, my dad and I . . . what else did we have in common?

Jane put her hand on Armand's shoulder. Both reached for the tissues.

"But," he suddenly and resolutely remarked, "let me focus on the good times we've had. It was one of those good times with Josh that brought the answer to my question about religious confusion.

"One afternoon, Josh was over for a visit. Sonnetta had a hair appointment. We decided to dazzle her, on her return, with a seven course vegetarian dinner. We'd have an appetizer, vegetable soup, an exquisite salad, a bean and nut dish with three vegetables, a fruit cocktail, apple crumble, and a cheese plate with chocolate-dipped strawberries. We started by cleaning the veggies and the fruit. It wasn't long before the kitchen counter was covered with pieces of broccoli, cauliflower, radishes, green onions, green and red pepper, zucchini, cucumber, carrots, apples, mushrooms, berries, you name it. But, while my hands were busy, and I chatted with Josh, my mind was pondering loftier matters. Interwoven with thoughts on the physics theory of chaos,

I was milling over the religious-confusion issue again. Jane, tell me when I lose you.

"This theory deals with closed systems in a state of chaos. Scientists use the word system for anything, from a leaking tap to a galaxy. The weather is a good example. It is classified chaotic because it has the three characteristics specific for chaotic systems. First, it is sensitive to initial conditions. A very small change may lead to a drastically different path of development. Theoretically, even the flap of any flying creature's wing could change its course. Second, it is governed by anywhere from two to many causes. Third, it feeds back on itself. Whatever the weather is at any given moment is the input for the next. And, I believe, religion is influenced in the same three ways. Are you still with me?"

"NO!" Jane bluntly replied. "Do I have to understand it all to get the drift? But never mind me. Just keep going. Who knows, maybe I'll catch on near the end. If not, Chris will have to repeat it, when we get home."

"So, here I was, looking at our chaotic vegetable/fruit counter, and pondering this theory. Suddenly it hit me. This was our kitchen and our counter. We had allowed this chaos to happen. But . . . no sweat! We knew the purpose of every veggie and every fruit. Sometime soon, this chaos would come together in a beautiful seven course dinner. Could it be, I asked myself, that a possible God, in his universe and on his earth, has allowed this religious chaos to happen? No sweat for him either. He knows the purpose of every train of thought. He knows, in the end, this religious chaos will come together into one beautiful, all-embracing, spiritual banquet. And the most amazing thing about chaos is: the state it can ultimately evolve into can be simple. Physicists call this final state 'the attractor.'

"Then, because I got excited, I asked myself out loud, causing Josh to stop slicing the red pepper, 'Could it be that our religious chaos, ultimately, also has an attractor, a 'Divine Attractor'? Yes, I had already christened it. Could a Divine Attractor be the catalyst of all of mankind's beliefs?

"We finished the seven course dinner. It was a great success. But, through it all, I had to forcefully control myself not to walk out of the dinner project, leave Josh alone, and start my search for this Divine Attractor. Are you catching some of my excitement?"

"Sounds interesting," is all I could say. Jane remained silent.

"What are you thinking, Jane?" Armand asked

"I think we should stop for coffee. I saw a sign telling a highway rest station is coming up. My system needs time to digest your seven course dinner chaos. Besides," she hesitated. "I hope Chris got it. He'll have to rehash it later. But, do me a favour, Armand. Please tell me, in plain English, what's the bottom-line of all this."

"The bottom line, Jane, is a twofold question. 'Could what we see as religious chaos, in reality be a wide spectrum of spiritual understandings? And, could this entire spectrum be brought together into one simple principle, which I named Divine Attractor?"

"What exactly do you mean by spiritual understandings?"

"It's the understandings religions have about spiritual issues relating to a possible God, the cosmos, and our human relationship with both."

While pushing Armand's wheelchair through the open door of the highway restaurant, Jane replied, "Is that the same as what I call 'horse-feathers?'"

It was uplifting to hear Armand laugh. We had almost forgotten we were on our way to a very sad funeral.

14

ATTRACTOR

"WELL, TELL ME," JANE asked Armand, even before I turned the key after our highway rest station break. "What's the purpose of me being dumb for lack of education and, forgetful now that I'm getting old?"

While helping Armand out of his wheelchair, and back into the passenger seat, she had noticed a truck driver giving his truck the once-over. Remembering the wheel that was on-the-loose during our Toronto trip, and still questioning Armand's conviction that everything has a purpose, Jane just had to pose that question.

"Jane, we can only speculate. Where your lack of education is concerned, every person has a different purpose. At the end of our earthly life, all we can do is ask ourselves; 'have I fulfilled my purpose?' But, that question only makes sense if we believe everything does have a purpose.

"About losing your memory? I can see some benefit in that for older people. It forces them to diminish their reliance on their mind, and become more sensitive to inner promptings. And, it also cuts down on possible pride because they become more dependent on others. But, again, to accept this, a person needs to believe in the reality of the soul/self."

"Soul/self? What's the diff between soul and soul/self? And how do I know I even have such a thing?"

"Jane, I love how you mince no words. My understanding is that you don't *have* a soul. You *are* the soul/self. You, in harmony with your body and its brain for processing the lessons you need to learn, are expected to fulfill your personal purpose. Your body is a small, wonderfully-intricate galaxy, of which the soul/self is lord and master. Your brain is the computer that controls every atom in your body and their interactions with every other atom. It also controls your galaxy's interaction with other galaxies—other humans. Your brain receives, stores, and processes all the data entering your body through its sensors. When I say an understanding should ring true in your heart, I really mean, it should ring true in your soul/self."

"Well, imagine I accept all that. Then, tell me, what, according to your understanding, is the purpose of this Jane-person sitting behind you in this 72-year-old body, desperately trying to use her mushy brain?"

"As I understand it, Jane, you are not *one* person but *three*."

"Well, well, well! Three Janes? Tell me about them."

"Jane one is the person your body projects to the outside world. It's the easy-going, down-to-earth, no-nonsense Jane.

"Jane two is the person your mind makes you aware you are. It's the insecure, hungry for affirmation and sensitive Jane.

"Jane three is the Jane as she is known in love by her creator.

"This trinity concept may sound strange to you. I struggled with it too. But, once I accepted its reality, I saw how this understanding affirms the belief that we are created in the image of our creator. He projects Himself outward as the Christ, in the person of Jesus. He knows Himself, as the great 'I AM.' And, His Spirit bonds these two into one, in wisdom and love.

"The scary part of this understanding is that, if this is true, I am as much an absolute truth as my creator is. Like Him, I, too, am two total opposites existing as one. I am soul/self and I am body. I am a spiritual being as well as a physical being.

"Realizing this, I dared to ask the question, 'If this possible God is real and I am real, what kind of relationship would I want to have with Him? Would I want to be His slave? Would I want to be His servant? Would I want to be a fully awake but indistinguishable part of Him? Would I want to be just a human being with a good attitude? Would

I want to be a member of a chosen race, excluding the rest of mankind? Or, did I dare to dream big and desire to be or become a little god myself, a child of God, his son? And for you, Jane, that, of course, means His daughter."

"Well, what did you choose?"

"If I answer that, you'll ask why. Then I have to explain my choice, which will bring us right back to my search for the Divine Attractor."

We either let him do his whole spiel from start to finish, I thought, or he'll keep evading issues. Ah well. I'll just let Jane deal with it. She's asking the right questions. At least, with Armand talking about his favourite subject, his mind will not be occupied with Josh's death. But this Divine Attractor business may be too much for Jane. Lucky for her, my recorder is humming.

"Well, I bet, when you start digging into this tractor-stuff, it'll be way over my head."

"The word is '*At*tractor'. But don't feel bad. Both words are derived from the same Latin word 'trahere', which means draw. And yes, it may be a bit heavy at times. But we still have a couple of hours before we hit Detroit. What do you think? Would it not be a good idea to fill your brain cells, the ones that were taken up by fear of religion, with better understandings?"

"I've always wanted to learn stuff but never had the opportunity. And, you're right, we do have time. But, please, keep it simple. And, don't get upset when I shout to activate your stop-button."

"Certainly not. Keep me in check. It's easy for me to get carried away. Apart from Sonnetta and Josh, no one else ever listened to my ideas.

"As you probably know; the number seven often shows up in the physical world. Seven colours of visible light, a seven-year cycle of the renewal of our body tissues, etc. So, I wasn't surprised to find there are seven major religions: Hinduism, Judaism, Buddhism, Confucianism, Taoism, Christianity, and Islam.

"When Sonnetta and I started our search for truth, we focused on finding a display of God's power in whatever religious gathering it would manifest itself. However, to find the Divine Attractor, I focused on finding the bottom line in each religion. But, right from the start, I discovered that not only the entire religious scene is one big chaos; every single religion on its own is chaos as well. What did I expect? On my kitchen counter, there was only one kind of tomato. But there are cherry tomatoes, currant tomatoes, gold nugget tomatoes, and many other varieties. It's the same with religions. My first job, therefore, was to look for the main focus of each religion, hoping it would help me in my search for this Divine Attractor.

"Islam, the youngest of the seven, was founded by an uneducated camel merchant named Mohammed. Born in 570 CE, in what is now known as Saudi Arabia, he became disturbed, while growing up, with the way priests of the existing polytheistic religion manipulated the people. His followers believe he received a vision from the angel Gabriel who told him there is only one God and His name is Allah.

"After I studied the Holy Qu'ran—Islam's Holy Book—it seemed obvious that 'submission', which is what the word Islam means, is the attribute every Muslim needs to strive for. It seemed reasonable to me, therefore, to conclude that Islam's bottom line was 'submission to Allah.'

"Christianity, the second youngest religion, is chaos supreme. There are too many different denominations to count. It receives its name from the son of a Jewish carpenter who, as his followers believe, was 'The Christ,' meaning, 'anointed one of God.' Known as Jesus, he preached neighbourly love, honesty and obedience to the laws God had handed down, 1500 years before his birth, to Moses, a descendant of Israel. Jesus claimed to be God's son. Christians believe he came from heaven to earth to lay down his life to save all mankind from the consequence of sin. The scholars of his day judged this idea blasphemous and they pressured the Roman authorities into crucifying him."

"Stop! What do you mean by sin?"

"To sin is to wilfully think, speak or act against the will of God."

"So, what's the consequence of sin we humans need to be saved from?"

"According to Christians, Jews and Muslims, the ultimate consequence of sin is eternal damnation in a place called hell. And whoever has a concept of this possible hell, should find it attractive to be saved from it."

"What's your idea?"

"Jane, if I'd elaborate on that, we'd be into information overload again. How about we first finish my search for the Divine Attractor?"

Jane is needling him good. She should have been around when I was still living with my stepfather. He certainly would not have evaded the hell issue. He would have given her a description that would have made Joan of Arc burning at the stake look like the dying flame of a tea light. But then, who knows? Armand may have some horror ideas about this hell as well.

"So, because Jesus allowed himself to be crucified, to pay the price for mankind's sin, I concluded the bottom line of Christianity most likely is sacrificial love.

"Taoism, the third youngest religion, was founded in 600 B.C. by a man named Lao Tzu. His name means 'Old Philosopher'. He taught that humans can remake their world by more closely following the way of the cosmos which he called 'The Way.' This led me to believe that 'searching for The Way,' could be the bottom line of Taoism.

"Confucianism was founded by Confucius. He . . ."

"STOP! Confusion! You're right. Confusion is what all this stuff sounds like to me. And how come you, at 84, remember these things, while I, at 72, have already forgotten most of what you've just said. Honestly, Armand, what you're spouting are just words to me. It's as if you're feeding me veggies while I'm hungry for meat. What do I care about smart, holy men who lived thousands of years ago? You have to understand, Armand, while I'm half listening, my mind is busy with my own issues. I'm sitting here in the back seat of this car, on my way to the funeral of your grandson. When I get there, I may be crying more than your daughter. She has faith. If Chris died like that, I'd fall apart. To me, dead is dead. For your family things are different; you believe in life after death."

"Yes, Sandra and Rachel believe the two boys are in heaven with Jesus."

"Well, there you have it. Why wouldn't they be with this Mohammed or with Mr. Tao, or with that confused guy?"

"Confucius."

"Whatever! Seven good men that started religions. Why doesn't anybody believe they're all in the same place welcoming us all?"

Wow, my Jane is on a roll. The last time I saw her tenacious like that was when our good friend, Jerry, tried to convince us the American moon-landing had been faked. 'Like how can a flag move in the breeze on a moon where there is no air?' He had argued. 'And how come the pictures they took never showed any stars?' Jane just wouldn't lay off. She kept firing questions, trying to poke holes in his theory. Only later did we learn the flag wasn't flapping, but moving slightly, because the astronauts had just touched it. And the stars didn't register because the moon reflects a lot of light, and the pictures were taken with super high resolution cameras.

"The answer to the question, 'why Sandra and Rachel believe Josh and his friend are with Jesus,' is; these boys invited Jesus into their heart at some point in their life. To your question of, 'why don't people believe that all the founders of religions end up in the same place after death,' I have no answer. Almost every religious person believes that anyone, who does not believe as he or she does, loses out on eternal life. So, nobody knows for sure?"

"Well then, what in all this religious bickering is for sure?"

"Religious bickering will probably never end. Inner assurance of spiritual realities, however, can come to anyone. When the soul/self desires to be a channel for divine mercy and opens its mind to an ever increasing intimacy with the divine, the divine will respond in kind."

"Well, whatever. My head feels like a jack-o-lantern with a fat candle burning inside it, and no holes to let the heat out. This spiritual stuff is too much for me. And, I hate to ask the question . . . but, if every believer believes that he or she knows things for sure, and yet they all believe different stuff, what makes your daughter's faith so special?"

"Jane, stop it!" I almost shouted. I thought we had enough. At least I had. I must change the subject. How about mentioning the moon landing?

"At times," Armand continued, giving me no chance to stop him, "Sandra has doubts about faith issues too. Josh had doubts. After he'd given his heart to Jesus, he questioned his so-called born again event. But, I believe, spiritual growth only comes by dealing courageously with the challenges thrown at us by 'the Accuser.'"

"The who?"

"Remember how I shared about mercy and judgment vying for the human heart? When anyone's soul/self starts leaning towards mercy, an inner voice starts pestering that person's mind with judgments. Day and night, it will stir up accusations from within. And, through the mouths of other people, it will rain judgments on that person from outside as well.

"That, Jane, is the voice of the Accuser."

15

ACCUSER

I AGREE; I LOST IT. On our way home from the funeral, about an hour east of Windsor, my anger got the better of me. Armand had stayed behind. It was just Jane and me. Out of the blue, Jane switched off the radio and said, "Well, I wanna talk." But we seldom talk when we drive. We let the chatterboxes on the air take care of that.

"What you wanna talk about?" I asked. Then the fireworks began. As if I was a dummy at a shooting range, she began firing annoying questions at me, all related to the funeral.

'What did you think of the service? Did you get touched by that song about God being a shepherd? Didn't you feel like crying when Armand played his clarinet solo to honour the boys? How did you like the sermon? Wasn't the pastor nice?' However, it was her last question, 'How about we try and find a nice church to go to sometime?' That did it.

It all started on the day of the funeral. We arrived at Sandra's Church more than half an hour before the service. Already then, we had to park many streets over. If Jane hadn't fussed forever and a day with her hair, we could have been earlier. Our hotel was ten minutes away. Besides, we had been awake all night anyway. At home, we sleep with a window open. In this place, the one small window, meant to give fresh air, was riveted shut.

Then, while walking from where we had to park to the church, Jane threw a fit. Intimidated by the highest church steeple she'd ever seen—eighty-five meters high, the tallest in the land, as we learned at the social afterwards—she needed a calming pill. After rummaging through her big, confusing purse for about as long as she had needed for her hair, she found the pillbox, took three, and clasped my arm. True, this Detroit landmark, built of limestone quarried in Canada, was an edifice of Gothic Revival grandeur. But, I mean, who cares. It was just another fancy building. I guess it was the entering through the massive, wide-open, oak doors that she dreaded. For her it was like stepping into another world. It was the first time in her life she had set foot in a church. Her jaw dropped. Mine did too. The entire front wall was covered with row above row of different-sized organ pipes. The crescent-shaped balcony, completely filled with people, and adorned with flags of many countries, made the place look like a theatre. As I looked up at the ornate hammer beams supporting a roof which, as we also heard at the social, was exceeded in width only by Westminster Hall in London, even I had to say, "WOW.' It's unbelievable what humans can build to honour a God they believe in.

Armand had insisted we sit with his family. But I knew, not having been in a church for over fifty years, and with Jane being a stranger to it altogether, we would be uncomfortable. We preferred sitting incognito.

The usher showed us a seat somewhere in the middle. That's when things began to irk me good. He tried to cram one extra person in every pew, regardless of anyone's bulk. The fat lady beside Jane—a down-the street neighbour of a friend of Josh's friend David's Aunt, as she confided to Jane—wiped her eyes every few minutes. I never saw a tear though. And a family of five, sitting behind us, talked incessantly, right up till the two coffins were carried in by classmates. Even then the mother kept whispering to her grown kids. Definitely annoying! But it was the sermon that really got me going. To use an Armand kind of metaphor, it unplugged my inner geyser of anger. Somehow able to control the spurt, I remained sensitive to the pain and sadness of my surroundings. But when Jane, on the way home, started firing her questions, the geyser had to have its way.

The pastor's talk had brought back memories from a funeral service for my best friend's mother. She died of cancer when I was sixteen. My holy stepfather went through his spiel, thanking God for taking this woman into his glory because she had been a follower of Jesus. Then, to remind me again of my dad's lot, he rubbed it in how those not lined up with Jesus would end up in the everlasting fire. While he was still hammering away at it, I snuck out a side door. The sickening injustice of this God he believed in was too much for me. To allow this woman to be happy for eternity while tormenting my dad forever in unquenchable fire was not only unjust, it was unforgivably cruel. As I walked circles around the church, I cried and swore. The deep, burning anger born in my heart that day, and directed at this God and his henchman, my stepfather, had never left me. True, Sandra had assured us at the social that this pastor opens the car door for his wife. He stands in line at gatherings to get her coffee. He puts his arm gently around her when they talk with members of their congregation. Yes, *their* congregation. But, what's the difference? Genuine pastor or freak in shepherd's clothing, all believe in the same vindictive God who is merciless concerning those who don't belong to the Jesus-club. No matter how exemplary their life has been, he burns them. My dad always opened and closed mom's car door gently. He opened every door for her. He often tenderly rubbed her cheek when she was stressed. When she was busy, he helped her so she'd have quality time as well. Not my holy stepfather. He expected to be served, hand and feet, as soon as he stepped in the door. And now, my own wife was charmed by this pastor, who was as personable as my stepfather had been. To her suggestion of finding a nice church, where we can worship this people-burning God, my answer was, 'No way. No way! No way! And . . . NO WAY!'

"It's always the same with you," I snapped. "You talk, while you don't have a clue what you're babbling about."

"Well, what's wrong with finding a nice church community? I'm sure Armand belongs to one."

Armand! Yes; Armand! It's because of him we're in this fight.

"Listen, woman, your friend Armand also picks up other people's litter, has sympathy for highway murderers, and hugs drug addicts. Is that the lifestyle we're after?"

"Now you're exaggerating. He didn't hug them."

"Pretty close. Anyway, he's starting to rub me the wrong way."

"Well, just remember, buster, you introduced me to the man."

"Yes, I should've said good-bye to him the first time we met. This is the second time you're picking a fight over this church-going nonsense."

"Who's picking a fight? If I feel like going to church: why not?"

"What's come over you? All our married life you've been calling this religion business 'horse-feathers'. Now, all of a sudden, you want to get involved with it. And, how come you coughed up this burning-at-the-stake story so easily for saint Armand? You've never told *me* anything about it. Here we are. Almost forty-five years married, and you're still hiding things from me. What other secrets are you keeping so you can confess them to your holy friend?"

I knew it was my anger that made me unreasonable. But somehow, I just couldn't shake it. It seemed to force itself up and out, from deep within, like a volcano spewing lava. Or was it puss oozing out of a re-opened wound? My mind had become more determined than ever to reject every thought connected with God, church, or religion.

"Well, *you* certainly never encouraged talking religion."

"Hear this! I've never encouraged my wife to talk religion. How was I supposed to know you were sitting on a burning-stake issue? Can't you just volunteer things, if they're such a load? Can't you just speak your mind when you have a problem, instead of waiting for me to second-guess you?

"Anyway, next time I see Armand, I'll tell him. No more religion. I want my peace back."

After a long, tense silence, I started again. "Why don't you say anything? Of course, you don't like the idea of breaking off with him. You like the man. He's a charmer. He had me in his web. But, in that funeral service, I made a firm decision. Religion is not for me. You go ahead. Have coffee with him and listen to his clever arguments. Maybe he'll take you to his church and get you involved with some wonderful, manipulating pastor. I'm quite capable of entertaining myself. I may even like the idea of having some freedom. I could start attending some live baseball or hockey games. Actually, the more I think about it, the better it sounds. You were never interested in any of those things anyway."

"Well, you never told me you like doing stuff like that."

"Did you ever ask me? No, it's always been what you wanted."

"Well, why didn't you speak up? You're right. Here we are: married for decades and still strangers."

"Yes, and now we'll do better still. You, on your own, want to get involved with some church. Who cares if that makes us grow apart even more?"

"Now you're unreasonable. Accusing me of making us grow apart, just because I feel like going to some church, is ridiculous. By doing different things, we'll at least have stuff to talk about."

"Accusing? Who is accusing? All I'm trying to tell you is that I'm not interested in you regurgitating some wonderful, long-winded sermon to me."

"You're talking as if I'm already a nun or something."

"Listen, woman; do what you need to do and, like always, I'll adjust."

"Accusing me of always wanting things my way, that's nasty."

"Nasty? Who's nasty? Who's telling me, in a round-about way, she's going to get her own social life?"

"Now you're really blowing stuff out of proportion. All I asked was, 'How about we find ourselves a nice church community to go to?'"

Deep down I knew; I was fighting this unjust God. My anger was directed at him. Thinking that he, through Jane, was trying to force me into doing things I did not want to do, was too much.

"Yes, and there's your big problem. Do you know what it means to just go to some church? It means you start looking around for a church where you like the pastor. Never mind what he preaches. As long as you like the man, you'll stick to him. Imagine, you start liking a priest. I bet you don't even know the difference between Catholics and Protestants."

"Tell me."

"First of all, according to some people, Catholics aren't even Christians."

"So, what's the big deal? I'm sure Buddhists aren't either."

"Be quiet. I'm trying to tell you something. This is how it is. Protestants believe that every word written in their Bible is a word spoken by their God. They're all free to read that Bible and figure out what God is saying. But Catholics believe those words are in such screwball language, it needs to be interpreted by someone smarter than them. That's why they have popes, bishops, and priests to tell them what to believe or not."

"So your stepfather was a priest."

"What kind of a dumb remark is that? Of course, he wasn't."

"Well, you told me he was always telling everybody what stuff in the Bible meant, and what people should believe or not believe."

"Listen, woman. Drop the stepfather bit. I'm trying to tell you what happens when you like some pastor. First he nails you to attend a mid-week Bible study. Next he'll hook you up with the choir. Then he'll ask you to volunteer for visiting shut-ins. Then he suckers you into helping him out with his social events, bake cookies, decorate the hall, do the dishes, make sandwiches, move the chairs, you name it. Before you know it, you'll pretty well be living in his church. I know. My stepfather was a master manipulator. If he'd been in Jesus' sandals, he would have had high priests, soldiers, and apostles organize fund-raising spaghetti dinners together. So, don't ever tell me again, you just want to find a nice church community.

"I also know, and you better listen to this very carefully . . ." I pounded my right fist on the dashboard out of sheer frustration over my inability to control this anger. Dormant for all those years, it was truly boiling over. Consequently, I jerked the steering wheel. We hit the graveled shoulder. Instead of letting the car ride it out, I over-reacted. I hit the brakes. Dumb. I know. The back wheels slid on the gravel. The car went sideways towards the ditch. Not deep enough to have a guardrail, but deep enough to make a car roll over, the ditch came up fast.

"OH MY GOD!" Jane shouted. Then . . . , a crash and the sound of crumbling metal. Slightly jolted out of my anger, I switched off the engine and stepped out. A kilometre pole had made a lasting impression in the car. But, I thought, these poles were supposed to snap on impact. Whatever! The damage was a deep dent in the right rear door, extending into the gutter-rail. And a right rear fender, jammed against the wheel.

I grabbed a hammer from my emergency kit and began to pound. It felt good. I pounded harder. It felt better. While pounding harder and harder, I realized that, even if I could free the wheel, I needed help to get back on the road. I called for roadside help on my cell, climbed back in, and avoided looking at Jane. She was staring out the window and remained silent.

"If everything has a purpose," I said after a while, forcing myself to speak slowly, "let this remind you, if you want to spoil my mood; all you need to do is start talking about God, church or religion."

16

FRANKIE

WHILE FOLLOWING THE ARROWS to the back door of the boarded-up, white stucco garage, with pieces of stucco missing, I dreaded the thought of going in. A piece of dangling eavestrough almost hit my head. The oversized chopper, with big, worn, leather seat, standing next to a dumpster spilling over with broken pieces of fibreglass and empty resin cans, was no encouragement. And my assumption that the little black flag, hanging limp from the chopper's rear fender, carried the skull and crossbones, made me shake my head. It reminded me of the flags of the world gracing the balcony railing of the Detroit church. That was where my bad luck had started. If there hadn't been a sermon reminding me of my miserable teens, I would not have gotten angry and there would not have been any accident.

When I carefully pushed the backdoor further ajar and looked in, I almost had a heart attack. Seeing a four-hundred-pound-plus, near naked, roman gladiator hunched over a car, I remembered the oversized chopper.

"Come right in," the human mountain thundered. He had spotted me in a mirror hanging from the ceiling. His head, with a greyish pigtail dangling at its side like that loose hanging piece of eaves-trough, was covered with a white polka dotted, red bandana. His body, dressed in flimsy undershirt and boxer shorts, was covered with tattoos and sweat. His biceps and neck were massive and solid, like the lowest branches of a mature oak. They seemed ready to snap the barbed wire tattooed around them.

Slowly, as if suffering from a back problem, he straightened himself out. Then, while turning and showing a big smile, he extended his right hand. Hand? That scooper bucket could have wrung my neck with two of its fingers while straightening my car door's dent with the other three.

"If I scare ya," he said with a laugh, "relax. I don't snack on people between meals." His laugh, and the sparkle darting from his eyes, gave me the courage to let my hand, reluctantly, disappear in his. "I'm Chris," I shyly said. His handshake was surprisingly gentle. "Frankie," he replied.

Frankie was the third body shop owner I visited.

The first body man had been rude. Making clear he was more interested in big insurance jobs, he had quoted a ridiculously high price. The second fellow gave me what seemed like a reasonable estimate. But, his timing was off.

I wanted the job done before Armand's return. I dreaded embarrassing questions. When I explained my hurry, he had sent me to Frankie.

After Frankie let go of my hand, I told him the reason of my visit.

Through a small office, covered with fibreglass dust, and without saying another word, he took me back outside again to assess the damage. Then, still beaming with some sort of happy-go-lucky smile, he asked the most ridiculous question that, I'm sure, has ever come out of the mouth of a biker: "What's your religion, man?"

Instead of speaking my mind and asking the colossus what his dumb question had to do with repairing my car, I realized, in time, I needed the man. So, with as pleasant a voice as I could fake, I replied, "interesting you should ask. I suppose different religions get different pricings."

"No, Sir, I treat everybody the same. I asked because you look like a Buddhist crippled by a heavy karma. But, who was your passenger?"

Slightly relieved by Frankie's explanation, I saw my way out from more dumb religious talk and quickly answered; "My wife. And, I am an atheist."

"Do you love your wife?"

"Of course I do!"

Then, cheer up, man. You need a new back door. If the pole had hit the passenger door, you could've needed a new wife as well." He laughed. I uttered some sort of hiccup.

"Now, for the price . . . ; give me a minute." He guided me back into the workshop, where he let me wait. After I had heard him make a phone call in his office he came out and said, "Let's say, the price depends a bit on how big a hurry you're in."

"The sooner the better."

He stuck his right palm in front of my face. It had numbers scribbled on it. "Here's my quote. If you say 'yes'; I'll get your beast in tomorrow. I'll need it for three days."

His quote was two hundred more than the one I got from the body man who'd sent me there. But, if I made up my mind quickly, Frankie could do it right away.

"If ya wanna think about it," he said, again bending his big frame over the car he'd been working on, "that's fine with me. So, you're an atheist eh?" You believe there ain't no God. How can you be so sure?"

He wasn't giving up. Desperately trying to figure out what tactic to use to cut off the religion nonsense, I replied, "Oh . . . , I don't think about this God-business. I've never seen him. I'm sure you haven't either."

Wrong answer.

"In Florida they have some pesky little bugs. They're called no-see-ums. I've never seen one. Yet, they're there. So, I figure, if there can be critters so small I can't see them, there could be a God so big, I can't see him neither. By the way, my ninth foster father was an atheist. The best foster father I've ever had. We got along great. He was the only one, of the twelve I had, whom I called dad. I was happy to be with him. He let me be Frankie. Not like number eight. He was a Mormon. 'Frankie,' this Mormon kept saying, 'if you try hard, you can be just like Jesus.' But you know something? I didn't wanna be like Jesus. I wanted to be Frankie. I liked myself. True, at times, I could be a mean bastard. But I knew I had a good heart. This Mormon, trying to make me into another Jesus, kept dragging me to his church. But I didn't want it. So, I made life hell for him and his family. That's why I ended up in this atheist home. What relief! But then, this dad got a brain tumour. They gave him three months to live. He was brave. We even joked about death. Then I saw him on his deathbed. That was ugly. Somehow there was a fight going on."

Frankie made as if struggling with his grinder.

"His face contorted." Frankie contorted his face.

"He screamed." Frankie let out a scream.

"He had foam on his mouth. The struggle lasted for over an hour. Then he calmed down." Frankie relaxed, hung the grinder on a hook suspended from the ceiling and, while leaning against the car, folded his arms.

"Some sort of peace came over him. My foster mother later told me, she had been secretly praying for him all her life."

Frankie unhooked the grinder again and switched it on. He had preached his sermon. Now he ignored me completely. It was up to me to ponder his quote and his words.

Unsure as how to break through the grinder's noise, I finally tapped him on the shoulder, making sure to hit his undershirt, not his sweaty skin.

He switched off the grinder and looked up.

"I'll take your offer," I said. "I'll have the car here in the morning." Then, trying to create some goodwill and pretend his preaching hadn't bothered me, I added, "I'm glad you're a happy Buddhist now."

Wrong remark again.

"I'm not a Buddhist. My tenth foster father was a Buddhist. That's how I know all about karma. He tried making me a Buddhist. If it hadn't been for his wife, he would have ended up a dead Buddhist. In those days I had a bad temper. There was no way he was going to make Frankie into an illusion. 'Try hard,' he'd say. 'Wake up to reality. There is no person named Frankie. You and I are one. Together we are one with all there is. We're one with the universe. And, in reality, there is no universe. Everything's an illusion. I'm an illusion. You're an illusion.' Imagine, anybody telling Frankie he's an illusion. But . . . , we've got a deal. See you tomorrow."

"Yes," I replied, glad to be leaving the place. Then, suddenly, the words 'bad temper' replayed in my mind. What if this giant does a lousy job? What if I need to draw his attention to it? Hesitantly I ventured, "How is your temper these days?"

He laughed again. "Completely gone," he said. "And you know, Mr., if you weren't an atheist, you'd probably love to hear my story. But, I've promised this car—he pointed to the car he was working on—to be ready tomorrow. I gotta quit talking and get to work. See ya in the morning."

His giant, sweaty paw reached for my white, small, office hand. "By the way," he said, "if you can arrange it some day, try to be at the deathbed of one of your atheist buddies. It might make you think. Seeing how my foster dad struggled on his deathbed gave me the creeps. It made me figure, there must be more to dying then meets the eye."

As I stepped out the back door, walked by the dumpster and the chopper, and climbed into my car, I remembered a suggestion made by Armand. He once said, 'Imagine, with far-fetched imagining, you are a physicist living some three thousand years ago.' How about imagining, with far-fetched imagining, I had known what I was in for when I offered to drive Armand to Detroit. In his spiritual dimension of purpose, you could say my intent was good. But, the consequence most certainly did stink. To get the fibreglass smell out of my clothes and off my skin would take standing in the wind for a week. I opened the three functioning car windows. So, this foster dad had a struggle on his deathbed. He probably didn't want to die. Who does? Nobody wants to die. Not even the churchy people.

They're sure those two boys are in a better place. Yet they cry and mourn like non-believers. How come they're not dancing in the isles, happy for those two lucky fellows who made it? It's because they're just speculating. They know; it's misery here on earth. So they dream of a better place out there . . . up high . . . wherever. Anyway, how on earth am I going to find a dying atheist who'll let me sit at his bedside? Let alone one who has been secretly prayed for?

*   *   *

Wednesday, February 8, 2012

I paid the cab that dropped me off at Frankie's. Spotting my fixed car, I went over to check the repair. The damage was invisible. An amazing job.

Frankie sat down behind his desk, on a double car seat mounted on two chair frames, and handed me the bill. I wiped the fibreglass dust from the only real chair and pulled up. As I started to write the check, he said, "Wait! I'll make you a deal. The other day you asked about my temper. If you wanna know what happened to it, you should come hear my testimony. Three weeks from this coming Sunday, I'm telling the folks in the Christian Fellowship Church how my life was changed. You're an atheist. You've probably never set foot in a church. So, I'm making you an offer. I know my price was two hundred higher than my buddy's. He called me right after you'd left him and told me. Now, I'm suggesting you write two checks: one for two hundred and one for the balance. I'll rip up the two hundred one after my testimony, if you show up with two more people to listen to it. How's that for a quick buck? When was the last time you made two hundred bananas just sitting on your fanny?"

Dumbfounded at Frankie's unexpected proposal, I quickly replied.

"No. That's not my style. Thanks for the offer. It's very generous. But I've heard enough church stories in my life. They don't do much for me. I'm happy for you though. I'm sure it's nice to be rid of your temper. I bet, with your muscles, it could get you into a lot of trouble."

"Yes, it has. My temper would flare up like a tempest. Whenever I thought I wasn't treated right, BANG." He lightly hit the desk with his fist. "I'd be like a cork jumping out of a champagne bottle. If you've never had a temper, it's hard to understand. My atheist dad understood. He had a streak of it himself. I guess *you* never had one."

"Ah, well, sometimes I do, just a bit. And . . . you got rid of yours, eh? Just like that. Interesting! Anyway, I'd rather write the whole check."

"So you're happy with my work?"

"Yes, as far as I can see you deserve the money, you did a great job."

"Then do me this favor. I'm not pushing you to come and listen to my testimony. I'm just asking for two checks. It'll give you time to think."

To get out of the place in an amicable way, I wrote two checks. Then he shook my hand again. This time he held it firmly between his two, as if locking it in a vice. Outside, glancing at the dumpster, I saw my dented door propped up behind it. And . . . the little black flag on the back of the bike now fluttered in the wind. "You must be kidding," I blasted so loud, I had to look back to make sure Frankie hadn't heard me. Then softer, "this is the limit." His black little flag bore a cross and a crown of thorns! "Absurd!"

Driving away, with all four windows rolled down to let out the fibreglass smell, I shook my head. Half singing, half shouting, I kept repeating,

"No way Hosee! No way!

"Frankie man, you can cash those two hundred bananas any day.

"Visiting another church; will never be on *myyyyy* agenda."

Thursday, February 9, 2012

17

LOGGERHEADS

"I CAN'T BELIEVE THIS," I said to Jane. "Three times I've been switched over and put on hold. For more than thirty minutes I've been trying to get through to the right person. Remember, we changed telephone companies. The old one is now charging us for ending the contract, for disconnecting the service, and for removing us from their files. That's robbery. I want to give someone a piece of my mind. But, they're all passing the buck. I bet, next thing you know, they'll be on the phone pestering us to use their services again."

"Well," Jane replied, standing at the door, impatiently waiting. "It's two minutes to eleven. We have a date with Armand. You were going to tell him; no more religion."

"I know. But I'm not hanging up now. I've spent too much time trying to get through. You go ahead. I'll join you as soon as I get off the phone. And, remember, not a word about the accident."

"Well, we'll see."

*   *   *

Ten minutes later, I was still on hold, Jane walked back in.

"Well, Armand had to unexpectedly go for blood work. They suspect prostate cancer. But, he gave me a copy of an email he'd received from some Muslim who works with Paul. Armand said that he had an interesting talk with the man at the social after Josh's funeral. He thought we might want to read it."

"What? Why would I want to read anything written by a Muslim?" I replied, hanging up on the last 'please hold-a-minute' lady. "I just paid an arm and a leg fixing our car because we talked Christianity."

"Well, who knows, maybe Muslims know something Christians don't."

"Like what?"

"Maybe they know how you can get your arm and your leg back."

"Funny!"

"Funny or not, one thing isn't funny, and that is how you stay stuck under the thumb of your stepfather. True, I was stuck in my fear because of that stake-burning horror story. But, I told you, I felt very peaceful during Josh's funeral service.

"A lot of people feel peaceful at funerals."

"Well, I've been thinking how nice it would be to be part of a community of people who care for each other. I'm no longer scared. I'm even looking forward to attending some classes, learning about Mohammed, or Buddha, or Jesus, or whatever nice guy's church I'll end up in. I'd love to join a choir, visit a few shut-ins and, together with other women, make sandwiches for funerals and stuff like that. It'll beat watching TV and having nothing to say to each other. So, I am telling you, either grow up and be willing to, at least, listen to some of Armand's stuff or I'll be listening to him on my own. Imagine, he's right about me being Jane, living in this body and, when this body dies, Jane will live on. If that's true, I want to know where I'm going. Right now, I haven't got a clue. If death is not the end of the line, I want to know. Remember that door of fear of the box I'm supposed to be living in according to Armand? Well, I'm kicking it open. I am tired of being clueless and feeling inferior because of it."

"Wow; woman! You're kicking the door all right. Did Armand, just now, give you a five minute pep talk?"

"No, he didn't. I've been thinking this out all on my own."

"You know, Jane, it's a good thing Jerry and Sylvia are coming for dinner tonight. I'm sure Jerry will get you to loosen up about this church nonsense. Right now, you're just too strung out."

"We'll see. But, before I am lifting a finger to prepare dinner, I'm reading this Muslim's email."

When finished reading, Jane slowly put the email on the coffee table. For a few seconds she looked at me; then said, "You know, Chris, maybe religion *is* for the birds. First of all, I don't have a clue what he is talking about. It's about some discovery that could prove how everybody on the planet is tangled up with everybody else. What I do understand, though, gives me the creeps again. Remember Armand saying something about the accuser. I had no idea what he meant. But, after reading this guy's ideas, I can just hear all those religious people belting each other with accusations. And, another thing, even this Muslim couldn't figure out Armand's religion. Anyway, it's a good thing Jerry and Sylvia are coming. To have some good laughs, without any religious hang-ups, is sounding pretty good again."

*   *   *

Monday, February 13, 2012

We had a lot of laughs with Jerry and Sylvia. Jerry and I even drank too much wine. While the girls were in the kitchen cleaning up, I told him about the two hundred dollar Frankie deal. I knew he'd keep it to himself. I didn't want Jane to hear about it. She might want to go and hear this Frankie. Although, after she had read the Muslim's email, she seemed to have caved in a good bit on her religion stand. I'm glad she is shopping again. That'll keep her mind from the church-business for sure. I'm curious though. What made her change her tune? I looked at my watch. Fifty minutes to hockey. I got up, went to the kitchen, unclipped the Muslim's email from the fridge magnet and read.

From: Prasanth's email address
To: Armand's email address
Dear Armand,

I appreciated and enjoyed our open and informative exchange regarding matters of faith. I was pleased to learn that you knew the difference, in that the Qur'an is a recital book for prayers and not, like the Bible, a historical narration. I also appreciated how you talked with equal enthusiasm about different religions. And, even though I am not ready to embrace your religious outlook, I am indebted to you for giving me softer judgment. I can now see how a person, born and brought up in, for example, the Hindu faith, can be completely spiritually satisfied by believing his faith to be richer than any other. If Hindu's Lord Krishna tells followers he welcomes them no matter what path brings them to him, for all paths are his paths anyway, then it will seem useless for such a person to change religion.

You seemed on fire about the beauty of the Hebrew language. You quoted, with what seemed genuine enthusiasm, sayings of the Buddha. And, you seemed sincere when clarifying some of the issues Muslims have with Christianity. You also seemed very knowledgeable about my faith. All this makes me wonder, what's your faith commitment? This question seems even more relevant after you declared your conviction that, on the whole face of our earth, there is not one human who truly proclaims or preaches the word of God. The best anyone can do, according to you, is to proclaim or preach his or her own personal understanding of God's words.

However, regardless of what this implies for you and for me, I thank you for sharing some of the excitement of physics. Most intriguing for me was the current debate about entanglement. This, according to you, is about the growing body of evidence that subatomic particles, like for example protons, once connected in one locality, will, in some way, remain connected even though they become widely separated. If this would prove to be true, and if this would then, in some way, be applicable to humans as well, our understanding of our human interconnectedness, even our entanglement, could drastically change. After all, as you said, each proton in every human body has an unbroken history back to the first ten micro seconds of the origin of our cosmos. It was there that they, and thus in some way we, originated. And if space and time are, in reality, not what we humans perceive them to be, the original entanglement of our common building blocks could then be just as true now as it was at the Big Bang or Big Flash as you preferred to call it.

Encouraged by your openness to wisdom and insights in other religions, I went on the internet to search other scriptures. I was amazed to discover how, in every major religion, the basic understanding is the same. The power which brings forth and sustains our cosmos, whether known as Allah, God, Yahweh, Brahma, etc., is one with all it sustains. Could a possible entanglement of particles and a possible entanglement of people, even for physicists, have implications that are yet unthinkable? Could this be part of a scientific route to mystical understandings?

I stopped reading. These two men were dreamers. Science and religion finding common ground . . . think again.

"Think again, Chris Smith," I said aloud to myself. "You have had it with this God and yet, every day, you let yourself get sucked deeper into his business. But, what is the alternative right now? Hockey? Not for another half hour." I picked up the email again.

You were right. There are similarities in the few verses about creation in our Qur'an and in the lengthy account in the Judean/Christian Bible.

Both books acknowledge the existence of a 'personal creator'. Both agree on a six day creation. Both can be read as to accommodate evolution. However, the lengthy description in the Bible makes it difficult for me to accept it as truth. I read it as a man-made story far removed from reality.

The Qur'an simply states, 'We created the heavens and the earth, and everything between them, in Six Days.' The Qur'an also acknowledges evolution, by saying, 'Allah created every animal from water.' Your explanation of the word 'day' as used in the Bible was an eye opener for me. This original word, you believe, is not a mistake in translation, but a difference in word value. I can see how translating the Hebrew language, which is poor in nouns, into any other language that is rich in nouns—for example English—is no easy task. Correct me if I am wrong, but this is what I heard you say. The Hebrew word 'yom' which has been translated into 'day' has a whole range of possible meanings. It can mean day, week, year, millennium or any unspecified length of time. The true meaning of a Hebrew word is determined by the context in which it is written. This, according to you, is the beauty of the Hebrew language. It accommodates mankind's evolving understanding at any time and any level. The translated words, 'day', 'morning' and 'evening' have served Jews and Christians well in the past. Today, with the discoveries of physics, they can now easily be read as, 'a length of time', 'a beginning' and 'an end'. I have no problem accepting this explanation. The Qur'an, as you were aware, justifies the use of the word 'day' in the creation account by stating, 'A Day with your Lord is equivalent to a thousand years in the way you count.'

But, despite this common ground, we have some glaring differences.

I cannot accept the Judean/Christian belief that mankind has been, is, or will be in need of a Saviour. My faith clearly states that there never was, there presently isn't, and there never will be a need for anyone to come down from heaven and pay the price for Adam's sin. Adam and Eve admitted their mistake when they said, 'Our Lord! We have wronged ourselves. If you do not forgive us and have mercy on us, we will be among the lost.' And the holy Qur'an clearly tells us, 'Then Adam received some words from his Lord and He turned (relented) towards him.' Jesus did *not* die on the cross. There was no need for it.

Again, the Qur'an makes that clear. It states, 'and their saying, 'We killed the Messiah, 'Isa son of Maryam, messenger of Allah.' They did not kill him and they did not crucify him but it was made to seem so to them. Those who argue about him are in doubt about it. They have no real knowledge of it, just conjecture.'

"Nuts," I said out loud, as I dropped the email on the floor, got up and went to the fridge to get a cold beer. "Religion is nothing but battle cries." I could just visualize my stepfather standing on one side of the street waving his Bible. Backed up by millions upon millions of Christians, he would loudly taunt, 'Jesus died on the cross. That's what God says in *my* holy book.' And, on the other side of the street would stand this Prasanth, waving his Qur'an. Backed up by millions upon millions of Muslims, he would then shout back, 'Jesus did *not* die on the cross. That's what Allah says in *my* holy book. So there!'

Who on earth, in his right mind, would want to get involved with these fights? This Armand must be losing his marbles.

With aggravation running through my veins, I switched on the TV. Hockey in two minutes. The good thing about watching competitive sports is, you can project your frustrations on your favourite players. Let them do the fighting. So what, if, once in a while, there's blood on the ice?

18

INTEGRITY

SITTING AGAIN IN OUR preferred corner of the café for Thursday morning's ginger tea, chocolate and coffee clutch, I had only one thing on my mind. Without upsetting Armand any more than necessary, now that he was facing possible prostate cancer, I was going to tell him; no more religion.

"Well, Chris," said Jane with a hint of malice in her voice. "Before you tell Armand about quitting the religion talk, why don't you tell him first about your two hundred dollar Frankie deal."

My jaw dropped.

"Two hundred dollar Frankie deal," I loudly and angrily replied. "How did *you* find out? Didn't we agree to leave the car issue alone?"

"Well, yes. That was before Sylvia told me what Jerry babbled about. Done in from all the wine you poured him,

Jerry tattled, on their way home from their dinner with us, about a two hundred dollar deal you made with Frankie."

Now I had to get mad with my best friend, with his wife and with Jane. Why can't people keep their mouth shut? But, by getting mad, I wouldn't save face right now. The beans were spilled. After giving Jane another dirty look, which I would follow up later, I reluctantly told the story. Of course, I left out the real reason of why I wrapped the car around that pole.

"Interesting," Armand enthusiastically remarked. "Now we have another learning experience coming up. What Sunday will he speak?"

"But I don't want to go."

"Well, that's not true. You and Jerry made a deal too. Jerry suggested you take me to that church. The emotional crap going on there, he said, would cure me of wanting to join some church. And, while getting me cured, Jerry said, you'd get your two hundred bucks back. For that money you're supposed to buy two hockey tickets. I think it's a great idea. If Frankie's church cures me, that's fine with me. What do *you* say Armand?"

"I'm game!"

I should have controlled Jerry's wine intake. Better still. I should have kept my own mouth shut.

"But I didn't want that deal. This Frankie-giant twisted my arm. I went along just to get him off my back. But, if it's a sure way to cure Jane of her church urge, it'll hopefully restore peace to our home. And Jerry and I get our night out. However . . ." I looked directly at Armand. "That Muslim's email clearly proves, religion is nothing but confrontations that nobody can win. Your Muslim friend and umpteen million other Muslims are one hundred percent convinced Adam was forgiven. And yet, my stepfather and umpteen million Christians are one hundred percent convinced Adam was *not* forgiven. You must agree. This makes the religious scene nothing more than a childish shouting match. Listen to it. Muslims claim Jesus did *not* die on the cross. Christians claim he did. Give me one good reason why anyone would want to get involved with futile religious battles like that? If you think you have an understanding that's better than all others, good for you. I'm not interested. If you find that breaking your brains on dumb riddles like these is a challenge, good luck. I prefer watching sports."

"Chris, if that's your free-will choice: fine. Personally, I'm convinced that the timeless realm of spiritual reality is the only true reality. If you're not interested in exploring it, I'll be the last one to force you.

"So, let's get back to the physical realm. I'm diagnosed with prostate cancer. I'll need to undergo tests, a biopsy, bone-scan, etc. Six weeks of radiation; five days a week. Coming together every Thursday will therefore be impossible anyway. But, before we close the book on religion, I'm glad we're still going to hear Frankie."

"Well, Chris and I are sorry to hear the bad news. Please, let us know when your PSW (Personal Support Worker) isn't able to drive you. I'm sure Chris won't mind taking a turn. As long as you promise, of course," Jane mockingly added, "not to talk religion."

"Thanks for the offer. But I have a new PSW. She's a wonderful Hindu girl with a beautiful spirit. All compassion. I nicknamed her Joy. She promised to be there for me, whatever my needs."

Expecting our discussion to be closed, I stood up.

"Well, I'm also sorry I won't be learning any more religious stuff. But, after reading the Muslim's email, I agree with Chris. It's all too ridiculous. I've been thinking, though, about your what-ye-me-call-it. I don't dare to say tractor because I know that's not it."

"Divine Attractor, you mean."

"Whatever! On the way to the funeral, I was uptight about landing in the midst of strangers. But later I thought; if that thing proves that all religions have the same bottom line; what's all this religious fighting about?"

"Good thinking, Jane. But let's not get Chris upset. What do you say, Chris? Shall I keep my mouth shut and talk to Jane about it some other time? Or, shall I finish my Attractor search story, making it as short as possible?"

I really wanted to leave. The problem was; whatever he would say had to be recorded. Jane wanted that. To understand his words, she needed to hear them more than once. If I left, there would be no recording. Jane's looks were clear. I knew my job. Dutifully, I replied, "Okay, if you promise to get to the point quickly, let's have it. What, according to you, is this Divine Attractor that underlies the fabulously intriguing religious chaos in our amazingly wonderful world?"

"Integrity."

After a long silence, Jane ventured, "That doesn't sound very religious."

"You're right. That's the beauty of it. I have thought about it for many years and entertained different possibilities. But, I couldn't come up with a better, universally acceptable foundation for all religious and non-religious belief-systems. Imagine, integrity being taught to every child, in every school, in every country around the globe. Imagine all the children of the world learning, from kindergarten on, about integrity in their relationships with peers, with parents, with those in authority, with the environment, in politics, in business and in every other interactive situation. No matter what religion or non-religion anybody has, every belief can be helpful in bringing integrity into practice. Who can find fault with that? Even the Almighty Creator himself, no matter what religion he favours, will be hard-pressed to find fault with men and women of integrity. It means honesty, sincerity, uprightness, wholeness, completeness, soundness. It means uncorrupted, original and perfect.

And, if there's a glorified life after bodily death, it's easy to accept that, anyone who hasn't tried to live a life of integrity on earth isn't welcome in the hereafter. Imagine, Chris, people on earth religiously filling out their tax returns with integrity. You couldn't knock that."

My back was getting up again. I had just told the man, I wasn't interested in hearing any more of his religious reasoning and now this. One half of me wanted to resolutely say, 'thanks for sharing and good-bye.' The other half of me wavered. Integrity? Imagine, with far-fetched imagining, that he was right. Imagine integrity being the measuring stick for admission to eternal glory, whatever that could be. Imagine I had been angry with this God because, thanks to my stepfather, I had judged him wrongly. Imagine all who sincerely tried to live with integrity, regardless of their membership in whatever religious club, would enter into whatever realm there might be after bodily death. Then, my dad would be there. And, let me believe this. Hallelujah: that holy pain-in-the-behind stepfather would not be!

"As I see it," Armand continued, "integrity was man's issue from the beginning. Integrity means honesty in relationships, not only with the world around us, but specifically with ourselves. This, I believe, means acknowledging the existence of a higher power and having the humility to obey its laws. Yet, the first question man asked when he faced a choice was, 'Does my conscience really prompt me to practice integrity?' And that's the question he's been asking ever since. But, by questioning the integrity of our built-in conscience, we question the integrity of the very source of life. We question the integrity of the cosmos that brought us forth. And by questioning the integrity of our built-in conscience and the cosmos we live in, we humans have spoken, and are daily speaking, *iniquity* into being."

"Well, if you're right and integrity is the bottom line of *all* religions, then why's everybody trying to convert everybody else?"

"I don't know, Jane. I guess, not many people see things the way they were meant to be seen. I can only speak for myself. For me, this realization has opened many doors. By using my experience in physics and applying it to this understanding, I could see how religious chaos was born. Physics tells us, when the forces that influence a system become more complicated, a bifurcation takes place. Don't panic, Jane. Bifurcation is a scientific word meaning, a fork in the road, a split. And that's exactly what I believe happened with religion. When the pressures of life continued to increase, mankind's understanding of absolute honesty towards the higher power and towards one another, kept dividing. It went from two, to four, to eight, to sixteen, and on to the thousands upon thousands of different religious understandings we have today."

"Well, who knows? Maybe your discovery of this divine thing can end all that ridiculous religious fighting."

"No such luck, Jane. Religious fighting happens because of those who are insecure, because of the hypocrites, bigots, chauvinists, pretenders, fanatics, manipulators and liars present in every religious rank. They even are in the ranks of atheists and agnostics. While loudly proclaiming their beliefs, the hearts of those who fight for them are often far from integrity.

"In one holy book, it tells how some religious big-wigs, as Jane calls them, on judgment day cry out, 'Lord, Lord, in your name we did good deeds and performed miracles!' The judging lord replies, 'I never knew you, away from me. It is not those who say 'Lord, Lord,' who will enter into my glory but those who do the will of the one who sent me."

I could see Jane's mind doing overtime. Leaning forward, she asked, "Well, what else did you find out about this religious bottom line stuff?"

Armand looked at me.

I waved my hand. "We're retired, remember. Whether I clock up hours here, or in the apartment, it's about the same."

"Chris, Chris," he said, gently laying a hand on my shoulder. "Could I tell you what I think right now while looking at grumpy you?"

"What?"

"According to the old school your grumpy looking body is made of some hundred trillion cells. Each cell is made of molecules with some hundred trillion atoms in each cell. In one second of your frowning, the molecules in your wrinkled eyebrow vibrated ten billion times. With each molecular vibration, the electrons within that molecule orbited a million times. These multi million actions continue down to the smallest atomic particle.

"And it is the soul/self of Chris Smith, who orders these trillions of particles to cooperate with one another to portray grumpiness.

"Now, just in case you care to know, according to the new school, as I told you earlier, these atomic particles aren't even real. What I really see is the characteristic, or property, called grumpiness made visible by cosmic energy or light through its obedience to the free will of Chris Smith."

"Hmm," I grunted. The fatherly friendliness of his touch—never mind the incomprehensible trillion particle business—the thought of my dad, maybe being okay and my stepfather not, made me add, "Just keep talking."

"So, after I decided that integrity could be the Divine Attractor, I thought of Moses. He must have learned about this religious bottom line idea at the Egyptian court where he was raised. After all, he expressed that same understanding by cleverly weaving it into the Adam and Eve story around the key question, 'does my conscience really tell me not to?'

Then, looking into Egyptian writings from before Moses' time, I discovered the mythology of Horus. With not enough time to learn the old Egyptian language, I had to rely on researchers who did take that time. Some of them found that certain peculiarities, 2500 years later, ascribed to Jesus of Nazareth, were part of that mythology. They compared the story of Jesus with the myth of Horus and with other myths showing up in religions much older than Christianity. Their conclusion: the story of Jesus is that same mythology retold and attributed to a make-believe person. And, that reasoning made good sense to me, even if this mythology had been attributed to a real person.

"You must be kidding," I gasped, looking at Armand with open mouth. "Are you now saying the story of Jesus, whom my stepfather used as his front and whom Josh supposedly gave his heart to, is a myth?"

"Yes, that was my understanding at that time."

"Man, you're something else! Instead of clarifying the religious scene, you're smiling broadly while making it worse. I'm glad it's lunchtime."

"Relax. It's not the end of the story. If you're willing to listen to how my myth conclusion became a solid part of my convictions, I'll buy lunch."

19

BALANCE

"F ASTEN YOUR SEATBELTS," ARMAND suddenly said, after he had finished his lunch and I hadn't. "Imagine you're strapped down in an Apollo spacecraft and we're taking off for the moon." Surprised by his crazy command, I almost choked on my second last bite.

The squash soup and beef sandwich had been great. While working our way through the food, my curiosity had increased. Armand's divine attractor had given me a glimmer of hope regarding my dad's lot. I was even a bit cheerful. Pondering the prospect of Jesus being no more than a myth would put my stepfather in his place for sure.

"But," Armand continued. "Because we're talking spiritual matters, time does not exist. Everything happens in the eternal now. We've taking off, we've landed, stepped out and walked to my favourite beach. Here we are, at the edge of the Moon's no-water, sea of Tranquility. Relaxing in our Muskoka chairs and drinking in the vista, we spot little earth." He pointed to nowhere. Yet, it looked as if he saw what he was talking about. Jane's eyes even followed his pointing finger.

"And, over there are the smaller and the larger planets."

I was opening up again to his boisterous imagining.

"While on the moon, we're circling the earth. Earth, moon and all other planets are circling the sun." Here he made a 360 with his right hand around his head. If there had been room enough, he probably would have done a 360 around our bistro table with his scooter.

"Now look," he said, with a wide sweep of his hand. "Look beyond all that, and allow yourself to be overwhelmed by the magnificence of the unfathomable universe."

The other four people in the café turned their head. Whether annoyed at the increased volume of his voice, or curious to see what loud mouth was up to, they stared at us. Armand lowered his voice. And, as they turned back to whatever they had been talking about, I saw one of them shake his head.

"If that doesn't leave you speechless," Armand continued, "what will?

"Thirty years ago, I imagined myself on the moon as well. I thought, if I distance myself from the earth, it might be easier to expand on the god/man myth. But look," he interrupted himself, pointing at the sunlit sky, visible through the café's big windows, "the sun broke through.

Why not make ourselves comfortable here on earth and soak up some life-giving sun while we pretend sitting on the moon?"

Outside, Jane and I sat down on the same bench where, four months earlier, I had been roped into Armand's spiritual ideas. Sitting on his scooter in front of us—face turned to the sun—he picked up where he'd left off.

"Thirty years ago, when imagining myself on the moon, I was convinced Jesus was a mythical figure. Hoping to get a universal perspective on the god/man myth, I drank in the incomprehensible vastness of the cosmos. Then, while looking into the infinite expanse, a question came to me. Why would this god/man story be playing itself out on an insignificantly little planet like ours? After all, its size is negligible in the infinite expanse of the cosmic theatre. Mulling this over, I realized that, regardless of the size of the earth, regardless of the size of the players, and regardless of the magnitude of the backdrop, the stakes of the play could not be higher. The god/man story, just like my own life story, is about a struggle for life, a struggle for life eternal. Who knows? Mankind's struggle between integrity and iniquity could very well be the struggle of the soul of our galaxy. And, with other creatures on planets in other galaxies, we could even be part of the collective soul of the cosmos. Looking from the moon at my earthly home, drinking it all in, I gave way to my sentiments."

And there, in the sun, as oblivious to his surroundings as he had been when we sang 'Blue Christmas', Armand let his warm voice fill the air with the well-known song, titled 'What a Wonderful World.'

Even I got in the mood when he, with a warm feeling of appreciation, sang about green trees, red roses, and how they bloom for all of us. We all three looked up when he sang about a blue sky with white clouds. And, when he softly sang how blessed a day can be and what tranquility a night can bring, it seemed as if some sort of hush fell over us. Then, when he raised his voice again to praise the beauty of the colours of a rainbow and express the wonder of how these colours are also visible in the faces of the people we meet throughout life, I was expecting Jane to get up and hug him again. Especially when he sang, right after that, how friends, by shaking hands, in reality express their love for one another. And sure enough, when he sang about babies that cry, and learn, and grow, I did see Jane wipe away a tear. But after Armand had sung the last line twice, a repeat of the title of the song, which encourages people to contemplate on how wonderful our world really is, he sounded sad. When finished, he didn't even pull out his harmonica. He just sat there. It was as if the sun had stopped shining on him.

"What's wrong?" I asked.

For a few seconds he looked at us both. Slowly turning to face the sun again, he started, "Yes, it's depressing. But it's true. Thirty years ago, as I sang those last lines, a bad memory popped into my mind. And, just now, the same memory returned. It's the memory of the answer my dad gave me when I, at age twenty, asked him, 'why don't you practice your faith?' His answer, 'How would you like to introduce yourself to the world with, I am that stinking Armand?'"

"What?" I gasped. "Why on earth would your dad say that?"

"He told me about a German, World War 2, a camp named, Theresienstadt. It was a pretend, idyllic community where Jews, especially those gifted in arts and science, were brought together, supposedly to be saved from the holocaust. It was a mockery. A former barrack town, meant for five thousand troops, was now jammed with forty thousand Jews. When asked for their name by any of the commanding officers, any Jew living in that community was forced to reply, 'I am that stinking so and so.'

"But, even though the memory made me sad, it also convinced me that the Jesus story had to be a myth. For if the story was true, our world would have been a better place by now. Then, while pondering this, I remembered another Judean/Christian scripture story. It was about Cain and Able, two sons of Adam and Eve. Cain murdered Able. Cain was jealous of Able who had found favour with his God because of his integrity. Cain, I concluded, must have judged his brother to be 'that stinking Able.' There was judgment by one human with regards to another and no mercy.

"Mind you, I do not assume the six million Jews killed during World War 2 were all men and women of integrity. I'm sure, just as there are schemers, wheeler dealers and people of questionable repute among any sizable group of humans, there were some of these among them. But, there was judgment without mercy by the murderers with regards to their victims. And this has been, still is, and seems to remain that way in our wonderful world. It's Cain and Able over, and over, and over again. Pale faces judge coloured people. Tutsis, Hutus, Sunnis, Shiites, Hindus, Buddhists, Muslims, Christians, all judge one another. Even members of the same persuasion hate and kill their own. All over our wonderful world, respectable men, caring women and adorable children are judging other respectable men, caring women and adorable children to stink. It is brother and sister repeatedly murdering brother and sister. They either wish them dead or kill them outright. If this isn't a mental disease, what is? Could this be a tumor of fear that has, to some degree, infected the hearts and minds of almost every human being? Whether we call it inherited cancer or original sin, it's there. Already in grade school, kids are judging each other to be either airheads or browners. And they know the word 'stinkin' just as well as adults do. Quick judgments and ill-formed prejudices foul our minds. In there, they lay around to fester and become food for the cancer cells of fear. If physical litter is disgusting, mental litter is worse. And the god/man myth perfectly shows how we, in our wonderful world, could cure ourselves of this cancer. By removing the mental litter of prejudice and judgment from our minds, we could starve this cancer to death! "And what is our fear? We're scared to learn, and to have to admit, that the stench we attribute to others often rises from deep within ourselves. We're scared to learn, and have to admit, that how we see ourselves is a far cry from how our creator in the spiritual dimension of purpose sees us.

"In the god/man myth, High Priests, Pharisees, Roman rulers and all those threatened by Jesus' words judged him as 'that stinking Jesus.' Lacking integrity, they wanted to see this self-proclaimed son of God crucified. By doing so, they hoped to permanently eliminate what they saw as his stinking integrity. Yet, he insisted: 'integrity, that's me. It's the only way. It's the only truth. And it's the only foolproof guarantee to eternal life.'

"Safely alone on the moon, I even dared to speculate the god/man myth to spell eternal life for all who practice integrity, regardless of their religion or lack of it. For the message of the god/man myth is simple. Love your neighbour like yourself, even if you judge that neighbour to stink."

"Well," Jane sighed. "That's a tall order. Who's able to do that?"

"Not many, I agree. It's impossible for us humans to muster true compassion at all times. But, there's good news in the god/man myth. It shows how those who live with integrity can draw from the higher power's infinite compassion by acknowledging the laws built into their conscience."

Now the gears in *my* mind were turning. If integrity truly is the measuring stick for becoming a little god, as my own dad had suggested we strive for, then my striving has the same value as everybody else's.

"Tell me, Armand, how do you expect anyone to agree with you? I mean; who on earth is willing to throw open this door of fear of the box we're all supposed to be living in? Maybe it's a good thing no one does. Even *you* are constantly changing your tune. First you make us feel comfortable about integrity being the religious bottom line. Then you throw in this monkey wrench. By reducing the Jesus story to a myth, you pretty well wipe out Christianity. Don't tell me that you, by digging into more old books, wiped out the other six major religions as well."

"No, but who knows what brainy schemes I would have come up with if I had been left to my own resources? However, while pretend sitting on the moon, another big question relating to the god/man myth still occupied my mind.

"Remember how I shared my understanding of God's complementary duality? How God is absolute judge and unfathomable lover at the same time? So, still reclining on the moon, with my mind wide open to whatever would come to me to help me better understand the myth, I asked myself this: Could it be that I, by using my free will, am meant to develop within myself that same balanced duality of justice and mercy? Could it be that, if I judge someone to stink, I then also need to show that person enough mercy to help him, or her, come up smelling like a rose, so to speak? And could it be that, if I judge anyone unfit to live, I then also need to be willing to lay down my own life in order to help that person to become worthy of life? Could the real meaning of the word integrity be, to have a heart and a mind *always* bent on balancing justice with mercy?"

Armand adjusted the angle of his scooter to get maximum sun. Jane had her eyes closed. Heaven knows what went through her mind. Mine was in turmoil. Figure this. If I accepted Mr. Know-it-all's understandings, then yes, my dad was saved from hell. But instead, *I* would be destined for the eternal Bar-B-Q. I had certainly judged my stepfather to stink. Yet I did nothing to help him become an air freshener. I also judged him fit for a fatal dose of rat poison in his mashed potatoes. Yet, I surely hadn't been willing to eat his puree. Keep dreaming Armand. Nobody on the face of this earth can swallow all his anger and muster that kind of sacrificial love. Especially not for someone who ruined your life. Although the bottom line for me was still this supposed God. It was he who allowed my dad to be killed. It was he who was keeping my dad on hot coals. It was he who had ruined my life. What nonsense, though. If I'm an atheist, what sense does it make to be angry with a God I don't believe in? And if I'm not an atheist, what am I? If I believe in whatever Armand has dreamed up, I'm certainly not destined for the eternal good life. And if I don't buy into his creed, I more or less have to go back to the drawing board and figure out my own pie-in-the-sky ideas. But, with umpteen thousand options, I'll need at least another 74 years of life to do that. What did he say again?

"Say, Armand, what did you mean by 'who knows what brainy schemes I would have come up with, if I'd been left to my own resources?'"

"Chris, when I finished coming to these impressive, intelligent god/man myth conclusions, the higher power threw me another amazing curve ball.

"But I'm ready for my afternoon nap. And I think that, before I share God's new score, we should first go and hear Frankie's story this Sunday."

20

CHANGE

"Jesus freaks messing with our chicks," Frankie said, as he looked around the congregation, "they must be stopped." Standing behind the lectern, ready to give his testimony, obviously nervous about facing a crowd this size, he even looked a bit normal. Wearing a light blue short sleeved dress shirt and dark beige pants, he made me wonder. Where had he found dress clothes his size?

Jane and I, instead of being crammed into a hard oak pew like in Detroit, were comfortably seated in ergonomically-shaped, theatre armchairs. With rows of seats rising stepwise from the front, this didn't just look like a theatre. This was a theatre. Theatre for the performing gospel, Armand called it. Every other row had an indent to accommodate a wheelchair or scooter. Armand, stationed right beside Jane, seemed right at home.

Up front, in four different places, screens on which the lyrics would be projected hung from the ceiling. I could have sworn this ceiling was twice the span of Sandra's church roof. No hammer beams here. This roof just was. This place had space. There must have been about a thousand people. All talking with animation before the service, they filled the church at 10 am sharp, with an instant atmosphere of quiet reverence when their choir walked in. Dressed like angels in bright yellow robes, this fifty-one member, mixed choir, then led the congregation with gusto in a non-stop song festival. Apparently inspiring almost everyone to sing from the heart, they changed the church into a concert hall. How could a possible God knock a worship session like that? Armand, too, sang his heart out, lifting hands high like many others. He looked as if in another world. Who knows? Maybe he was in his spiritual dimension of purpose. As for me, I thought it would never end. "Finally," I sighed when the pastor stepped forward, and announced Frankie.

"Yes, Jesus freaks messing with our chicks must be stopped," Frankie repeated. "That's what I angrily proclaimed, four months ago, at a party. The usual biker girls were there, except Chickadee. Chickadee—I still don't know her real name—was a sweet little prostitute who knew her trade. A week earlier she had walked into your church to try to find a hypocrite who owed her money. And, three hours later, according to one of her girlfriends, she had come out a different person.

"By the way, copies of what I'm sharing this morning are at the back of the church. One of your elders helped me put this testimony together.

"As I was saying, Chickadee had fallen, as we saw it, into your religious trap. At the party where we missed her, I suggested to two biker buddies that we go attend your next Sunday meeting and stir up some hell. Just to let your pastor and all of you know we meant business.

"That Sunday morning, the three of us, bent on raising Cain, drove our souped-up choppers like a blast of thunder into your parking lot.

"Power, my one buddy, wore his army greens and soldier's helmet. With nine notches on his tank, representing the cats he flattened because he aims for them when they try to cross the road, he was ready for another kill.

"My other buddy, Phisto, wearing his black skull and crossbones shirt, was loudly singing the non-repeatable names we'd given your pastor. For the heck of it, he'd put a black patch over his one eye.

"I wore my sleeveless jacket showing off muscles and tattoos.

"And you?" Here Frankie made a gesture to include the whole assembly. "You were all dressed in your Sunday best. So was Chickadee. She later told me how she ran to your pastor to beg him not to let us in.

"'My child,' your pastor said, 'if anybody had stopped *you* from coming in would that have been wise? Let's bring this situation before our Lord.'

Then Chickadee and your pastor prayed together.

"As we walked into your church, a few greeters stepped up to us saying, 'Welcome! Welcome! We're so glad you're here.' We knew full well, they were lying. Seeing us walk in made many of you have the shakes. Some of you may even have wet your pants. And, most of you probably prayed hard for God to make us leave.

"Six ushers tried to seat us in the last row. Ignoring them completely, we headed straight for the front. There, being truly obnoxious, we plunked down, laughing, kidding and making a racket. We'd come to stir the pot and were determined to enjoy doing it.

"After what I thought was a crazy long time of singing, there was a collection. With much hullabaloo, we each put a penny in the bucket. Then, suddenly, Phisto leaned over and said to me, 'I'm sick to my stomach. I have to throw up.' The beer, the pizza, the fries, the eggs and the sausages we had killed for breakfast were coming back to life. Phisto never chews his food. Resurrecting that stuff wasn't hard.

"'Great,' I said to him. 'Barf it up right here. Spread it nicely all over the carpet. It'll make a perfect mess.'

"He must have been too sick to see the fun of that. With Power steadying him, he hurried out, leaving his stinky mess on the pavement in front of your church. Then they both took off. I still don't know why. But it didn't bother me. I have raised hell on my own before.

"'Some kids grow up,' your pastor started his sermon, 'in homes where there's little or no real, caring, parental love.'

"His words caught my attention. He explained how this hardens the hearts of young people. How it forces them to develop attitudes that are protective shields. How they hide behind these shields to hide their pain. For a minute, hearing that, I forgot why I was here. 'Deep down,' your pastor said, 'they all cry out for someone to notice them, someone to care about them, someone to love them simply for who they are.'

"It was as if he was talking straight to me. I couldn't help but listen. Nobody, except my eighth foster mother, a Buddhist woman, had shown me real love. Born to a single, drug-addict mom, who pretty well left me to die when five months old, I was put into a foster home by Children's Aid. By the time I was sixteen, I had moved through twelve different homes. To effectively deal with Frankie had been impossible for everyone. They all tried to change me into somebody I didn't want to be. The Mormons wanted me to become another Jesus. The Buddhist wanted me to realize I was an illusion. The agnostics wanted me to smarten up and just be like them. But, I wanted to be Frankie.

"The good thing about all these foster homes was that each foster father taught me a different skill.

The bad thing: I became a master manipulator. Playing the members of each family against one another, I was able to create hell on earth in every home.

"At twenty, I joined a biker gang. Suddenly I was accepted, appreciated and respected. Suddenly I had real friends. I belonged. We trafficked in drugs, partied, made trouble, hung out together, drank, cursed and swore, and outdid each other in being tough.

"'What's your name, my friend?' your pastor suddenly asked while looking at me. Caught off guard, because I had drifted off into my hurts, I automatically answered, 'Frankie.' But, instantly, snapping back to reality I quickly added, 'and get this straight, preacher-man, I am not your friend.'

"'Frankie,' he then said. 'Think back in your childhood. Are you the Frankie you've dreamed of being? Or are you a Frankie locked in by brick walls? Could you be honest with yourself and dare to admit you're hiding a lot of hurt inside that tough biker body?'

"Hey, I thought, this smartass is trying to needle me like he must have done with Chickadee. He's making it easy for me to give him a piece of my mind. 'Look, Mister,' I replied while standing up. 'If you think you can push me around like you did one of our chicks, I got news for you. It's none of your darn business—the word I used spells differently—what kind of Frankie I am. But I can show you. I can break your preaching stand in half with one hand. And, if you mess any more with any of our girls, I can do the same with you.'

"Ten ushers suddenly surrounded me. I laughed at them. 'Touch me,' I said. 'I'll beat the holy whatever out of each of you.' I can't repeat every word I used because your elder censored me.

"Turning to your pastor again, I said, 'Just remember, mister. Never again put your religious hands on one of ours.' With that, I turned around, and started up the isle towards the exit.

"'Frankie, my son,' your pastor very gently replied. I stopped. Expecting a shower of verbal abuse, in response to my parting words, I hesitated. The voice I heard sounded like the voice I'd often dreamed of hearing: the voice of a loving father. But my mind hissed, 'fuddle-duddle him. Just get your lower back out of here.' Yet, I turned around. Confused, and angry about being manipulated, I snarled, 'What?'

"'Son, would you like to experience a miracle?'

"'Hah,' I laughed. 'You bible thumpers make me puke. But, eh! If you can show me some holy hocus-pocus; by all means, do your thing.'

"'Brothers and sisters in Christ,' the pastor then said, 'please rise and, if moved to do so, unite yourself with me in prayer by stretching forth a hand towards Frankie.'

"He prayed this simple prayer: 'Heavenly Father if you find an opening, however small, in the deep recesses of

Frankie's heart, let your Holy Spirit, in the person of Jesus, enter in. We ask this, in the name of your son, our Lord Jesus Christ.' Then you all agreed with him by loudly saying, 'AMEN.'

"It was at your 'Amen' that something inside of me snapped. No, something gave way. I sank to the floor on the same section of carpet I had suggested Phisto to throw up on. It was as if a flood gate had been forced open. I began to cry. Two couples walked up and knelt beside me, one on either side. They started praying softly. Their prayers sounded like warm oil gently flowing into my hurting heart. Lying on the floor, I heard, soft, sweet, and peaceful singing. Your choir was reverently worshipping. Oblivious to my surroundings in some way, but also very much aware of where I was, I cried, cried and cried. It was as if my tears were flushing my heart, washing away layer after layer of pain. There was the pain of being rejected by my real mother. There was the pain of foster parents who, unable to crack my shell, had given up on me. And there was the gnawing pain in my heart of not being able to become the Frankie I so desperately wanted to be. I cried for a long time.

"Then, when I thought I had cried out all my pain, a new surge of pain washed over me. This pain was worse. It was the pain I had caused my foster parents who had tried so hard to help me. The pain I had caused the girls I had misused and abused. 'Oh, my God,' I cried out loud, 'forgive me. Forgive me. How can I ever make up for all these pains I have caused?'

"Then your pastor knelt beside me. And, in the same gentle voice, he asked, 'Son, are you sorry for all the pain you have caused others?'

"'Yes. Yes. Yes,' I groaned.

"'Son, did I hear you ask forgiveness? How do you think you can be forgiven unless all these hurts have been properly dealt with?'

"'I don't know,' I stuttered. 'I can never make up with all these people.'

"'Son, Jesus has compensated for it all, by sacrificing his life for you.'

"'Why would he do that for a piece of sh . . . , I mean misery like me?'

"'Because he loves you. He longs to come and live in your heart to help you become the Frankie you were created to be from the beginning.'"

Armand was checking his pockets for a tissue. Jane was mesmerized. I was thinking of Jerry's reference to emotional crap. My stepfather never had testimonies. But then, nobody ever fell down and bawled their eyes out in his church either. So, what was there to testify about? I wondered if this was the moment when Frankie got the sparkle in his eyes. I bet my dad had a sparkle. I don't. I know. No joy bubbling up in me.

Meanwhile, Frankie had come to the end of his story. The pastor had taken over. He invited anyone who needed prayer, for whatever reason, to come down to the front. While he was talking, some twenty pairs of men and women had lined themselves up to minister to the onslaught. I'd never seen anything like it. I realized that's why they needed all that space between the podium and the first row. While the choir quietly sang, more and more found their way to the front. For us, the show was over. What would happen, I wondered, if these one thousand people would all stretch forth their right hand towards me and, in unison, pray, 'in Jesus' name, anger be gone.' I got up and stepped into the isle. Right away, Jane got up too. She slipped her hand into mine and, while she looked at me with beaming face, she whispered, "I'm coming with you."

"Why?" I asked, surprised at her sudden warm affection. "I can handle it. I'm just going up there to make sure Frankie rips up the cheque."

"Oh," she sighed, sounding like a deflating balloon, while taking her hand back. "I thought you were going up for prayer."

21

FOOLISHNESS

"WHY NOT GO FOR lunch and share thoughts," Armand suggested while we walked out of Frankie's church. "I know an Austrian Bakery and Deli where the treats are fabulous."

And, Austrian it was. Each small square table, covered with a red and white checkered tablecloth, had a small vase holding fake Edelweiss. A tiny note, stuck between the fakes, read, '10% off, if you can yodel.' The padded chairs, either red or white, were okay. No match, though, with the comfort the church had offered us. A larger table, in front of a bay window overlooking the waterfront boardwalk, had just become empty. After we'd each ordered 'a sausage on a bun with sauerkraut' at the counter, I could hardly wait to sit down and give my take on Frankie's tearjerker.

"Wow, that preacher was smoother than my holy stepfather. True, it doesn't take a shrink to figure out how a guy like Frankie was deprived of love in his youth.

Everybody knows that most tough guys have had love starved childhoods. And to start a sermon from that angle in order to hook a guy like Frankie is common sense. But, to respond to Frankie's angry outburst by gently saying; 'Frankie, my son,' that was brilliant. I bet he used the same line with this Chickadee. I can just hear him softly say; 'Chickadee, my daughter.' When spoken in the right tone, such words could even give me a goose bump or two."

Neither Armand nor Jane responded to my assault.

"You know, Armand," I continued after an uncomfortable silence. "I wouldn't be surprised if these two converts will be back in their old rut within a year. I've seen it in my stepfather's church. People say they're sorry for their sins. They join the congregation, take part in prayer meetings and programs and then, after a while, you never see them again."

I was determined to prove Frankie's conversion to be nothing more than emotional nonsense. In no way could a guy like him have such a drastic change in attitude simply because a group of people say, 'Amen.' If that were true, a lot more churches would use that formula. My stepfather never talked about Jesus coming into anybody's heart. Outside, on the boardwalk, a long-haired guitarist fiddled with a mouth organ, trying to attach it to a neck brace. Meanwhile Jane and Armand persisted in their silence.

"Tell me, Armand, how can you make Frankie's story fit into your Jesus-myth idea?"

"I can't. Remember how I also told you on Thursday that God, after I had come to my god/man myth conclusion, threw me a scoring curve ball? But," he added while eyeing the plates that were set in front of us. "I'm eating my European specialty first." He folded his hands and silently prayed. Embarrassed, I looked around, hoping nobody in the half-filled Deli would notice.

"What about your money?" Armand asked after his first bite.

"Oh, up front, Frankie was surrounded by people eager to shake his big hands. He'd seen me coming. Looking over their heads he held up my cheque, demonstratively ripped it in half and gave me the thumb up sign."

Armand took his time finishing his plate. Finally he shoved it aside empty, wiped his mouth and started, "So, here is God's curve ball.

"One Saturday morning, in the early eighties, Sonnetta and I found ourselves attending some breakfast meeting in a hotel banquet room. Friends, who knew about our earlier search for a manifestation of God's power, had conned us into it. And, if it hadn't been for politeness sake, I would not have entered that room. Filled with hand-clapping, foot-stomping, arm-raising, country gospel-singing men and women, it made me cringe. Seeing how these people believed in a real Jesus while I was convinced he was a myth, I knew I did not belong. But Sonnetta's friends had entered behind us and I saw no gracious way out. Annoyed about this waste of my time, I insisted we sit as close to the back door as possible. I wanted the option of sneaking out if things got on my nerves.

"We had landed in a breakfast meeting of the Full Gospel Business-Men's-Fellowship International. Here, away from a church setting, men with wives and friends met every first Saturday of the month. They came to listen, after singing, praying, and eating, to a fellow-businessman giving a testimony of how he'd found Jesus. Or, rather, how Jesus had found him.

"Over cold toast, soggy scrambled eggs and lukewarm tea, I learned how this organization had been established in the U.S.A. in 1954 by a dairy farmer. On his knees, in the living room of his home in Los Angeles, California, in the early hours of December 29, 1952, this farmer had received a vision. God had shown him people of different denominations, of all races, all over the world, raising both hands high in worship and opening up to the in-pouring of God's Holy Spirit. It had taken the man much persistence. But, when we walked into this Businessmen's fellowship, on December 11, 1981, it had some 3,100 chapters, in 91 countries.

"The speaker that morning came from England. He opened by saying, 'There is a big difference between knowing *about* God, and *knowing* God.' Born Catholic, this man had started at an early age to question his Church's teachings and decided to find 'truth' by studying theology.

"One day, when deep into the Bible, some words hit him hard. Jesus said, '*no one knows the Father, except the son, and those to whom the son chooses to reveal Him.*' This, he concluded, was extremely unfair. It meant that, even if he received a divinity degree at every university on earth and learned the secrets from every religious fraternity, it would benefit him little. If Jesus chose *not* to reveal the Father to him, he would still not know God. If this was true, he was wasting his time. But, being too close to his degree, he shut his mind to this possibility and kept studying. He got his degree. However, not convinced of anything he'd learned, he kept searching.

"By then, I was all ears," Armand added with emphasis.

I was ears too. Not all, but some. While desperately wanting to deny the reality of whatever I had heard in Frankie's church, I needed more hard facts to prove my case against it.

"A London cab driver, with no education, had given this man his next clue," Armand continued. "This cabbie, eagerly witnessing for his faith, had said, 'Sir, if you want Jesus to reveal God the Father to you, you need to first ask God the Father to forgive you for your sins. Then you need to accept his forgiveness. Then you need to invite Jesus into your heart. And then, both God the Father and God the son will come to make their home with you.'

"And that," Armand said while crumpling his napkin, "was the advice the man up front repeated at the end of his testimony."

"Well, did you?" Jane, taken in by the story, asked right away.

"When I heard his invitation for anyone, prompted from within by God's Spirit, to come forward and follow the cabbie's advice, my analytical mind sprung into high alert. 'This is an altar call for brain deads,' it yelled. I had read about those things. It was similar to what the pastor did this morning after Frankie's testimony. 'Stay seated!' my mind commanded. 'You're in a good spot. You're in the far back. Don't make a fool of yourself.' But, at the same time, my heart was whispering, 'imagine it is true.' 'No,' said my mind, 'it is hogwash! They're just looking for gullibles to join their club.'

"And so, my heart and mind battled. Finally, I stood up. Sonnetta happened to stand up that same moment. Her left hand found my right and, together, we started walking up to the front.

"'IDIOT!' my mind yelled in total panic. 'You know better than this. You've gone to all those different religious places, read all those religious books, talked to all those ministers, priests and gurus. And you, great thinker, have come up with this brilliant universal understanding. What on earth are you doing? God's power won't show forth just because some hand-clapping, foot-stomping, emotionally questionable country gospel-lovers sing and pray. Use your mind! Drop Sonnetta's hand. Hang a left, and head for the washroom.

"Sweating profusely and ready to head for the john, I loosened my grip on Sonnetta's hand. Then, for one split second, I saw to my right, suspended in mid-air, the crucified Christ. It stunned me and kept me going straight. Up front, I faced a big man. I later learned he was a Pentecostal block layer. While praying silly words, he gently laid his right hand on my left shoulder. I sank to my knees and my embarrassment was complete. Now everybody knew; I wasn't even a Protestant. For, as a rule, they don't kneel.

"I wanted to get up. I couldn't. My body was numb. Something was happening to my heart. It felt warm and peaceful. And, while a cloud of sweetness seemed to engulf me, it was as if warm, soothing, oil was poured over my head. Flowing down and bathing every part of my body, it flooded my heart and soul. Was I, at last, experiencing the touch of the power of a living God?

"And, how wonderful. Sonnetta, at my side, experienced the same."

Armand stopped talking. Dead silence.

"Bingo," I said to break the dreaded silence. "Armand the physicist became a Pentecostal."

"No," he chuckled. "I became a super confused physicist. Used to reasoning everything out, never allowing feelings or assumptions to influence my thinking, I was at a loss. I went home denying the experience. I tried to chalk it up to mass hysteria. I tried to explain it psychologically. Yet, all the while, down in my heart, I felt warm, loving and peaceful. My heart wanted to enjoy this peace. But my mind wouldn't let me. My mind was merciless. It kept insisting, I'd lost control and I'd better admit it. I had fallen into an emotional trap set up by an excellent, manipulative, speaker. And, truthfully, as a man of reason, I knew that whatever I'd experienced could just as well have happened with a mythical Jesus. Yes, the room had been filled with people who believed in a living Jesus. Yes, I had been touched by some extraordinary power when prayed over by a believing block layer. And, yes, I did see the image of the crucified Jesus. But, all that proved nothing. The crucified image could have been conjured up by my own imaginative mind. I'd read enough about Jesus. And whatever overwhelmed me could have come from the higher Power that permeates the cosmos without the need for a living Jesus. Besides, the faith of the people in that room in their Jesus was probably not much different from the kind of faith Muslims or Hindus have in *their* prophet or messenger.

"And then," Armand thoughtfully added, "I did what comes natural to me. Back home in the privacy of my own backyard, while looking up at the blue sky, I made another deal with God.

"But let's first order a hot drink with a baked goodie. That baking, in the showcase underneath the counter, looked very tempting."

Imagine a God who makes deals! I should have made a deal with him when I was young. 'Possible God,' I should have said. 'If you rid me of this stepfather, I'll become a believer. Believer in what, though? Not in my stepfather's God for sure. And not in Frankie's God either. Emotionalism is not for me. But then, my fits of anger aren't all that rational either.

Strudel for Armand. Mocha slice for Jane. Peach crumble for me.

"So," Armand continued, "standing in my own backyard, under my own blue sky, I said, 'God or Jesus or whoever you are, I'm still convinced my understanding of the god/man myth is right. But, if I can experience that same overwhelming holiness one more time, here by myself, in my own space, I'll reconsider the issue. And, let Monday bedtime be the deadline.'

"Monday bedtime came. Nothing had happened. My mind was happy. It now had proof. Jesus was a mythical figure. Feeling dumb, deflated, relieved, and annoyed, all at once, I said to Sonnetta, 'I'm off to bed.'

"I went upstairs, stepped into the bathroom, picked up my toothbrush, turned on the tap and opened my mouth. Then, like a tsunami, a wave of sheer compassion washed over me. A feeling of great inner joy took hold of me. The water running from the tap sounded like a choir of angels. I couldn't help join their singing in, what sounded like, silly words."

My eyes fell again on the little sign, saying, '10% off, if you can yodel.'

"I sank to my knees in front of my bathroom sink. My singing became heartfelt worship. Time stood still. I have no other words at my disposal than to say, I was submerged in holiness. Was I with God or was God with me? It didn't matter.

"Then, slowly, after about fifteen minutes, my toothbrush regained its place of priority again. The happening was over. Its memory was imprinted on my mind forever. I knew I had received 'the Baptism of the Holy Spirit'. A fellow across the table at that breakfast had talked about it. According to him, this Holy Spirit baptism gives power to the recipient to do, at times, what Jesus did. Heal the sick, drive out evil spirits, prophesy and hear the small voice of God in words of knowledge."

Out on the boardwalk, the long-haired guitar and mouth organ musician reminded me of Armand's Adam who sang the blues after he'd been kicked out of paradise.

22

HELL

"FRANKIE CALLED," I SAID to Jane, as she walked in with groceries. Trying to sound casual from behind my newspaper, I added, "His church family told him, he can go to hell."

"WHAT?" she gasped. Stepping up to me, she pushed my paper aside. And, ignoring the tomato that fell out of her bag, making a mess on the floor, she threatened, "Don't pull my leg like that. Get serious. Why on earth would Frankie call you?"

"Okay, okay," I chuckled, "they're telling him he can go to hell or, he can not go to hell. It all depends on whether he goes back to his former biker buddies or not. Now he wants to have coffee with me somewhere. He remembered I was an atheist. And the only foster father he'd ever trusted was an atheist as well. He doesn't know what to think of these churchy people warning him about this hell business."

"What are *you* gonna tell him? You don't even believe in that stuff."

"You're right. I most certainly don't buy into any devil and hell baloney. But Frankie sounded desperate. I couldn't say no. It won't hurt to meet the man. I'll just tell him to loosen up about the hell nonsense. Maybe that's all he needs to hear."

*   *   *

Thursday, March 1, 2012

Frankie looked smaller than I remembered. He wasn't all that cheerful either. No sparkle in his eyes this time. But, he was happy to see me.

"I could cry again," he started, as soon as we were seated in one of those a-dime-a-dozen coffee franchises. The difference in this one was; I knew the lady behind the counter. She was a retiree from our complex, working to pay for non-covered drugs prescribed to her bedridden husband.

"Yes," Frankie repeated. "I could cry again. But now it's out of despair. I need my buddies. I go crazy at night being alone. I tried slaving sixteen hours a day in the body shop. That made me more depressed. I tried attending prayer meetings and bible studies. I can't take it anymore. I need to have a good laugh again. I need some rowdy talk and, just hanging out with the guys. But these church people keep needling me, 'Frankie,' they say, 'it's the devil that's making you feel this way. He's playing with your mind.' This devil, they tell me, wants me to get back into my old lifestyle. If I believe everything they throw at me, this devil-joker is poking up his fire just for me. So I ask them, 'if this creep is doing all this to my mind, why isn't Jesus coming in between to tell him to get back into his cozy hell? I even prayed with the pastor, 'Jesus, if you're for real, and if you truly did come into my heart, how come I'm feeling lonely and miserable again?'"

"I'm sorry, Frankie. I don't have answers to your questions."

Frankie thought for a moment. Then he sighed, "I didn't think you would. But, you know, when you came into my shop, I was still full of this warm, peaceful, and joyful feeling that had overwhelmed me on the Sunday I broke down. When you left my shop, I started thinking. He's an atheist. He seems to do okay without Jesus. Who knows, I thought, maybe that morning when I went to raise hell in the church I'd been drinking too much. Maybe I was overtired. We had a good party the night before. Maybe this pastor got me good because he knows how to manipulate people. Now I feel empty, lost, and totally abandoned by both my biker buddies and Jesus. And there's nobody in that Church I can hang out with. Chickadee is in the same boat. It was a good thing this elder and I wrote up my testimony earlier. I just read it as I'd promised. But, even while reading, these doubts kept twirling in my head. Tell me, you don't believe in any of this hell and devil gibberish, do you?"

Frankie looked at me with apprehension, desperation even. As his eyes met mine, I felt at a loss. I knew nothing about the devil. What did I really know about anything, besides tax returns and sports?

"No," I answered slowly. "I don't believe in any of it. I guess it's all part of that big religious chaos we humans are living with."

"Religious chaos? What do you mean?"

"Remember the man on the scooter who was sitting beside us during your testimony? He's a retired physicist. I met him half a year ago. He's worked out his own understandings of the religion business. But, they're pretty philosophical. I couldn't repeat them. Come to think of it. I've never heard him talk about the devil. But then, he still has more up his sleeve. I wonder what he's figured out about hell.

"Listen!" I said after a few moments of thinking. "I have an idea. Next time my wife and I get together with this Armand, I'll ask if you can join. Then you can pick his brains on hell and the devil. Right now he's having radiation treatments for prostate cancer five days a week. Who knows? If he can get enough rest on Saturday, he may be willing to meet with us on Sunday. Leave it with me."

When I called Frankie that night to tell him Armand loved the idea, he hesitantly asked, 'Could Chickadee come too?'

*   *   *

Sunday, March 4, 2012

Armand's apartment was about the size of ours, but his kitchen was part of the open living room, which was ideal for him to move around in on his scooter or wheelchair. No carpet anywhere, of course. To make his movements easier still, there was hardly any furniture. Standing in the living area, against one wall, was a large couch with a stack of fold-up chairs beside it. Some of them were unfolded this Sunday morning because of us, his visitors. Pushed against another wall was a large table, stacked high with piles of papers and books, seemingly in total disarray. Was this his desk?

After I told Armand about Frankie's dilemma, he had insisted we get together this Sunday morning. Chickadee's joining was no problem. But, even though he'd slept most of Saturday, he looked exhausted.

Jane, busy cleaning a corner of the table/desk to put cups, saucers, sugar and some sweets she had baked, got a jolt when the buzzer rang.

Frankie walked in first. Chickadee was second. Wow! Well-shaped, medium build, dark black hair, and with features that reminded me of a gypsy, she was dressed in the uniform of her former trade: low-cut blouse, tight, black leather miniskirt and high heels. Her face wore the marks of drug abuse and her eyes looked sad. No sparkle. She was nervous, shy, and hardly spoke when we introduced ourselves. When she came to Armand, sitting on his couch with pillows supporting him, she hesitated. He, however, instead of simply shaking her hand, asked, 'Can I give you a hug to show you how welcome you are?' She giggled, consented, bent over to him with her low-cut blouse and all, and seemed more relaxed after that. Armand, despite his weakness, even insisted on hugging the Frankie colossus. Some production that was. The giant needed two chairs to sit on. Chickadee, for whatever reason, chose to sit on the floor, resting her back against a wall. Jane and I were sitting apart. We had a bit of a tussle before we came. If it hadn't been for Frankie, I would have stayed home.

"Is the devil for real?" Armand asked for openers, digging right in after we finished the small talk. "And, why is Jesus withdrawing himself after first giving you this wonderful experience of peace? Thirdly, did Jesus really come into your heart?"

Then, for several minutes, he was quiet. When he finally spoke again, I had to admit, even I was curious about what we would hear.

"Apparently, Frankie and Chickadee, the church people have given you explanations that do not fully answer your questions. As you now have experienced, there is more to the 'Jesus coming into your heart event' than meets the mind. But, in order for you to relate to whatever I will share, I'll have to elaborate. This means, you have to make a choice. We'll have empty banter right now, with coffee, tea and cookies, after which I can do no more. Or it'll be Armand's home church for this Sunday and three more. I need to pace myself. I can deal with only one question at a time. Today is the intro. Next Sunday we'll deal with the question of why Jesus seems to have left you. The Sunday after that I'll share how I understand the person of Jesus. And, on the fourth Sunday, we'll deal with the devil."

"If you have answers," Frankie instantly responded, "answers that'll get us out of our nightmare; we'll be here. Right, Chickadee?"

Chickadee nodded.

"All right, last question first. Yes, I believe what happened to you in the church was real. But the question is, did Jesus, who is spirit, enter your heart or did something dormant within you get activated? My answer is that you did experience the activation of God's kingdom within you. The kingdom of God is dormant within every human being, regardless of a person's faith. But, like a seed, it needs nourishment to come alive. In you, it came alive for two reasons. Reason one was your own unspoken desire to be genuinely *you*, and not some put-on. Reason two was the faith and prayer power of the pastor and his congregation. They gave the kingdom seed its first spiritual watering."

"Where then," Frankie impatiently interjected, "is this Jesus now?"

"As I understand it," Armand replied, "Jesus is the embodiment of 'the Christ.' I will share more about that, Sunday after next.' He is king of the kingdom that is dormant in us all. The seed of His kingdom has sprung to life within you. In some small measure, you have become part of the living Jesus. You gave him permission to be born in your heart. It was both your personal Christmas and your spiritual rebirth."

"So, why has Jesus left me?" Chickadee asked aggressively. "Why do I feel cold and abandoned? Cheated even."

For a moment I thought she would start to cry. Then she added, "I came dressed like a whore, because that's what I am. I wanted you to know that. My life was a mess and it's just about to become as big a mess again. I hate myself. I hate. Hate. Hate. Why didn't this Jesus take the hate out of me? If it was him who set me free from my drug addiction, then why didn't he set me free from this choking hate?"

We all remained silent. All waiting for Armand.

Then Armand did something ridiculously stupid. He reached behind him, grabbed an envelope from his desk and said, "instead of giving you more answers now, Chickadee, I'll give you this." He held up the envelope and added. "You have no income right now. This will tie you over."

How dumb can a man get? Who'd keep check on this trollop? Who was going to make sure she wouldn't blow it on more sexy clothes?

Slowly Chickadee stood up, walked over to Armand and, I guess because she was used to taking money from men, accepted his gift.

"What makes you so understanding?" she softly asked.

Armand smiled. "I'll tell you next Sunday. For now I suggest that you and Frankie, sometime this week, read the Exodus story in your Bible. I'm sure the church gave you one. Read how God set a tribe of people free from slavery and how he, right after that, tested them heavily."

He turned to Jane. "Please serve the refreshments and bring out the sweets. I've had the biscuit." Clearly done in, he sank back in the pillows.

Jane stood up, looked at Chickadee, smiled her biggest smile and, without consulting me she made this crazy suggestion:

"Well, Chickadee and Frankie, how'd you like to come to our apartment this Wednesday night? We could study this Exodus stuff together. Chris is going with a friend to a hockey game."

Great, my mind muttered. A has-been biker and a former floozy are going to sit on our spotless sofa. It's like a soap opera. First I meet this Armand who's looking for a sounding board for his ideas on religion. Then these two social outcasts roll into my life. Or did I roll into theirs? What did it matter? Unless I made a stink, I now had to sit through Armand's gospel hour for the next three Sundays. If I didn't, how would I be able to give Frankie my views on what Armand was going to feed him?

I could just hear Jerry's crackle of a laugh. He'd call me a sucker for punishment. 'Let people fly their own kite,' he'd say. 'Live for yourself.' Jerry never opens a door for anybody. He doesn't even hold the door for the next person coming through. My nose remembers.

"So, we'll see you Wednesday night," Jane said, while giving Chickadee a farewell hug and shaking Frankie's scooper bucket.

I bet the sofa won't take his weight. But I wouldn't want him to wreck my high-back chair either. I should borrow two fold-up chairs from Armand. And, with their history, I better make sure there's no money or jewelry lying around either.

"Say, Armand, could we borrow two fold-up chairs for Frankie to sit on next Wednesday?"

"Well, Chris, I don't think we need them. Our sofa is big enough."

"Jane, listen . . ."

"No, *you* listen; they're gonna be *my* guests, not yours."

23

HARRY

CRAZINESS! IF I HAD known what we were in for, I would have stayed home. For starters, my wife has a new friend: a former biker chick. Apparently this Chickadee and my Jane hit it off at their Exodus meet last Wednesday. Then, on the Friday after, Frankie called Armand and asked, 'Could a man named Harry join us this Sunday?' Harry, as Frankie had explained, was a well-versed-in-the-Bible elder from a non-denominational Christian Church. While having bodywork done to his car, he had also been invited to come to hear Frankie's testimony. Not in need of conversion, he just went out of curiosity. But, after Harry had heard Frankie's story, he had returned to the body shop, enticing Frankie to come to *his* Church instead. His Church's teachings, Harry had explained, were solid. No emotionalism. And when Frankie told him that, as far as Armand was concerned, the seed of God's kingdom is dormant in every human being, regardless of a person's faith, Harry got his back up. 'I want to challenge this man,' he had said. And, of course, Frankie had the nerve to call Armand to ask if Harry could join.

So, there I was, Chris Curmudgeon, setting up an extra chair and grumbling, 'Next thing you know, they'll send me out to rent a hall.'

But that was just the prelude.

Frankie walked in first again. Wearing the same clothes he had worn at his testimony and the Sunday before, he looked uptight. Chickadee, like last week, came in half hidden behind him. However, this time she was modestly dressed in a white crew neck sweater, light grey pants and shoes with much lower heels. And Harry was third. With polished black shoes, dark pants, light grey jacket, light pink shirt and a darker pinkish tie, he looked impressive. He had brought the other two with him in his car. As they came in, Armand welcomed them again with hugs. Harry preferred to shake hands. He seemed a bit uneasy. Instead of putting his Bible on the big table right beside him after he sat down straight as a pin, he held it on his lap. Chickadee, to his right, sat on the floor again. And Frankie, on his two chairs, was on his left. Jane and I, this time next to each other, were sitting across from him to the side of Armand's couch.

Comfortable with his pillows and looking slightly better, Armand suggested we sing 'Stairway to heaven' as an opener. Harry turned rigid. While Jane handed out the lyrics, Armand explained, "Making joyful music together makes it easier to relate to spiritual issues. But, I know, you're not comfortable with singing. So I suggest we do what some churches do; we only sing the first two verses."

After playing the melody a couple of times on his clarinet, he raised his pleasant voice and sang verse one.

Yes, I had heard the song before. But it wasn't of my time: too modern. Not my kind of beat. On top of that, it had psychedelic lyrics, if you ask *me*. They sounded like nonsense the first time I heard them and they sounded like nonsense now. Some lady, who believes everything that glitters is gold, is buying a stairway to heaven. But . . . , to please Armand, we tried singing along, except Harry. He looked disgusted. Judging by this crazy song, though, I could see how he had a problem with Armand's ideas. Weren't we supposed to focus on the spiritual business, instead of singing a song of some far out rock band? Listen to it. We're singing about a sign on the wall, about words that can have two meanings, about a tree, a brook, a songbird and whatever. And, all put together, these things are supposed to make us wonder; yes, make us wonder.

No sooner had we finished, even before Armand had put down his clarinet, or Harry blurted, "You'll never hear a song like that in my church."

"Why not, Harry?" Armand inquired.

"It's written and performed by unbelievers."

For a minute or so Armand remained silent. "What," he finally asked, "does the Bible say about unbelievers?"

"It says, 'What does a believer have in common with an unbeliever?' It's in second Corinthians, chapter six, verse fifteen."

"Isn't it interesting how each different denomination finds its strength in different Bible verses, often at the expense of neglecting others?"

"What do you mean by, at the expense of neglecting others? My Church doesn't neglect anything. It believes every word in the book."

"Then, maybe, you could share how your Church reconciles the verse you just quoted with a warning written somewhere else in the same book. It warns not to judge others so *we* won't be judged."

When Harry did not respond, Armand turned to Chickadee.

"Chickadee, what name were you given at birth?"

"Gloria," she timidly replied.

"That's a beautiful name. Would you prefer we call you that?"

"I'm a whore, remember? I'm not worthy of that name. My mom loved it. She loved me and I loved her." Tears came to Chickadee's eyes. She wiped them with the sleeve of her sweater. Oh, no, I thought. Not more emotionalism. But, emotionalism it was. Chickadee began to cry. Armand handed Jane a tissue box while pointing at

Chickadee. Jane took it, went over, knelt beside her and, like a caring mother, put her arm around the now rather distraught-sounding woman sitting on the floor.

In between sobs, Chickadee shared how her mom had died of cancer when she was twenty-four. Her dad had gone off the deep end, left her with an aunt and disappeared. Her brother, nineteen at the time, moved out west. Gloria, they thought, would be able to hold her own. At the time she was in a relationship and had a good job. But, she had felt abandoned and lost. Within a year she was an alcoholic, a drug addict and a prostitute.

Harry blew his nose, scraped his throat, kept re-gripping his Bible and rearranging his legs.

"When you were born in the spirit, a month or two ago," Armand said after a few seconds, "you *were* set free from your addictions. For a while you were feeling great. Now, life's a struggle again. The hate that remained in you, which you talked about last week, probably entered into your heart soon after your mom died."

Chickadee nodded.

"Would you like to be set free from this hate?"

"I'd love to." Then, looking up to Armand with a mixture of surprise and fear, she asked, "But how can I be?"

"Focus your mind on Jesus, in whatever form you're comfortable with. He'll take care of it by using unworthy me."

To everybody's amazement Armand stretched out his hand toward Chickadee and said, "I claim the power of the shed blood of Jesus to cover and protect you, Chickadee, and all of us present in this room."

If I hadn't noticed Harry's open mouth, I would have let my own bottom jaw drop. Like a tribal witch doctor, this man was covering us with blood, even the blood of a Jesus whom he himself had claimed was no more than a myth. What on earth had I gotten into? This was the last time for me.

"I take authority over you, spirit of hate residing in Chickadee," I heard him say. And without raising his voice even the slightest he added, "In the name of Jesus I bind you and in His name I command you to depart from her now and go to the foot of the Cross where Jesus will deal with you with authority and with justice. For Jesus is Lord."

Chickadee convulsed as if having to vomit. She let out an ear-piercing shriek. Her body went limp.

"And I ask you, heavenly Father, to fill the void created within Chickadee by the departure of this spirit of hate with your spirit of compassion and love. Thank you, Father, for giving us this authority in the name of Jesus. Amen."

Slowly, Chickadee regained her posture. Her face had changed. Making sure nobody saw it, I pinched my arm. It did hurt.

Her eyes had softened. And strangely enough, she now seemed to radiate some sort of peace. When she finally spoke, her voice was gentle and warm. "Thank you, Jesus," she said. "Thank you. Thank you." Then, after slowly looking around the room and finally focusing on Armand, she softly added, "Yes, I would love to be called Gloria again."

Harry's mouth was still open. Jane looked frightened. Frankie had his eyes closed and his hands folded. I was shaking my head. This was unreal.

"Yes, thank you, Lord Jesus," Armand said. Then, while trying to meet the eyes of one person at a time, he added, "Relax! I simply did what Jesus promised I would be able to do if I believed in Him."

"This," Harry stuttered, "this, this is of the devil. The authority to do these things was only given to the apostles. When they died, it ceased. Besides, Frankie told me you believe people can be born again even if they don't believe in Jesus. That's not what Jesus taught. Jesus said, 'No one comes to the Father but through me.' John fourteen six. I'm leaving."

"If you're uncomfortable, Harry, by all means—feel free," Armand said in an accommodating tone. "But you may be better able to guide Frankie in his faith if you give me a chance to first explain my understandings."

Harry, already standing, hesitated.

"Yes," said Frankie, "please stay. If you leave, who will be able to warn me when Armand starts twisting words and meanings?"

Harry sat down.

"Thanks Harry, I appreciate that. And now, Gloria and Frankie, why has Jesus seemingly left you after he was born in your heart? The reason, as I understand it, is simple but hard to accept. As long as you're functioning on His grace, you're not building your faith. From the Exodus story, which you read with Jane last Wednesday, you learned how the Israelites were set free from slavery. You were set free from slavery to sin. The Israelites, after gaining freedom, had to endure many tests. They had to prove that they trusted Yahweh, their God. You are being tested to prove your faith and your trust in Jesus. From the moment the Israelites were set free, they had to struggle for forty years in the desert in order to arrive in their promised land. When you were set free, you embarked on the road to your promised land, which is heaven. But Yahweh promised the Israelites he'd be with them all the way. And, in the person of Jesus, He promises the same to you. But, like the Israelites, you need to learn to recognize your Lord's presence.

"Did you recognize his strong hand, a few minutes ago, when he used me to cast out that spirit of hate? Everything that happens to you from now on is meant to build your faith. If you return to your former life, Jesus will do whatever is needed to bring you back into a meaningful relationship with him again. He may have to use tears, sweat, and suffering."

Harry was still rigid. He had put his Bible on the table and was now just fidgeting with his keys.

"I chose 'Stairway to heaven' as our song, because it holds messages which you will hopefully remember. Verse two tells us that words sometimes have two meanings.

"The Bible is full of stories and parables that have important hidden meanings. Jesus spoke in parables. His heavenly Father even had the lessons, which contain His messages, acted out in the lives of real people and especially in the descendants of Israel. The Exodus story is a great example.

The verse, '*She's buying a stairway to heaven,*' means the lady believes she can buy her way into heaven by giving, out of her abundance, lots of money to the Church or other charitable organizations. But she knows, if that doesn't work, she can get what she came for simply by 'a word.' The supposedly unbelieving rocker who wrote these lyrics tries to tell us what the lady deep in her heart knew to be true. Namely, it's only by living according to God's word that she can find her way into eternal glory.

"And the words, 'Ooh, it makes me wonder,' will hopefully encourage you, no matter what you'll read or hear regarding earthly or eternal life, to always, like a child, do just that: wonder."

After Armand closed the session with a short prayer, Harry stood up. Half-heartedly thanking Armand for allowing him to attend, he said, 'I'm very uneasy about what happened. I'll discuss it with my pastor.' Then he excused himself to Jane and me, nodded to Frankie while avoiding looking in Chickadee's, I mean Gloria's, direction, and stepped out the door. Jane had already promised to bring Frankie and Gloria, home.

With Harry gone, we were all more relaxed.

Gloria seemed in another world. She tried to be ahead of Jane in serving Armand, spoke very little and, as if trying to wake up, kept closing and opening her eyes. Partly to make conversation, partly out of curiosity, I asked Armand, "Why didn't you cast this hate demon out last week when she told us about it? I mean, why let the jerk needlessly have his way in her for a whole other week?"

"Last Sunday, my physical and spiritual strength were low. I needed time to deepen my intimacy with the giver of life and, through prayer and fasting become more in tune with *His* spirit. I needed added power from outside of me to be able to set my face like flint against the creep."

24

ENRICHED

TOSSING AND TURNING, THE night after Armand's conjuring trick of changing a Chickadee into a Gloria, I tried to figure out how to permanently disassociate myself from the man. Without creating a major scene with him or with Jane, I wanted out. The implications of remaining part of his religious variety show seemed too much. Didn't even his Muslim friend agree? This man talked with equal enthusiasm about all sorts of religions. He was on fire about the beauty of the Hebrew language, quoted sayings of the Buddha with enthusiasm, was excited about quantum understandings in Hinduism and could clarify whatever issue a Muslim had with Christianity. But now, we had landed in Frankie's Christianity, with the casting-out of demons and the works. Where would it end? After he gets us all converted to whatever, I can just hear him say, 'BUT . . . , this is not what it's all about.'

However, the bare naked facts were; Frankie and Gloria had been set free of some undesirable attitude issues. And, talking about undesirable attitude issues, I still had this anger. I knew it was directed at God and, consequently, at the religion business as a whole. So, if I removed Armand and his abracadabra from my life, I'd have no more reasons to get angry.

After sneaking out of bed for the third time and not wanting to disturb Jane anymore, I decided, at 3 a.m., to sleep on the sofa. Thank God, the springs had survived Frankie and the Exodus business. Jane and Gloria had sat separately, I was told. Although that wouldn't have mattered much, for on that night Gloria had still been her old self, this feather light Chickadee. Anyway, why did God and the religion business continue to stir up my anger? It was because, if he existed, he was unfair. Armand, of course, kept insisting God is playing by his own rules. Lousy rules, if you ask me. Sure, I could just let Armand talk about his pet subject and allow Jane to join a Hallelujah choir. But it wasn't that simple. There were harder facts than a changed Frankie and Gloria. The whole religious scene is rife with confusion and contradictions. It's not just chaos. It's madness. Judging by the media's coverage of religion, it's all about infighting, back-biting, power struggles, hatred, proselytizing, boycotting, ethnic cleansing, wars and you name it. Anything causing pain and misery, religion has been guilty of it. No matter what Armand says; religion still seems to poison everything. And with all his religion, like a salesman working on commission, he now has his foot in my door. I must decide. Do I let him in with his spiritual deals or do I politely ask him to withdraw his foot? Or, do I just shut the door hard and the heck with his foot?

I must have drifted into sleep. When the phone rang that Monday morning, I still hadn't made a firm decision about Armand's foot. The call was from his support worker, Joy. Her car wouldn't start. Would I be willing to drive Armand to his radiation appointment?

*   *   *

"All-right," I said to Armand, while turning my car onto the main road to the hospital. I hope you'll excuse me, but I lost a lot of sleep last night over yesterday. You gave me the creeps. You sounded like a shaman sprinkling chicken blood on his patients. And then you tell us, 'Relax. It's nothing. I'm just driving out a demon.' How on earth can you justify that kind of language? Covering with blood—even the blood of someone whom you, only a short while ago, claimed to be nothing but a myth. Sure, you changed your mind on that issue when you were zapped by some supernatural power. But did that make you suddenly accept as truth the whole gamut of this religious sacrifice-business?"

Resting comfortable against the back of his seat, with hands folded on his lap as if praying, Armand kept looking ahead. He did not respond. I knew by now, this was his way of saying, 'I'm listening, let me have it.'

"Listen, friend! Half a year ago you got me entangled in this spiritual web of yours. Even to this day you're keeping us in the dark about your own religion. You got my back up by indirectly giving my wife this idea of finding a church. You destroyed my peace by preaching about those clever understandings you've had. You reasoned out your conclusion for a god/man Jesus myth. Then you changed your mind because of some spiritual awakening. Remember how you were sitting right beside me, just like this, on the way to Josh's funeral? Remember how you sang and recited how great God is? Are you blind to all the pain and misery mankind has suffered because of this great God of yours? Are you blind to how, in reality, God isn't great at all and how religion poisons everything? And . . . ," I took a deep breath and opened my mouth again to spout out more, when Armand began to laugh his warm, joyful laugh.

"Oh, Chris," he finally said. "Watch your driving. And loosen up. Life's too short to get worked up like that. You are who you are and I am who I am. And, it is true. Since we met, I've tried to make you sit next to me on my personal, religious, roller coaster ride. But, you're impatient.

"Sixty years ago, I was an unbeliever like you. I made my Sonnetta-deal with a supposed God. In that deal, both

God and I won. He gave me my girl. And I, many years later, hoping to find out what to look for as proof for his reality, checked out all these different religions. But, during my search, I never experienced anything extraordinary. So my search for God's reality was moved to the backburner. In fact, some years later, I removed it from my stove altogether. My reasoning mind had built up this water-tight case for a mythical god/man. But, lo and behold, out of the blue, in an environment where I would have never looked, I was overwhelmed by this unexplainable power. My scientific mind fought the experience while my heart drank it in. More confused than ever, I made another deal with God."

"Armand, please quit right there. Yes, you've tried to make me join you on your religious roller coaster. But I've told you, I'm not interested and I'm tired of it. Show me your end-stop and *I* will decide if I want to join you there. Right now I don't see the use of figuring out all these contradictory religious issues. Even you are changing sides like a drunken soccer player. Every time you've come up with a new understanding, you tell us you've used solid reasoning. I've lost faith in your clever arguments."

"Clever arguments, you're so right. I thought I was smart in discovering that almost all prophecies regarding a possible Jesus can just as well be applied to the descendants of Israel as a whole. I also thought it clever of me to notice there seemed little solid evidence of a historical Jesus in any first century writings. And, I considered myself very bright in picking up on how St. Paul, the man whose wisdom Christians use in defending their faith, hardly mentions a physically alive Jesus. The only argument that didn't take a lot of brains was the fact that the four main books, referring to a supposed living Jesus, were picked from a larger number of writings. This, to me, was putting them very much in question. Yes, I even thought I had a touch of brilliance for coming up with the mythical god/man Jesus solution."

"Okay, okay," I butted in. "Then, unexpectedly, you get doused with holy power. You thought you saw a crucified Jesus and, bingo: all these clever arguments go out the window."

"Wrong. After I had been doused, nothing went out the window. As I told you in the coffee shop after Frankie's testimony, the power that overwhelmed me at that breakfast meeting only confused me. Even though my heart wanted to open up to it, my brain convinced me to shut it out. Nothing in my mind would have changed if God hadn't followed up on the deal I made with him after that. And follow up he did. I told you how he, in my own bathroom, in front of my own sink, drew me for the second time into an experience of holiness, the memory of which has never left me."

"Hmm! So what was this covering with blood all about?"

"I did not say, 'I cover you with blood.' I said I cover you with *the power* of the shed blood of the living Jesus.

"I know this sounds crude to whoever cannot relate to it. But, as I understand it, the explanation lies in the spiritual dimension of purpose. It is in this dimension that this spiritual power exists. It is the spiritual power generated by the sacrifices and the blood shed by those who have been, who presently are, and who, in the future, will be persecuted and suffer on account of integrity. I planned to elaborate on that next Sunday morning."

"So, after your Holy Spirit experience, you ditched the mythical Jesus idea and got yourself a living Jesus instead. How long did that last?"

"Wrong again. I didn't ditch anything. After that event, I came to understand the spiritual dimension of purpose better. More important still: I became convinced of the reality of complementary duality. Complementary duality manifests itself, as I shared before, in the smallest energy part of a beam of light—the photon. The photon is, simultaneously, a particle and a vibration. Assuming that complementary duality also explains the basic attributes of the creator of that light, his perfect judgment and his merciful love, I asked myself this question: could complementary duality be the stone of wisdom with which to solve all spiritual riddles?

"Could the myths of god/men, as they appear in different cultures, be just as relative to our spiritual evolution as the actualization of the myth in a living Jesus of 2000 years ago? Could it be that, because the creator wanted the story of the living Jesus written under the guidance of His Holy Spirit, no writings about Jesus can be found until many years after his death? Is it possible that he wanted the story of the flesh and blood god/man to be brought together through both the memory of those who had known Jesus and the past understandings of all mankind? And, could it be that everything prophesied about Jesus is equally applicable to the nation of Israel and its descendants collectively? After all, the promise of a flesh and blood Messiah, 'the Christ,' was fulfilled in and through them.

"And, is it possible for complementary duality to explain why the gospels focus on Jesus, the flesh and blood human in whom 'the Christ' fully lived? This while the apostle Paul focuses on 'the Christ', who is the personification of our collective righteousness, which is meant to come alive and become active in every human being.

"In other words," I grumbled. "No matter what conclusions you drew during your roller coaster ride, *your* goose got never cooked. Always able to reconcile an old understanding with a new one, you just got smarter. That's where I lose, I guess. Yesterday, when Chickadee changed into Gloria, *my* goose got cooked officially. I can no longer deny what my own eyes have seen. Her face, mean and tight, became relaxed and gentle. Her voice, harsh and angry, became soft and warm. So, the possible God you keep talking about showed forth his power and channelled it through you."

"Remember, Chris, how I talked about the cosmic dance? How I envision people from all persuasions to step onto that dance floor, on which is written: Enrich me. Enrich me. Enrich me. There's no goose cooking on that floor. Whenever I came to different insights, my understandings were enriched. Why wouldn't that work for you?

"And your remark, 'God isn't great', is an oxymoron. God, in whatever form, with or without intelligence, represents what is greatest. A mere human cannot claim there is nothing great in or about the universe. But you're right. Some religions have pictured God as a cosmic monster. Man's unwillingness, or inability, to freely open up to the workings of this God's power has changed the meaning of religion. As I see it, true religion still is about a relationship based on integrity between me, the higher power and every other human being. And, interestingly enough, physicists are discovering that, instead of sub-atomic particles, the only thing that may be real could very well be the relationships that exist between the different expression of energy or light.

"And about the poisoning; I believe it's the lack of integrity in the relationships of the odd leader and many followers that poisons religion. Those are the issues the media tries to draw our attention to. Deceit, ignorance, greed, hunger for power, manipulation, or lives filled with empty practices can suck the spiritual wonder out of any belief system."

"Man, it's a good thing we're at the hospital. I need a break."

"I'm sorry, Chris. I can't help myself. My mind seems to be bursting with a desire to verbalize the entire cosmos.

"But, why not forget about everything I've told you so far and only remember this. My greatest enrichment came when I was doused with God's Holy Spirit in front of my bathroom sink. There, my relationship with the higher power changed.

"The cosmic power, this breathtaking phenomenon I had tried to analyze, became a personal, loving and caring entity as well. There, on my knees, I sensed and experienced complementary duality. I came to know how I truly am God's offspring, God's son, and how He is my loving Father. Mind you, getting to know Him as my Father was one thing. To think, speak and act as my heavenly Father's child, as his worthy son, that turned out to be a life-long challenge."

"We're here. Tell me, Armand: while they nuke your prostate does your mouth busy itself with verbalizing the entire cosmos to the nurses?"

He grinned, squeezed my shoulder and said, "Thanks for taking me."

25

FRICTION

Here we go again. I had arranged to pick Armand up at the hospital main entrance after his treatment. From a distance, I already noticed how he had parked his wheelchair away from people traffic and, of course, facing the sun. As I approached him from behind, I couldn't believe my ears. He was animatedly babbling to himself about majestically white, cumulus clouds, and heaven knows what. I knew he had no cell phone. If that wasn't dementia, what was it? Hoping to hear things that would reveal another side of the man's character, I quickly switched on my pocket recorder. Unreal! The man was praying. These were his words. "Thank you, heavenly Father, for the coming of spring, for new life and all the miracles of your creation."

I know, I should have respected his privacy and switched off my gadget, but I just couldn't resist.

"Thank you, Father, for nature's abundance of fractals and how they remind me of how I am a fractal of you. Thank you for the cosmic dance of randomness and order which we experience as chaos. Thank you for the gift of life and for the gift of eternal life. Thank you for the measure of health I have. Yes, I would like my cancer cured. Sandra and Paul have taken the loss of Josh hard. For them, I'd like to be around a little longer. Regardless, help me to be a worthy photon in your marvellous light. I surrender to whatever pain, discomfort, or inconvenience I need to suffer. I offer it up to obtain graces and blessings for those of my cosmic siblings whom I bring before you every day in prayer.

"Bless Jennifer, the nurse who cares for my comfort while I am having these treatments. Bless her teenage son, her daughter, and the husband who left her. Put it on Jennifer's heart to return to the faith community she belonged to. Bless Dawn, the head nurse, her husband John, her brother the drug addict, and her mentally-challenged sister. Bless all who are involved in treating me. Better still, Father, pour out your blessings on all who enter through the doors of this facility; doctors, nurses, employees, patients, and visitors alike. I know, papa God, these are many. But for you, there is only one. Each person is your beloved child with whom you desire to have a personal relationship.

"Bless Chris, Jane, Frankie, Gloria, and Harry. You . . ."

Then my conscience kicked in hard. It was wrong for me to listen in on this man's private conversation with his God. I flipped the switch and quietly backed away. Papa God? Maybe it's Alzheimer's. When I first met the man, he talked about God's seven spirits bundled up in light. Today he's talking like a baby snuggling on God's lap. Who knows, tomorrow he may be imagining himself to be God's majestic, cumulus clouds coordinator. And, he explained chaos to me. But what on earth are fractals?

Walking up to him from the side, ready to play whatever game was needed, I pretended I had just arrived. "Hey, big man," I cheerfully greeted. "How'd ye make out? Did they treat you right? How do you feel?"

*   *   *

While driving home, curious to find out if there was an onset of mental disorder, I was first to speak. Never comfortable with silence in the first place, I just had to open my mouth. Of course, I would have liked to talk about anything but the God-business. But, with the demon demo still fresh in my mind, I was also getting more and more curious as to where this man's religious roller coaster ride would end. On the other hand, his words, 'I'm bursting with a desire to verbalize the entire cosmos,' still rang in my ears as well. Hoping against all odds that, maybe, on this short trip home, he would finally take me to the end of his quest, I asked, "After your Pentecostal block layer encounter and God's power-shower follow-up at your bathroom sink, did you decide Pentecostal was the way to go?"

"Yes, thirty years ago, that's what I decided. And for a while I was comfortable. But I discovered that, for some people, this baptism of the Holy Spirit, just like Josh's born-again event, wears off. And then people start pretending. They participate in worship services while their hearts and minds are not at all surrendered to the will of God. Having their own agenda, they begin to fake their spirituality. No, Chris, finding my way in the Christian chaos wasn't simple."

"Just keep talking." It was either stop him or let the verbal flood flow.

"My next experience was at another Full Gospel Business Men's breakfast meeting. Because these meetings were inter-denominational, I found myself, at the breakfast table, sitting across from a Protestant pastor with a Catholic priest to my right. Sonnetta was sitting with women friends.

"The priest's name was John. The pastor's name was Gregg. After we'd sung some worship songs, there was, as often happens, prophecy. That's when people who supposedly are in tune with God speak a message which God desires to give through them. This time, like almost every other time I had attended this particular chapter, this lady stood up and gave her usual, 'Oh my people, you are my people. It is you my people whom I am blessing among all other people.' Anyway: my people this, my people that, and nothing new.

"When she finished, I said to the priest, 'a penny for your thoughts?'"

"'Oh,' he answered, 'let her babble. By speaking words that sound like prophecy, she probably wants to impress the people at her table. It's not uncommon. There's a charismatic in my church who does the same. I believe these people, even though baptized in the Holy Spirit, still are in some kind of bondage. But, if I'm honest,' he hesitated before he added, 'I'm still in a bit of bondage myself. I struggle with pride.'

"At the time, I didn't know what a charismatic was. The priest explained. It's a person who has received one or more supernatural gifts, called 'charisms'. The word charism is Greek for 'gift of grace.'

"After the priest's explanation, the pastor remarked, 'John is right. People like that are one of the reasons why my church wants to have nothing to do with this Holy Spirit baptism. It's too hot an issue. These supposed supernatural gifts can cause a lot of trouble. Encouraging hypocrisy is one of them. Besides, this Holy Spirit baptism almost always causes division.'

"Hearing all this, I became excited. Here were two learned men from opposite sides of the Christian spectrum.

I expected an interesting dialogue and enthusiastically hooked in. 'Tell me, John, what brings you here? I thought Catholics believe they have the corner on truth.'

"'You're right,' he answered. My Church does believe it has the truth. What does your church believe?'

"In those days, I attended a Pentecostal church, but already had second thoughts. I knew, of course, Pentecostals are convinced that *they* have the truth, so I told him. I also confided my growing uneasiness in that denomination. The priest then turned to the pastor and asked him the same question. Gregg, probably sensing the trap, was slow to reply. But he confirmed that yes; his church was also convinced it had the truth.

"'So,' the priest laughed, 'we have nothing to discuss. Each of us believes his church has all truth. Although you, Armand, you're having doubts. You want to share?'

"'I have experienced some hypocrisy and fakery,' I said.

"Again the priest laughed. 'Good man, when you find a church where there is none of that, let me know. In my experience it's a permanent part of the human scene in both the religious and secular world. Therefore, when I visit other denominations, I commit myself to focus on what is genuine.'

"Am I boring you with my pastor-priest story, Chris?"

"Will it finally give Jane and me an answer to what your religion is?"

"Impatience! Impatience! I told you before. If I tell you straight what my convictions are, you will undoubtedly ask, 'how on earth did you come to believe that?' Then I have to tell you this whole story anyway. So why not relax, sit back, listen, and along the way, draw your own conclusions?"

I sighed, looked sideways at the man and couldn't help but smile. He had his answers and was determined not to shortcut his spiel. Did I want to hear it? I couldn't talk sports with him anyway. Why not let him have the floor? At least there wouldn't be any dreaded silence.

"Okay, have it your way. I won't interrupt anymore."

"The next remark the protestant pastor made got the ball rolling fast. He said, 'as long as a Christian Church teaches from scripture alone, it has at least the foundation of truth. And,' he slowly added, 'this, as I understand it, is not the Roman Catholic approach.'

"Then the priest asked Gregg where it said in scripture that scripture alone can be trusted and not scripture *and* tradition? I was lapping it up. These two men knew their stuff. Gregg right away fired back, quoting verses they both knew by heart; verses that, apparently, are very important in the Protestant-Catholic dialogue. If you can call it a dialogue, that is. Since then, I have hashed them over so many times that I now know them by heart as well. So, this is what Gregg quoted, 'all scripture is inspired by God and profitable for teaching, for reproof, for correction, and for training in righteousness that the man of God may be complete, equipped for every good work.' And, without a pause, he quoted another verse in which Jesus rebukes the Pharisees saying, 'Why do you break the commands of God for the sake of your tradition?' Of course he added chapter and verse number to each quote. But those I forgot.

"What I didn't forget was how the priest readily answered, 'John, the verse you quoted says, '*all* scripture,' not '*only* scripture.' And Jesus condemned the Pharisees for their *corrupt* traditions, not for *all* traditions? Scripture also says, 'brethren, stand firm and hold to *the traditions* which you were taught by us, either by *word of mouth or by letter.*'

"And, just as I'm having the time of my life listening to their scripture skirmish, Gregg spoils it all by saying, 'I shouldn't be discussing Catholic-Protestant faith issues while eating bacon and eggs. There are too many teachings of that church that give me heartburn.'"

No kidding. Here was Armand again delighting in another religious fight. I could even sense his excitement in reliving this two-clergy battle. So I asked, "What's the matter with these Protestants? I now know, thanks to Jane, that Catholics burn heretics. But that, according to you, was done by religious manipulators who were messed up themselves. So why this Protestant antagonism towards Catholic beliefs?"

"It's the nature of the beast, so to speak. To be protestant means to be 'protesting' against any issue of faith originating in Rome."

"What was the priest's response to the pastor's heartburn?"

"'Let's drop the subject,' he replied. 'I don't want your breakfast to be spoiled on account of my faith. I came here because I love being with brothers and sisters in the Lord. These discussions don't bother me. I'm used to them. Whenever I attend an interdenominational gathering, I always have to defend something. That's why I have written down some Catholic apologetics. You can have a copy if you like.'

"'Thanks, but no thanks,' the pastor shot back. 'I've had my fill of Roman Catholic theology: purgatory, indulgences, Mary worship, praying to Saints, etc. etc. When I received my pastor's training, I was clearly shown what's wrong with it all. I have no need for more clarifications.'

"'Too bad,' I said. 'I'm searching for truth and you two seem to know what you're talking about. You certainly can quote scriptures.'"

"The priest laughed again, 'Fooled you good, didn't I? I only know fourteen verses by heart. Two for every one of the seven most common faith issues protestant people keep challenging me on. Of course, I've studied scripture in the seminary. I read from it every day during my meditations and when I say Mass. But I'm not able, like many protestant pastors, to quote verses at random and tell you where exactly in scripture they are.'

"Determined to profit as much as possible from this religion bout, I asked for a copy of the priest's apologetics and fired another question.

"'John, tell me, what's your church's answer to those who claim there's no solid proof that Jesus ever lived?'

"'We believe there's ample proof. But, even if there wasn't, we always have the one artefact that proves everything. It proves Jesus lived. It proves he was severely scourged. He was crucified. And it proves he rose from the dead. It's all imprinted on the Shroud of Turin.'"

"'The what?' both Gregg and I exclaimed."

And, while Armand and I drove into our retirement community's underground parking garage, I exclaimed the same, "The what?"

"Thirty years ago, Chris, I had to go to the library to find out what he was talking about. You, Chris, can go online, type in 'Shroud of Turin,' and get as much info as you can stomach."

"Hmm! And what's a fractal?"

"A fractal is an object or a shape, like the branch of a vine or of any tree, where a small part resembles the whole. Fractals in nature make it easy for me to see how I resemble the higher power from which I sprung forth."

26

ABBA

"WAIT," I SAID, AFTER I parked the car, turned the key and eyed how Armand groped for his door handle. "Why don't you have prostheses?"

"The amputation wounds keep opening up. They don't tolerate irritations. Caring for them is a full-time job. But, in my apartment I get around okay. I strap pads to my stumps so I can walk. Like a midget, I adjust to my surroundings. My son engineered a fold-away twenty inch high aluminum bench that slides out of the way under my table. When it's time to cook, I unfold it in front of my kitchen counter."

Slightly reluctant, for whatever reason, to end my time with him, I put both hands on the steering wheel, looked at him sideways and said, "I just don't get it. I'm sorry, but I overheard you pray when I came to pick you up. The first day we met you asked if I recognized the existence of a higher power greater than me at work out there in the universe. We're talking trillions of stars, millions of galaxies. We're talking powers and distances that boggle the mind. And you, you call this incomprehensible power 'papa God.' True, you asked me to forget everything we've talked about and try to only remember the most memorable experience you ever had. The one, when the unfathomable cosmos showed you, in front of your bathroom sink, the other side of its duality. It was there, you said, this phenomenon named 'cosmos', suddenly became a loving and caring entity as well. The power, overwhelming you at that sink, revealed itself to you as a father. But how on earth can you call this cosmos-filling power, bigger than a zillion hydrogen bombs blowing up, 'papa'? How can your rational mind possibly reconcile a fourteen-billion-year-old universe with a Michelangelo rendition of a bearded, old man living in the clouds, wearing a hospital gown?"

"Tell me, Chris, why did you love your dad?"

"Simple. He cared for me. He did things with me. He showed he loved me by treating me like his son. And . . . , I guess, I felt intimately connected to him because he fathered me: flesh from his flesh, so to speak."

"So here is this incomprehensible power that brings forth and sustains the universe. I, a mere earthling, try to relate to it. Physics has learned about the interconnectedness of all that is. Personally I feel, taste and see how this incomprehensible power surrounds me with everything I need to enjoy earthly life. It makes it possible for me to co-create with it. It gives me the space and the freedom to learn my lessons, often the hard way, like a wise father would. And, through whatever creative or evolutionary process, I have received life; ultimately, this cosmos has fathered me. Therefore, even though its grandeur is incomprehensible, I am its offspring. Why then would I not express my love for this life-giving power and address it as, 'dear dad'?"

Through the windshield of the car, I looked up at the concrete ceiling of the garage. The galvanized water pipes of the sprinkler system, hanging from it, directed my mind back again to Armand's running tap story. Okay, so he had some sort of experience that made him see things differently. How crazy can you get, though? Claiming to have an intimate relationship with the Big-Bang and its aftermath and call it papa, that sounds like lunacy.

"Tell me, Armand, why not call this higher power 'mama'? I mean, talking to the cosmos as if it is one big womb sounds equally ridiculous."

"There you have it again, Chris: complementary duality. The willful power that brings forth is the father aspect. The mother aspect is the universe in which it all takes form. This became crystal clear during my running tap experience. But, talking about a running tap; that radiation treatment sure made me thirsty. How about a visit to the coffee shop? I'll treat."

*   *   *

12.45 p.m. Wrong time for coffee shops. Every table was taken.

"Why don't we go to my apartment?" Armand suggested. "I can brew you a lemon-ginger tea, with lemon wedge and honey, the likes of which you've never tasted before."

I accepted the invitation because, during his cosmic papa explanation, a rather direct question had formed in my mind. The privacy of his apartment seemed a better place to ask it.

The apartment was as we had left it the night before. All fold-up chairs neatly stacked beside the couch. However, the low aluminum scaffolding he had mentioned was now standing unfolded in front of the kitchen counter. I watched how Armand strapped on his pads, slid out of his wheelchair, mounted his kitchen runway and went about making tea for me and hot chocolate for him. It looked effortless. Yet, the ease he displayed must have come from dogged perseverance. When he finally wiggled himself onto the other end of the couch, placing between us a basket with muffins he had baked before breakfast, I complemented him, "You're amazing."

"I guess you've never seen a foot or mouth painter at work. They're a lot more amazing than I am."

Then, looking him straight in the eyes, I asked, "Tell me, Armand, what did you say to your loving, heavenly papa when you held your suffering, dying wife in your arms? And, what did you say to him when they wheeled you out of the hospital minus two legs?"

He didn't wince. His eyes remained open. But for a long time, he did not respond. Finally he said, "Chris, like every other human being in deep pain, I asked 'why?' However, my asking was not a cry of desperation. It was my hunger to understand. Already then I believed that every explanation, of whatever happens in our life, lies in the spiritual dimension of purpose. Measured backwards in time, it covers all intents of past events in our life, in the lives of our ancestors, and in the lives of those who have influenced our growing up and maturing. It also covers all consequences. The problem we humans have in finding answers is that we cannot possibly know the myriad intents and consequences that influence every happening. Only the cosmic computer can keep track of them all. Good and bad intents, and far-reaching good and bad consequences, all mixed together, bring forth our joys and sufferings. With regards to the why of my dear Sonnetta's death and the amputation of my legs, I have no answers; only speculations.

"As I understand it, my human purpose is to become tuned in to the will of the higher power. Everything in the cosmos obeys its laws automatically. I, however, do not. I have been given an intelligence of my own and a free will to choose. Whether I want to obey those laws is my decision. And, I believe, in order to procure my total obedience to those laws, I need to acquire an Abba-consciousness within my soul/self. The receiving and cultivating of such a consciousness comes about through the ways in which I respond to whatever happens in my life. I decide how I deal with the life I'm living as a result of those innumerable intents and consequences. By the way, the word 'Abba' is Aramaic for 'dear dad' or 'papa'. Tell me, Chris, what do *you* believe the purpose of our challenges is?"

What a question? I don't even believe my troubles have a purpose. They just happen. Why dwell on them? Most of them can't be changed anyway. But then, Gloria got a healing. But then, she was a mentally screwed-up addict. Suddenly an alarm bell went off in my mind. "Hold it," I said. "Are you trying to lead this question and answer game to the place where you can point at my occasional anger and say, Chris, you've got a demon?"

"Have another muffin," he replied with a chuckle. "You sound like some Pentecostals I've met. No, Chris, I don't see a demon in every corner. But we could try to figure out why you have this anger?"

"No need. I know why. I am angry at whatever higher power is responsible for my dad's death and . . . I'm angrier still if I'm told he, she or it, has dumped my dad in some heavenly campfire. And when someone tries to assure me that my holy stepfather is sitting, smiling broadly, on a golden throne in some air-conditioned heavenly mansion,

I'll boil over for sure. So, tell me, how did you know for certain this Chickadee had a demon?"

"With her it was easy. When anyone displays hate, anger or fear that's unreasonable or out of proportion to the situation at hand, that person must be channeling extra negative power from an outside source. Likewise, when someone displays compassion, acceptance or love that exceeds their own normal human ability, that person must be channeling extra positive power from an outside source as well. When the extra power increases the negative, I believe it shows a connection to the source of spiritual evil—a demon at work, so to speak. The person is in bondage. When the extra power displayed increases the positive, I believe it shows a connection to the source of spiritual good. Angels at work, you may say. The person is in a state of grace. So, next time you flare up, *you* do the math. Or, root out the cause. The quickest remedy for you might be to forgive your stepfather for having his misconceptions about God and imposing them on you."

"Imagine," I said with a heavy hint of sarcasm. "My friend Armand has all the answers." My eyes were resting on the aluminum runway made by his son, the engineer. That son probably loved his dad unconditionally. Never had any need to be angry, feel bitter or be depressed. How many mornings, after I had left home, had I woken up in that dreary apartment and considered downing a bottle of sleeping pills or go and jump off a bridge?

Slowly I stood up. "If Joy's car still isn't rolling in the morning, feel free to call me. I'll be awake and ready."

Speaking to my back, as I walked to the counter with my empty cup, he replied, "Remember, Chris, how on the first day we met, I asked for five more minutes to share my excitement about the miracle of colour? How about giving me another five to share my excitement about the miracle of the human heart?"

"How about getting to the point in, say, two and a half minutes?"

"Set your watch. White light, with seven colours hidden within it, shines on every fruit and vegetable. Each one absorbs and reflects it in a different mixture. But no matter what the mixture, the same light gives colour to all. Similarly, I believe that, in the spiritual dimension of purpose, the light of spiritual life shines into every human heart, into every soul/self. But every soul/self absorbs and expresses its own unique mixture of the seven spirits hidden in that one spiritual light. My mixture is different from every other human being's mixture. Yet, no matter what mixture of beliefs each human absorbs and expresses, the same Spirit gives spiritual life to all. And this Spirit, when we allow it, will nurture the seed of eternal life in us and quicken our Abba-consciousness. Only with an Abba-consciousness can we see all other humans as our cosmic siblings. Thanks for listening."

"Thank you for using big words again to express your pie-in-the-sky ideal. I guess the older one gets, the farther one moves from reality. It's nothing but a pipe dream to think that humans all over this world could see each other as siblings, as brothers and sisters of the creator's family. To accomplish that, everybody would need to denounce the religion they belong to. Religion is all about exclusiveness, about being chosen, about being set apart, about being right while everybody else is wrong."

"Wrong, and wrong again! Remember how you said, 'whoever thinks he understands the sub-atomic realm probably didn't get it?' Remember how I replied, 'many, who think they understand their religion, probably didn't get it either?' I also shared a while ago how I believe that most religious people have their minds dictate religion to their heart. Abba-consciousness will, instead, prompt our hearts, our soul/self, to sing the kind of spirituality to our mind that will help us see one another as brothers and sisters."

"Good for you. *My* heart certainly isn't singing spirituality to *my* mind. My heart and mind seem to specialize in cooking up criticisms and ridicule."

"Chris, Chris, how come you don't see what I see?"

"See what?"

"The multifaceted grandeur of our cosmos. My mind and soul are overwhelmed by its infinite greatness. To believe that one religious understanding can do justice to the entire spectrum of cosmic spirituality seems a rather restricted way of thinking to me."

"I'm sorry, Armand, I don't see it. Remember how you took us to the moon one day. Remember how you, while looking down on earth, talked about people judging others as stinkin these and stinkin those? And remember how you believed that even kids in the schoolyard, if they can get away with it, happily add the word 'stinkin' when they judge the mentally slow as airheads?"

Armand burst out laughing and blurted, "I knew you and I would get along great!" In control again, he added, "Know though, Chris, I'm not judging you. I simply want to see you live in a box with a wide open door, enabling you to live a life without fear of listening to others."

"Whatever!" I thoughtfully replied as I looked at my watch and walked to the door. "We're into overtime. Both your ginger tea and your muffins were state of the art." With the knob in my hand, I turned around, showed him a grimace of a smile, and assured him once more, "don't forget; call me if you need me."

"I will. And you, Chris, don't forget to check out the Shroud of Turin."

27

MYSTERY

"HALLELUJAH, PRAISE WHATEVER," I exclaimed, smiling contently. "The Shroud of Turin, the supposed burial cloth of Jesus, is a fake." That's the beauty of the internet. You can almost always find what you're looking for.

Armand had not called on Tuesday morning. Joy's car must have been purring again. After breakfast, I played Jane the recordings I had made on Monday's hospital run with Armand. When finished, she tried to cajole me into searching out the Shroud business on the web. But with the demon affair on Sunday, two sermons in the car on Monday, plus another sermon at his place and the re-runs for Jane on Tuesday, Religion was, so to speak, coming out of my ears. Even when Jane left that Wednesday morning to meet Sylvia, I still had no desire to dive back into the faith-business. I decided to forget it all and get back to reality by reading the paper. But, whatever I read, my mind kept going back to that Shroud.

After half an hour or so, I dropped the paper, went to the man-made super brain and switched it on. What I found made me happy. The article clearly stated: 'The Shroud of Turin was man-made.' It further stated that, even though many believers are convinced it is the burial cloth in which Jesus was wrapped after his crucifixion, it now has been proven to be bogus.

Yes, this rectangular piece of cloth, composed of flax fibrils measuring 4.4 x 1.1 m (14.3 x 3.7 ft.), holds the front and back image of a Caucasian man, about thirty years old. Heavily flogged, and with all the wound marks of having suffered crucifixion, the image is real. But, artists have been able to reproduce the image, using materials and methods that were available in the 14th century.'The report was based on research funded by the Italian organization of atheists and agnostics and a 'debunking group.'

"Hmm," I mumbled. "Debunkers, agnostics and atheists eh? All people who've probably never seen a Chickadee change into a Gloria."

The only fair thing to do was check more sites. I shouldn't have.

Wishing Jane the pleasure of becoming independently confused, I fed my findings to the printer. I figured, if she could read it all herself, she wouldn't have to badger me with questions.

The Shroud, preserved and guarded in the Cathedral of Saint John the Baptist in Turin, Italy, is the most studied and most controversial ancient artefact known to man. The image on the cloth has been imprinted by a power no scientist has yet been able to identify.

In 1978, a group of scientists working under the name STURP, (Shroud of Turin Research Project) analyzed the shroud for five days around the clock. Some of its members would be working while others slept. Their final report, the result of 150,000 man hours of investigation and analysis, was published in 1981. This group, led by a nuclear physicist, included a thermal chemist, a thermo-dynamicist, two electric power experts, a forensic pathologist, two photographers, an optical physicist, and a biophysicist.

Their official consented conclusion: 'the Shroud image is that of a real human form of a scourged, crucified man, and is not the product of an artist. The question of how the image was produced is an ongoing mystery, and remains unanswered until further studies are done.'

But . . . in 1988, other scientists used radiocarbon dating and found that the cloth was made in the 13th or 14th century. Conclusion: it's a fake.

Then, in 2005, a chemist discovered the piece used for the 1988 radiocarbon dating had been cleverly sewn in by nuns to repair some of the damage done to the Shroud by a fire in 1532. This same chemist showed that the Shroud could very well be from 2000 years ago.

Noteworthy characteristics of the shroud are:

* The image on the shroud, put on the cloth long before the invention of photography, is a negative.

* On each of the eyes is the image of a coin. It is the widows-mite, a coin issued between 29 and 33 CE.

* A two-dimensional photograph of the two-dimensional image produces three-dimensional information; information where it cannot possibly exist.

* If, as some have suggested, the image was made through the use of a laser, this laser beam must have been much more powerful than today's technology is able to produce.

* The imprint on the part of the cloth that was underneath the body does not show any pressure points. This means the body was suspended in mid-air when the imprint was made, and thus, not subject to the law of gravity. It also means that the image of the body was projected upwards and downwards from a center interface.

* By slightly changing the focus of a camera's lens, different information is revealed at different depths of the image.

* Further evidence of the cloth's authenticity is the fact that, blood marks on the head of the image on the Shroud perfectly correspond with blood marks on the burial cloth wrapped around Jesus' head. And the history of this head-cloth, kept in a small chapel attached to the San Salvador Cathedral in Oviedo, northern Spain, is undisputed.

*   *   *

Thursday, March 15, 2012

While bringing a spoonful of crispy flakes, swimming in velvety smooth milk, to my mouth on the morning after my Shroud search, I suddenly had a brain wave. Wise-guy Armand's complementary duality understanding of two absolute-opposites does not fly. For, if God is a universal truth, he must then, simultaneously, be perfectly good and incorrigibly bad."

When I nailed him on it over the phone, he laughed and said, "talk about idea exchange, Mr. Masochist. You know how I like to elaborate."

"Hit me back. I'm in my favourite chair with a morning coffee."

"Chris, good stands on its own. Good, in itself, is comprised of the two absolute opposites of perfect justice and unfathomable mercy. It is the eternal attribute of God. Bad, on the other hand, is not comprised of opposites. It is *not* eternal. Like us humans, it is subjected to time.

"And, Chris," he right away added. "Did you check out the Shroud?"

"I did. And, while we're at it, if that Shroud embodies a truth what, according to your scientific mind, are the absolute opposites it then holds?"

"If it's a fake, it is both an ordinary piece of cloth and a master piece of human achievement. It then is a testimony to the artist's faith, as well as to his genius. Passing it off as the genuine cloth, must then have been the work of some greedy wheeler-dealer who might have bought it from him cheap.

"If it is the real burial cloth of Jesus, again, it is just an ordinary piece of cloth. But to find the absolute opposite of an ordinary piece of cloth in that situation requires going out on a non-scientific limb.

"First of all, what do you know about holograms?"

"Holograms are made by splitting a laser beam in half and letting one half fall on the photographic plate unaltered. The other half of the beam is first made to reflect off the object to be imaged, and then on the plate. Together these two beams form an interference pattern of stripes and swirls which can produce a three-dimensional image named hologram."

"Sounded like you read it out of a dictionary."

"No. I remembered. I looked it up after my internet Shroud party."

"Then you know that the word 'hologram' means 'whole message' and that all the information of the whole hologram is present in each of its parts.

"Now, as for me going out on that limb, hear I go.

"Science says, 'the Big Bang was the beginning.' They can even study it today by analyzing the info they receive from the microwave background that surrounds our cosmos. Science also says that all things originate from that Big Bang. But . . . , as I've probably said before, in the beginning there was nothing to carry sound waves. Therefore it must have been a burst of light, which equals energy. It must have been a Big Flash.

"Scripture tells us, 'In the beginning, God said, "Let there be light."' It also tells us, 'In the beginning was *the Word* and *the Word* was with God and *the Word* was God. Through *the Word* all things were made and without Him nothing that was made has been made.'

"By believing in both science and scriptures I, for starters, feel confirmed in my understanding of the Big Flash. Secondly, I am tempted to conclude that the Big Flash and *the Word* are one and the same. Scripture even calls *The Word*, the light of the world.

"So, when scripture says, '*The Word* lived among us in the person of Jesus,' I am equally tempted to conclude that, in Jesus, the Big Flash lived among us as well. After all, Jesus claimed to be fully God and God calls Himself the 'I AM.' In this name, I hear God say, 'ALL that truly is, is me.' And, of course, this includes the origin of ALL, the Big Flash, through which, according to science, ALL things were made.

"Now if the Christ who resided in the body of Jesus also personified the Big Flash, then we have our absolute opposite. For if one small part of a hologram can hold the information of the whole, there is no reason why that one minuscule part of the Big Flash, living in the body of Jesus, wasn't holding all information pertaining to the whole Big Flash. It even implies that if the kingdom of God is within *me*, as scripture says it is, then you and I, and all humans have, within them, a minuscule part of the Big Flash, a minuscule part of the 'I AM.' And, I believe, this minuscule part of the Big Flash within you and me is the very power of life. If true, this would explain how Christ Jesus could say, 'I am *The Life*.'

"After some miserable humans had tortured this Jesus' human body to death, that part of *The Life* vibrating within Him, burst free. Instantly changing all atomic structures back to their origin, it imprinted His very nature, as part of the whole Big Flash, on the burial cloth. Then, wrapping Himself in a body made up of photons, He again took the form of Jesus, walked through walls and appeared and disappeared at will.

"When our bodies stop functioning, they decay slowly over a period of time. The body of Jesus disintegrated in a flash.

"And listen to this. Whatever information may be locked up in the Shroud is more readily available from the photographic plates made in 1931 than from all the digital photographs made since. It's because in 1931, in order to make a photographic plate, the object photographed needed to have a much longer exposure time. The extended exposure has apparently drawn out an incredible amount of information. In a holographic laboratory in Eindhoven, in the Netherlands, this data has been retrieved and digitally stored. Today's physicists don't have the tools to read it. But, once they do have the tools, that digitally stored information may blow their minds."

"Blow my mind, that's what you're doing.

"Where'd you get this info thirty years ago without a world wide web?"

"It took some digging! And, Chris, one more thing. Those who doubt the Shroud's authenticity must incorporate, in their judgment, the understanding we now have of light, space and time. At the speed of light, time stands still. We humans merely observe and participate in illusions created by energy and light in an ever-expanding cosmos where the value of time changes with speed and location. Whatever our eyes see as real is constructed from particles that cannot be regarded as real. Who are we to judge what is possible regarding the time-subjected body of the one who says, 'I AM WHO AM.' It's a name that sounds to me like, 'All that truly is, that's ME.' In the eternal NOW of this entity, which also claims to be the Alpha and Omega, the year 33 CE is as near as the Big Flash.

"Through deep-field, space telescopes, cosmologists are now looking down the tunnel of time, right back to the 13.8 billion year-old microwave background of the Big Flash. Through different colour-blocking lenses, they are constantly obtaining more information about the birth and life of our cosmos. So, why can't we expect to develop, in the future, instruments that will enable us to look down the tunnel of time in the subatomic realm? As one of the researcher of the Shroud said, 'for those who study the possible burial cloth of Jesus, it seems a link to another dimension.'

"The conclusion, drawn by debunkers who've probably never even touched the Shroud, holds no value for me. I have more confidence in scientists who have studied it extensively. By honestly reporting what they found, they have left the door wide open for further research. With them, I would rather hear people say, 'how the image was produced is an ongoing mystery. It remains unanswered until further studies are done.' Chris, it is not about reproducing the image. It is about deciphering the wealth of data locked up within it.

"I have been called old geezer before. But, I believe that one day we will learn that the unexplainable burst of light, which produced the Shroud's image, is intimately related to the Big Flash of the beginning."

After Jane woke up, made her gooey oatmeal and settled at the kitchen table; I read her the printouts and replayed the telephone conversation.

"Well, what's a debunker?" she then asked.

"It's a person who exposes false claims."

"Wasn't that *your* job at Revenue Canada?"

I looked at her. How come I hadn't made that connection myself?

28

DEATH

"GLORIA, PREGNANT!" I EXCLAIMED, way too loud for apartment living, as I walked in the door. Even forgetting to take off my boots, wet from a dusting of snow that morning, I added not much softer, "How on earth can a woman of ill repute allow herself to get in that kind of a fix?" One boot had already made a puddle.

"Well, that's how it is. And, not another step before you . . ."

"Okay, okay, I'm sorry. But how did *you* find out?"

"While you were helping Jerry move his pull-out couch to the basement, Gloria called. I told you before; we got along great on our Exodus night. That's when I said to her, call me anytime. Anyway, she explained how, some time ago, this hate thing she coughed up at Armand's got the better of her. All screwed up, she let herself get pregnant. A child, she hoped, would become someone in her life she could learn to love. Desperate to try a new kind of living, she knew that having a child would get her on the welfare list. But, since this Jesus stuff and now rid of her hate, she's thinking abortion."

"And what business is that to us?"

"Well, her church friends are giving her the same, 'the devil will get you' line they gave Frankie. She has no family and no real friends. That's why she called me. She figures, since she feels no more hate, a new life might be easier to start without being stuck with a baby. She was hoping that Armand, nice as he was to her with the money and all, could help her sort this out. But she was uneasy about asking him. With all his religion, she was afraid he'd be dead set against abortion. So, she asked me to feel him out. Well, I called him. And, guess what? He's pro-choice. He'd love to discuss it with her."

"Good for him. No woman should have to carry a baby she doesn't want. Problem solved."

"Well, not yet. When Gloria heard Armand is okay with her choosing, she asked for a get-together before Sunday, preferably tonight. And she wants you and me to be there. 'I want you guys' opinion too,' she said. But she doesn't want Harry to get wind of this."

*   *   *

"Of course, I'm pro-choice," Armand started in his usual direct way. "How can I not be? Being human means having a free will to choose. I believe it's our birthright to choose between life and death. By obeying the laws of the cosmos, we choose life. By disobeying them, we choose death."

"So," Gloria hesitantly ventured. "What if I go to a pro-choice clinic?"

"A pro-choice clinic?" Armand asked with surprise in his voice. "Where on earth will you find one of them?"

We looked at him. Had he lived in a cocoon for the last thirty years?

He smiled his usual disarming smile. "I know what you're thinking. You mean a pro-death clinic. A pro-choice clinic would consist of a group of agencies brought together under one roof. A pregnant woman would walk in there and be able to get information and advice on all the options she has. Yes, there would be an office wherein people will explain how her child can be executed in a legal and presumably civilized manner. But . . . there would also be a number of other offices wherein she would find people ready to explain alternate solutions. In one office there would be someone eager to tell her how she, by offering the baby up for adoption, could bring unspeakable joy to a woman unable to conceive. In another office someone would be able to explain the different ways in which she could get assistance, if she kept the baby. In another office again, she would find someone able to connect her with older and often lonely women and grandmothers who would love to help, assist, and even financially support her. That would be an honest pro-choice clinic."

"So," Gloria asked after a lengthy silence. "What are you saying?"

"I'm simply affirming your right to choose. But, in order for you to do that, you should first hear all the different options and understandings. After all, to be pro-life means nothing unless there is the ability to choose. In the same way, to be pro-choice means nothing unless there are choices and an equal respect for those women who choose to keep their baby. As it is, once you walk into a pro-death clinic, even if with hesitation, they assume you've chosen their solution. Don't expect a loving and caring elderly person to sit down with you, put her arm around you and say, 'my daughter, you must have had a terrible time coming to this decision. One minute you probably wanted to keep and love this little miracle, while the next minute you hated it with a passion. One minute you wished to carry it in your arms some day soon. The next minute you detested its very existence. How would you like to explore, together, solutions that will be edifying for you and for all who will be affected by your choice, including the child?' No, Gloria, there'll be none of that in a pro-death clinic."

"You're talking about some cosmic laws people need to obey. What law is there that tells me, I can't abort this thing?"

"I believe there is a law, right across the board, for all intelligent life in the cosmos. It commands us not to do unto others what we don't want done to ourselves. Ask yourself. Would you like to be murdered? I ask this because I see life as a gift. I see it as part and parcel of the Big Flash of 13.8 billion years ago, known to science as the 'point singularity'. I see a human being's moment of conception as that human beings' point singularity. The miracle is this, Gloria. There were no solid forms, in the pre-embryonic state of the cosmos. After the Big Flash there were only a multitude of sound waves. These sound waves carried all the information of the cosmos' origin and of its future. Likewise, all information from past generations and all information determining this new human being's sex, characteristics, and physical features, are present in the pre-embryonic fertilized cell. The very essence of the cosmos was present in its point singularity. And, I believe, so it is with a human being. The fertilized cell is, from its very beginning, the temple of the creator's spirit. It's a newborn trinity of body, mind and soul. In the eternal now, this fertilized cell is, simultaneously, a new beginning and a complete human being."

"Come on! This thing isn't a human being yet. I'm only one month."

"I know. This is hard to agree with.

"However, science knows that the linear reality of time in which our physical bodies live is embedded in the absolute reality of the eternal now. Living, as we all do, in this apparent reality of time, many people see the human fertilized cell as an insignificant beginning. They feel, it can't be much, because it doesn't look like much. They forget how ridiculously insignificant a grown human looks compared to the cosmos. They also think, no matter what choice they make, nobody cares. So, why worry about what lies ahead when they can hardly cope with the present. But if the eternal now is the ultimate reality, then all intents and consequences regarding any fertilized cell are fully known at the moment of conception. Intents and consequences are the two parameters by which the purpose of every creature is determined. But this is *my* belief. It would be unreasonable for me to expect that you, Chris, Jane, or anybody else on the planet, automatically shares this understanding. It requires the realization that the omnipotent higher power, which upholds the cosmos, is also a loving father with whom every intelligent being can have an intimate father/child relationship."

It all sounded very lofty and, who knows, maybe he was right. But it annoyed me no end how he was dealing with the issue.

"Listen," I butted in, "what good is this scientific philosophizing for a woman who's pregnant and struggling with the choice of whether to let it happen or not?"

"I made a big mistake," Gloria sighed. "When I went out to let myself get pregnant, I was only thinking of myself. Now *you* tell me, I have to think about this thing as well. I don't want it. I want to start a new life without any hindrance. I let myself get pregnant because I wanted to learn to love. Why wasn't I set free from that spirit of hate before I decided to get pregnant? Why? Why? Why?"

Both Jane and I looked at Armand. *We* sure didn't know how to answer her whys. It seemed like he didn't either. He didn't say a word. To end the dreaded silence, my mind started reeling to find something sensible to say. Would I say something to lighten things up? Or would I speak some sort of opinion of my own? Or would I put Armand on the spot so he would air more of his ideas? After all, she'd come for *his* advice.

But it was as if Armand knew. Gloria had more on her heart. "If only there was a man beside me helping me to make this decision! Listen, Armand, if you're so sure there's some higher power holding all the cosmic strings, why didn't it arrange things differently? Why didn't it make me meet a guy who could also be happy about having something to be real about? Now I'll have to make this life/death decision on my own."

"Gloria, many women in this situation, even though they do know the father, are as alone as you are. Men, unable to deal with an unwanted problem like this, often tell themselves to ignore it. But the greater guilt lies with those in authority in communities, municipalities, provinces and nations. They ignore their responsibility to provide easily accessible counselling clinics, where young people can walk in without fear. Pro-death clinics are no solution. The emotional and spiritual implications of a pregnancy are just as serious, if not more so, than the physical ones.

"But, Gloria, you're not alone. You now have Jane, Chris, and me.

So, ponder what I've shared and choose. If you choose death, the child will simply become a number calculated into the tens of thousands of babies aborted each year in Canada and into the 1.3 million aborted across North America. If you choose life, he or she, can become a blessing to someone."

Gloria shook her head. Looking Armand straight in the eyes, she said, "You know, Armand, six months ago I would've called you a 'holy idiot.' How can you say, this thing will become a blessing? If the kid finds out mom was a whore and dad an outlaw-biker, it'll more likely become a curse."

"Gloria, if you accept this child, nourish it with love, sweet words, and proper food, I dare say it *will* become a blessing."

Turning to me, he said; "Remember, Chris, how you once asked for the possible purpose of 800,000 people killed by a tsunami? I promised an answer if you'd explain the purpose of millions of people being killed in genocides and wars. What do you think? If we define genocide as the systematic killing of a large number of humans seen as a burden, and thus denied personhood, how does that compare with abortion? And, if physical size is the measuring stick, how do *we* measure up to the cosmos?"

"Whatever, Armand! If you're trying to tell us there's a connection between masses of people that are killed in natural disasters and man-made genocides, I'd say, you're off your rocker. Volcanic eruptions underneath the sea floor cause tsunamis. Earth quakes are caused by the movements of earth's tectonic plates. Volcanoes will not quit erupting and tectonic plates will not stop moving just because we humans stop murdering one another."

"Did you ever see a flock of birds dancing in the sky as one? There is an instant transmission of info taking place between these birds. It's called entanglement. What if there is an entanglement in the spiritual dimension of purpose between all members of the human race? What if there's a spiritual entanglement between the earth and its inhabitants? For birds, entanglement works. They live their purpose. What if our purpose is to learn to dance together as one in our commitment to integrity? What if the innocent blood we spill cries out from the ground as it did when Cain murdered Able? After all, volcanic lava can flow down the left slope where people live. It can also flow down the right slope where it causes no harm. Shifting tectonic plates can unleash their crushing forces in a place where it'll create havoc. They can also be muffled by the earth's pliable crust. True, as long as what's genocide to some is just another day on the job to others, dancing as one is impossible. For that, we all need to believe that life has a purpose."

"Well, purpose, purpose," Jane sighed. "Don't get me wrong, Armand, I think you're a nice guy. But your big words and this purpose stuff is beyond me. I'm still clueless even about my own purpose. And I'm sure; all your smart-stuff isn't helping Gloria either. Gloria's got a problem. All she's looking for is help to make the right decision."

Armand wiggled himself from the couch into his wheelchair. He wheeled over to Gloria and gently put a hand on her shoulder. Turning, he said, "Jane, if Gloria chooses to visit the pro-death clinic, and if you're willing to go with her for support, that might be one of your purposes this week." Then, smiling warmly, he turned to Gloria and said, "Consider yourself my sister. If you choose life, I'll financially support you until the baby is born."

Then, speaking to all three of us, he added, "As I understand it, the purpose of your child, Gloria, and of each of us, is the same. Our soul/self is meant to magnify universal integrity. And the spirit that gives life to our soul/self is meant to seek, find and rejoice in the freely given gift of eternal life."

29

APOLOGETICS

"WELL, HOW DO YOU like my purple hair," Jane asked, twirling around like a model, as she walked in the door that afternoon.

"Ridiculous! For a woman your age, it's crazy."

"Well, don't get uptight. I can wash it out. I thought, just in case Gloria wants me to go with her to this you-know-what clinic. I don't want those young nurses to think I'm some grey-haired woman living in the past. Because . . . , I agree . . . , anything is better for a pregnant girl than having to go to some back-alley dive to get her thing poked to death with a straightened coat hanger."

"I guess so. Having the thing ripped to shreds by a state of the art vacuum cleaner should be less traumatic than having it randomly perforated by a primitive poker. When will she decide?"

"Well, she's not sure. She's waiting to hear tomorrow what, according to Armand, Jesus has to do with it all.

And," Jane looked at the paper in my hand, "what are you reading?"

"Oh, more confusion," I reluctantly replied as I eyed her purple hair again. Imagine; white light, containing seven colors, hits her head. And, because the atomic structure of the hair-dye is the same as the atomic structure of a red cabbage, only purple reflects.

"Remember how Armand, on the way home from the hospital last Monday, told me about a Catholic priest he met at some businessmen's gospel-breakfast? And remember Armand asking the priest for a copy of the explanations of his beliefs? Yesterday, after you left to bring Gloria home, he gave me a copy. Here, read it yourself."

With purple hair and all, Jane sat down and read.

Dear brother/sister in Christ,

With this letter, I hope to clarify some of the beliefs on which you may have challenged me. It is written in scripture, how Jesus said to Peter, (a name meaning rock) 'you are Peter, and on this rock I will build my Church.' (Mt.16:18) The Roman Catholic Church takes Jesus at his word. We also believe Jesus confirmed Peter's appointment, by adding, 'I give you the keys of the kingdom of heaven.' (Mt. 16:19)

We also believe that the leadership of Peter was confirmed by the following facts: After the apostles received the baptism of the Holy Spirit, it was Peter who addressed the unbelievers. (Acts 2:14-41) It was Peter who performed the first miracle in the name of Jesus. (Acts 3:6) It was Peter who addressed the Sanhedrin. (Acts 4:8-12) And, it was Peter who received the vision that opened up salvation for every human being. (Acts 10:11)

Just because we call the Pope 'Holy Father,' does not mean the Pope—a word meaning father—is holy. The title, 'Your Worship,' given to the mayor of a city, does not imply this person is worthy of worship.

True, leaders and members of my Church have many times been guilty of deplorable sins. Their conduct can be compared with that of leaders and members of God's chosen people, the Israelites. Greed, idolatry, abuse of power, immorality, etc. have been at work in human minds, hearts, and lives, throughout history. But God, in his unfathomable mercy, did not withdraw his covenant promises from the Israelites because of that. Neither did God, according to our belief, ever withdraw the covenant he made through Jesus with his Church and, through his Church, with all mankind.

Regarding Papal infallibility, this only applies when the Pope, in his role as head of the church, makes a statement to solve a debatable faith issue. Throughout my church's history, this has been done twice. Other statements may be binding for church members but they are not infallible.

I have no problem accepting the doctrines of my church. They have grown out of her tradition. True, not all are specifically mentioned in scripture. But St.

Paul states, "So then, brethren, stand firm and hold to the traditions which you were taught by us by word of mouth or by letter." (2 Thessalonians 2:15) This, my church believes, means both Scripture and tradition are carriers of truth.

I am well aware that those who, around 1500 CE, initiated the reformation believed that only Scripture can be relied on for truth. The Reformers also taught that it is by faith alone that people are saved. Yet, St. Paul writes, 'I can have faith to move a mountain, but if I have no love, I am nothing.' (1 Cor. 13:2) And St. James tells us, 'as the body without the spirit is dead, so faith without works is dead.' (James 2:24-26) We understand this to mean that people are saved through a faith expressed in works.

And yes, my church believes that I, through my office as a priest, am a channel of God's forgiveness. Jesus said to the apostles, 'Receive the Holy Spirit. If you forgive anyone his sins, they are forgiven, if you do not forgive them, they are not forgiven." (John 20:22-23) Jesus had authority over sin and he bestowed this authority on his apostles and, through them, on the priesthood. (Luke 5:24) However, forgiveness only comes to those who are truly repentant. And, in order for our sins to be forgiven, we must first forgive those who have sinned against us. (Matt. 6:14-15)

Do I worship Mary? No, I venerate her. She is my spiritual Mother. God is God of the living. (Matt. 22:32) Mary lives with Jesus and with all who have entered God's heavenly glory. I love Mary as my mother. If Jesus, my brother, loves her, what should keep me from doing the same? Asking my spiritual mother to intercede is as valid as asking my physical mother here on earth to intercede. We believe Eve is the physical mother of all mankind and Mary is the spiritual mother. While dying on the cross, Jesus said to his beloved disciple, John, "Behold, your mother!" To Mary he said, "Woman, behold your son!" (John 19:25-27) With these words, Jesus asked us all to receive Mary into our hearts and homes as our universal mother. By using the word 'woman,' Jesus emphasized Mary's connectedness to Eve. And, when I speak with Mary in prayer, I start by quoting scripture, saying, "hail Mary, full of grace, the Lord is with you, blessed are you among women and blessed is the fruit of your womb." (Luke 1:28, 42) Accepting Mary as my spiritual mother deepens my faith in the sanctity of the family. It is through the holy family of Mary, Joseph, and Jesus, that salvation was brought to mankind. We believe that our heavenly Father does channel special graces through families that imitate this sacred family relationship.

Why then am I not married?

I am. My marriage is a spiritual one. I am a member of the bride of Christ, his Church. And, by his grace, my heavenly Father has made me the spiritual father of a small segment of his Church family, my parish.

Do I struggle with sexual temptations?

Of course! But, judging by what happens in my parish family, my struggles do not seem to be more difficult than the struggles of married men. The *temptation of adultery, lusting after other partners, and the desire to view pornography does not seem to go away when a man is married. I believe we all, myself included, will have to spend some time in Purgatory.*

Where does the Bible mention Purgatory?

It does not directly. It's a doctrine grown out of my Church's traditions. It states that, when I leave my mortal body, I most likely need to be purified and cleansed before I can enter God's holiness. In the Old Testament, God reveals himself many times in fire; the fire of his infinite love. This fire of His love will burn up everything that is hay or straw in my soul to reveal what is gold. Only the gold in me is worthy to exist for eternity. Believing in Purgatory is synonymous with believing in my heavenly Father's infinite mercy. Many die, unfit to enter His glory. Yet, they're not wicked enough, to deserve the alternative. But . . . Purgatory is not a place. It's a process.

The most questioned practice of my church is the Eucharistic celebration, better known as the Mass. This celebration, we believe, was instituted by Jesus at the last supper. There, he took bread, gave thanks, broke it, gave it to His disciples and said, "Take and eat; this is my body given for you; do this in remembrance of me." Then he took the cup, gave thanks, and offered it to them saying, "Drink from it, all of you. This is the blood of the covenant which is poured out for many for the forgiveness of sins." (Matt. 26:26–28) Again, my church takes Jesus at his word. His disciples did. After Jesus had gone up to heaven, they continued to come together the first day of the week to break bread. (Acts 20:7) And, "anyone who eats of the bread and drinks of the cup without recognizing the body of the Lord; eats and drinks judgment on him, or herself." (1 Cor. 11:29)

By taking Jesus at his word, my church believes that bread and wine, consecrated in remembrance of Him by an ordained priest, transform into His body and His blood. (Luke 22:19) The appearance of bread and wine remains, while their reality changes.

I would love to hear a Protestant pastor share his understanding of verses fifty-two to sixty-eight, of the sixth chapter of the Gospel written by my name-sake.

Sincerely, Father John.

"This is too highbrowed for me," said Jane, talking to the back of my chair, as she put the letter on the coffee table. "Even if I did understand this kind of religious stuff, it wouldn't make any difference to me. As long as nobody can tell me why those religious guys can't hack it out among themselves, there must be horse-feathers in there somewhere. If all this stuff is really written down somewhere, how come they have to fight about it? It's either true or not true. You'd think they're grown men and women who are all interested in finding out what the story is. So what's their problem?"

"Honey, how do I know what their problem is? I always thought the whole religion business was a baloney problem. But you and I saw the Chickadee overhaul with our own eyes. And we both read about this Shroud business. Didn't Armand, with that stairway to heaven song, suggest we should keep wondering? When you asked me, last Wednesday, if my title at Revenue Canada had been, 'Debunker,' I thought it a silly question. But, while lying awake last night and wondering, I saw how I've been looking for false claims in the religion business ever since my holy stepfather moved in. I couldn't see how his heavy-duty preaching had anything to do with reality. Treating me like a nuisance, and a damned nuisance at that, he made each godly sermon sound like a farce. Debunking became my favourite hobby. Last night I realized that, by constantly seeking ways to prove Armand to be an off-beat dreamer, I have simply been honing my debunking skills. Meanwhile I haven't really heard half of what he has said. So, I decided to loosen up a bit and listen better. I might even replay some of his rhetoric. After all, if he, who's done all this research, figures religion is chaos indeed, then, who knows, maybe it is. And if he concludes that underneath this chaos there is a bottom line, which most religious people don't realize exists, who am I to knock it? This priest's letter threw me for a loop though. There's no way this guy can be right. I figured his church probably knows how to twist words to make them sound right while, in reality, they're written differently. Or, maybe, they stick unrelated verses together in order to make them prove what they preach. So I called Armand and I asked him, 'why on earth did you give me this letter? I don't know enough to shoot holes in it. Or am I all wrong again? Is this your end stop? You're a Catholic.'"

"Well, what did he say?"

"He laughed his hearty laugh. 'Chris, Chris,' he said, 'have you lost your cheater-chaser nose? Just because you're retired, you're not suddenly accepting as truth everything written on paper, are you?'

"Imagine! I had decided to be less debunky and here is Armand telling me to be less gullible. 'Refuting the priest's beliefs had been a piece of cake,' Armand said. By simply sending the letter to the protestant pastor and asking for his views on the issues, the priest had been knocked out cold. By having all his Catholic convictions ripped apart as if by a shredder, the poor priest had been left, like Armand, with not a leg to stand on."

"Well, did you get a copy of Mr. Shredder's stuff?"

"No! Armand wants us to first decide if we're having fun getting more and more confused? According to him, every denomination, persuasion, sect, or cult is able to justify its beliefs by quoting some verses from some holy scripture. Twenty thousand Christian denominations are all able to hang their individual hat on a few or a slew of Bible verses and fly with them. 'Although,' Armand said, 'it would be better to say, 'and nail that door of fear, of their box, shut with them.'

"So, are we having fun getting more and more confused?" I asked while looking over my shoulder in order to face Jane.

"Well, are we?"

"I wouldn't call it having fun. I'd still much rather watch the playoffs. But, we're deep enough into this religious quagmire to want to see the end of it. Besides, it might be interesting to read how pastor creams priest. For now, let's just wait till we've heard what Armand has dreamed up about Jesus after he discarded the 'Jesus is a myth' idea.

30

THE MESSIAH

I<small>T WAS NO WONDER</small> Harry had a problem with Armand's ideas. Propped up on the couch like the previous week, Armand had opened our churchy Sunday morning meeting—the second last according to what he had warned us for from the start—by joyously singing **Ya ha deedle bubba deedle dum.'** Considering our subject, this line from the song 'If I Were a Rich Man,' out of the musical 'Fiddler on the Roof,' even sounded sacrilegious.

"Of course, you're wondering why this song," he chuckled at the end of the first verse. "But I'm not telling until we're done this morning."

Although Frankie, wearing his you-know-what clothes, had settled down comfortably on his two chairs with Gloria beside him on the floor he looked ill at ease. And she, also wearing the same clothes as last Sunday—white crew neck sweater, grey pants and low heels, was depressingly quiet. Harry, sporting a darker jacket and tie and occupying the chair closest to the door, looked about as serious as humanly possible. Add to this my own dubious yes/no religious fun attitude and the recipe for a heavy mood was perfect.

Pretending to be unaware of this heaviness, Armand had Jane hand out song sheets. Slowly overcoming our inhibitions, first reading, then, one after another, shyly trying to sing, we joined in as he sang it a second time. Harry didn't try. He kept re-arranging his legs. Nevertheless, as our volume went up, our heaviness lifted. Frankie even asked for a refrain repeat. Armand seemed to itch to act out Tevye's dance in the barn. And our final *'deedle, bubba deedle dum'* was loud enough to annoy the neighbours.

"Messiah," Armand said as soon as we'd finished, is Hebrew meaning 'Anointed one.' In Greek the word translates into 'Christ.'

"A while ago, I shared with Chris and Jane how I, some forty years ago, saw the religious scene as total chaos. Here you have to know, physicists use the word chaos for the condition of a system wherein there is interplay between order and randomness. This kind of chaos can ultimately evolve into a simple final state which is referred to as 'the attractor.'

"Because physical chaos has an attractor, I theorized that, maybe, our religious chaos could have an attractor as well. I baptized it, 'Divine Attractor.' This Divine Attractor, I then theorized, could be 'integrity.'

"Some years after drawing that conclusion, I was overwhelmed by an unexplainable power in a Christian setting. Critical physicist that I am, I questioned its reality and asked the Christian God to repeat the experience in the privacy of my own home. He did. This prompted me to take a closer look at the Christianity. And to my great surprise I found that, by replacing the word *integrity* with *righteousness*, the Judea/Christian scriptures seemed to confirm my understanding from beginning to end. They even affirmed my concept of God's complementary duality. The Old Testament is about God's judgment. The New Testament is about His mercy.

"But, let's get out of this stuffy apartment and imagine ourselves on the moon on my private beach bordering the dry sea of tranquility. From here, let's spy on tiny planet earth by using our super-duper binoculars.

"Many little creatures living on that earth claim that, at a certain moment in their history, a very special person, named Jesus, was born in their midst. And, even though he grew up to be the same insignificant size as they were, they believe he was the son of God who came from heaven to earth to redeem all humans from their sins. Of course, I realize, I'm one of those insignificant humans. But the truth is, even though we humans are insignificant in size compared to the stars, we are incredibly more complex than they are. Stars shine in proportion to their physical size. If they, and we, would emit light in proportion to our complexity instead, one human brain would outshine them all. The biggest galaxy would be no more than a nightlight bulb and one human brain would be visible across the universe. This makes us very special. And, according to Christian belief, this Jesus, also known as 'The Christ', was more special still.

"If we ask: Who was this Jesus? Those who believe in him will reply, 'He was the only begotten son of God. He was with God from the beginning.' Then we can ask: What beginning? Was that before the Big Bang, or Big Flash, or was the Big Flash that beginning?'

"As a physicist, I know that everything that was needed to bring forth the entire cosmos was contained in the spark of the Big Flash.

"As a scientist I know that the power embedded in this beginning needed to either have intelligence or be brought forth by intelligence. After all, the DNA (Deoxyribonucleic acid) of every living creature born out of it is encoded. And, as any computer programmer can testify, only intelligence can produce a code. Random mutation cannot. So the code, dictating the evolutionary process in all its intricate steps, was engrafted unto the spark of the Big Flash. Why then would the omnipotent intelligence, when engrafting this spark, not have included in this powerful beginning the potential for it to evolve into a worthy end product, a creature so pleasing to him he would be delighted to call it his beloved offspring? I believe it did. I believe mankind's collective righteousness will evolve into a perfect and righteous 'Son of Man.' And I believe it was this 'Son of Man' who, some two thousand years ago, stepped out of the eternal now into the dimension of time. He even called himself, 'the Son of Man.'"

"Hold it right there," Harry said, standing up.

"You can't be right. You're twisting scripture to accommodate some weird idea. Jesus clearly said; 'I am the way, the truth and the life.' Nothing in these words says anything about him being some kind of incomprehensible, collective or composite human being."

"What then, Harry, did Jesus mean by those words? Furthermore what did He mean when he said, I *am* the bread of life, I *am* the light of the world, I *am* the resurrection, I *am* the beginning and I *am* the end?"

Harry sat down and looked like he was going to reply. Then he changed his mind. I bet, if anyone had dropped a pin, we would have heard it fall. After a while, when the silence became too uncomfortable, he said, "I don't have a theology degree, but my pastor does. I'll have an answer next week."

"Okay, Harry, then ask your pastor a second question. Is it possible that our increased knowledge of the universe warrants an expanded understanding of the power that brings it forth?"

Harry nodded half-heartedly.

"All founders of all religions tell us what they see as the spiritual path on which we humans should walk. They share their convictions on what they believe is the truth. They also give their understanding of the promise of eternal life. Jesus is the only one who did not.

"Jesus declares, *he* is the way, *he* is the truth and *he* is the life. Doesn't this imply he knows himself to be the embodiment of universal realities that transcend and simultaneously incorporate all physical manifestations? For him to be '*the way*,' doesn't that imply he is part and parcel of the entire evolutionary journey from creative spark to the Son of Man sitting at the right hand of the majesty in heaven? And isn't '*the way*,' clearly described to us as 'the path of righteousness?'

"When we believe Jesus to be fully human and fully God, do we see him as just another human being operating under the power of a divine spirit? This may be a concept we can relate to. But if Jesus is fully human and fully God; doesn't this imply he must personify within himself the righteousness of all mankind as much as the complete righteousness of God?

"When Jesus declares, *he* is the truth; doesn't this imply he knows himself to be the personification of all truths? Isn't there a measure of truth, however slight, in the heart of every free thinking creature in the cosmos? Could it therefore be possible that, whatever is true in you, in me and in any human is, in the eternal now, part of the eternal truth which was, is and always will be personified in the representative known to us as Jesus?

"And when Jesus states that *he* is the life, doesn't this imply he knows himself to be the personification of all life, from the begetting of the basic building blocks of life in the spark of the Big Flash to eternal life in all who will partake in the resurrection of the righteous?

"After all, the collective will of a nation, after a war, can rebuild itself to new grandeur. Why then could the collective *practiced* righteousness of all mankind, past, present and future, not beget one righteous representative?

"Note: I said, practiced righteousness. For it cannot be those who simply say, 'yeah, yeah,' who would be part of Him. No, it would only be those who put righteousness into practice. And, I believe, the omnipotent intelligence that brought forth the spark of the Big Flash would gladly say of such an offspring, 'This is my son with whom I am well pleased.'"

"Well," Jane said with a sigh, "I'm going back down to earth. I'll start the coffee. It's all over my head anyway."

"Maybe it's over everybody's head," Armand replied, disappointedly.

"I want to hear you out," Gloria softly responded.

"Okay, Jane, you fly back and start coffee. But, this representative of the human race was prophesied. Around six hundred BCE it was written that, from a certain line of ancestry, a righteous branch would grow from which the Lord, *our* righteousness, would be born."

"Armand," Gloria asked, "I don't understand how your Christ can be present 13.8 billion years ago in the spark of the Big Flash, walk the earth two thousand years ago in the person of Jesus and, at the same time, be the collective righteousness of the whole human race, past, present and future? How can he be there, here and everywhere?"

"Gloria, time is relative. For example, when two people move away from one another, time has a different value for either one. If the space between them increases at the speed of light, they would each measure the other person's time as standing still. Knowing this, how hard would it be to accept that time and space pose no restrictions for the power which created both? In its eternal NOW, past, present and future, here and there, all flow together. Existing inside and outside of all these parameters, it can manifest itself in the dimension of time at any moment in history, anywhere and in any form. In its eternal now, righteousness can be present, right here on the moon, in you, in me and throughout the cosmos in anyone, anywhere.

"And, as I see it, Gloria and Frankie, here lies the answer to the question of your spiritual struggle. Yes, in the dimension of time, the personification of our collective human righteousness was crucified 2000 years ago in the person of Jesus. Yet, this same Jesus is despised and rejected whenever anyone stands up for righteousness. Wherever and whenever any human life is taken for righteousness' sake, regardless of the victim's faith, it is a crucifixion. Anywhere, anytime, when a human being lines up with righteousness, that person's struggle begins. You both experienced that after you invited righteousness, personified in Jesus, to enter into your heart. To be righteous, in the face of unrighteousness, is a struggle in any persuasion. Doesn't it make a lot of sense that we all, throughout life, by choosing to either line up with righteousness or not, are making our own eternal bed?

"But let's go back to earth and join Jane in my stuffy apartment."

"Still, I don't believe you," Harry exclaimed in an even tone after we had landed. "If life is simply about living righteously, why did Jesus command us to spread *his* good news?"

"As I understand it, Harry, his good news is this. The incomprehensible higher power desires to have a Father/child relationship with everyone. He so loves the whole of his creation, he sent the crowning glory of that creation to pay the price for all unrighteousness. In him, everyone who comes to believe in righteousness can find forgiveness for their unrighteousness and have eternal life. Harry, you be the judge. Who deserves to delight in the grandeur of the cosmos for eternity? Should it only be the members of your church or should it be all who, right across the entire religious spectrum, hunger and thirst for righteousness during their life on planet earth?"

"How's coffee coming?" Frankie sighed. "I still don't know why we sang, 'if I were a rich man' with that crazy deedle-bubba-dum refrain."

"Frankie, the song is about material riches. We sang it to make you think of spiritual riches. These, according to a certain spokesman for the cosmos, are ours in abundance, in the Christ we talked about. He personifies the treasury of spiritual riches accumulated by all righteous humans.

"And about the *deedle, bubba, deedle dum,* line? I think; it perfectly expresses the fleeting value of worldly riches."

Harry stood up, quickly told Frankie he'd drop in later that week, excused himself and was out the door. Gloria was quiet. Not a word about the yes or no of the abortion issue. Jane, as usual, catered like a mother.

While Jane drove Frankie and Gloria home, I put the apartment back to normal. When done, I took a folding chair from the stack, plunked it down with its back facing Armand, straddled it and, with arms leaning on the backrest, I said, "Okay, man. We still don't see this religious confusion as fun, especially not after today's heavy homily. Jane prefers shopping and I'd rather watch competitive sports. But, I am curious to read how the pastor knocks out the priest. I'd like to read that rebuttal."

"Exciting fight, isn't it?" Armand chuckled. "How about placing a bet?"

So I did. Just for fun. One toonie on the shredder.

31

PROTESTING

IT HAPPENED AFTER LUNCH that Sunday. Jane and I were sitting next to each other on our spotless sofa with the intent of together reading the shredder's letter. She was happy I had again taped Armand's morning rhetoric. And, this time I was happy about it too. The man's understanding of the Christ wasn't in my league either. Besides, we both felt happy and warm because it had been a long time since she and I had sat together like this. I usually resort to my high-backed window seat and Jane loves her den with flowerpots and knick-knacks. Realizing how unusual our sitting together was, we smiled at each other. She moved closer, pressed her left arm and shoulder against my right, and said, "Well, you know, Chris, even if I don't understand half the stuff Armand's talking about, at least we've got some excitement back in our life. I'm dying to know what Gloria will decide about her whatever. She didn't want to talk about it, not even when I asked her while driving them home. Frankie said she hadn't been feeling well. I'm sure this complicated Christ-talk wasn't much help to her. I just listened to Armand and figured, I'll replay the stuff when I'm by myself. I can't concentrate with people around me. Armand's stuff is always too highbrowed anyway. Yet, I still hope I'll catch on someday. If I keep replaying the recordings and keep re-reading those letters, who knows, maybe one day I will see the light, whatever that is. I bet Gloria understands everything. She's a lot smarter than me."

Even though warmly aware of Jane's snuggling up to me, I still asked the dumb question of, "Why don't I first read the letter of the priest to you one more time? That way the pastor's knock-out punches will make more sense."

She leaned over, kissed me on the cheek, moved her lips to my ear and whispered, "Why don't we first have a nap?"

How could I resist? I chuckled, put down the letters, stood up, took her right hand and pulled her up from the sofa. No sooner was she standing than she led me. And, as we both walked to the bedroom, she began to sing:

"If we were a rich pair," I joined in with a laugh. Then, attempting a few dance-steps together, and with about half of Frankie's last refrain volume, we sang *'Ya ha deedle bubba deedle dum.'* Jane even remembered the words about not having to work hard and being able to biddy bum all day long, if we were a wealthy pair.

*   *   *

Two hours later, when sitting in Jane's den, ready to watch a movie together, I, with hot ginger tea in one hand and Jane's soft hand in the other, had a crazy thought. "Imagine," I chuckled. "Four hours ago, Armand unsuccessfully tried to get us both excited about our spiritual oneness with his Christ. And, hardly two hours later, you and I successfully tried to get each other excited about our physical oneness as man and wife. I wonder how that's to fit in Armand's complementary duality gospel."

"Well . . . ," Jane slowly replied, "if getting religion means I have to feel some kind of shame whenever I like to snuggle up to my very own husband, I don't want religion."

Monday, March 19, 2012

"You know, Chris," Armand said with a laugh when I told him over the phone about Jane's remark, "Your Jane has more theological sense than many a puritan preacher. The word 'religion' means to express respect for what is sacred. To be fully human means to realize and celebrate as sacred, both the physical intimacy between you and your wife and the spiritual intimacy you are meant to have with the source of life. We're not just intelligent animals. We're spiritual beings. And, we're not just spiritual angels either.

We're sexual beings. And from experience I can say that Sonnetta and I, after we had interiorized the richness of this duality, truly sensed the fullness of the all consuming power released during our marital intimacy by the mini Big Flash within us. When *life* would burst forth in me and explode inward to every nerve ending in my body and outward into her, I not only felt as one with *her*. I also sensed, as in a triangle of love, our common oneness with the source of life. At that moment I would be deeply aware of all three: my Sonetta, our cosmic source—known to us both as the lover of our soul/selves—and me, Armand. I believe it is disconnectedness from this cosmic source that cheapens our human, God-given sexuality. I also believe that the human body, male and female together, when fully understood in relation to one another and to their source, embodies the true theology of our cosmos."

After I hung up, still irked by his hint about Jane and me not getting enough bang or flash for our sexual buck because we weren't hooked-up to this spiritual, cosmic power supply, I happened to glance at the sofa. Jane had gone shopping again. Staring at me, from where we had left it, was pastor Shredder's letter. "Okay," I said out loud to a cold, uncomplicated, mid-day beer, "let's be witness to the decisive round between two religious heavyweights."

Dear Mr. Huete,

The Roman Catholic Church claims that Jesus installed the Apostle Peter as Pope. This interpretation helped them establish their hierarchical structure. But before Jesus said, "You are Peter and on this rock I will build my church," he asked Peter, "Who do you say I am?" Peter responded, "You are the Christ, the son of the living God." (Matt. 16:16-18) This statement, made by Peter, is the rock on which the church was built. The name Peter in Greek is Petros. It is masculine. It means a small stone which, like Peter, can easily be shifted. Tottering between affirming Jesus one moment and denying him the next, Peter certainly was no sure foundation. The second word Jesus used is Petra. It is feminine. It refers to a rock that's immovable. This is Peter's declaration that Jesus is the Christ.

Yes, Jesus entrusted Peter with the keys of heaven. And, yes, he told him, "whatever you bind on earth will be bound in heaven and whatever you loose on earth will be loosed in heaven." (Matt. 16:19) But it is the power of the Good News, which every disciple was commissioned to spread (Matt. 18:18) that will keep people either bound or loosed from their earthly burdens. The gospel messages are the keys to heaven.

The belief that God installed an earthly Father, a Pope, as head of his church, contradicts Jesus' warning when he said, "do not call anyone on earth 'father,' for you have one Father and he is in heaven." (Matt. 23:9)

When the reformation came, the Roman Catholic Church no longer showed any resemblance to the simplicity of the early Church. New doctrines had been declared, new traditions had been instituted, and new laws had been added. To say that the infallibility of the Pope only applies to specific faith items may be the official definition. In practice, the contrary is clear. Whatever comes down from Rome, is law for its entire Church.

Regarding the belief that a priest has the power to forgive sin, Scripture again refutes it. When Jesus says, "forgive and you will be forgiven" (Matt. 6:14), it is clear that we are all able to forgive, not just the priests.

This called for another beer and . . . pretzels. This was a good fight. I liked the way this pastor minced no words. No fancy foot work. Every blow was an upper cut. More confusion: no doubt. But, now that I was into this religious chaos, I should have a team to root for. And, judging by Armand's readiness to share this pastor's rebuttal with me, it looked like he and I were cheering the same team.

And how can they call Mary the Mother of God? Scripture never calls her that. Mary was the mother of Jesus' humanity, not of his divinity. It is illogical to call her Mother of God. God existed before she was born. Besides, Jesus never called her mother. He called her woman. (John 19:26)

Romanists also call Mary a mediatrix. They attribute mediating power to her. Yet, St. Paul clearly states, "There is one God, and one mediator between God and men, the man Christ Jesus." (1 Tim. 2:5)

Be assured, I too believe in family values and God's special blessings for those families that fear Him. But the stranglehold the Roman Church has is unscriptural. By instituting seven sacraments, Roman clergy have their foot in the door at every major family event from the cradle to the grave.

Scripture, on the contrary, only justifies two sacraments. The one is the Lord's Supper, instituted by Jesus before his death. (Luke 22:19) The second is baptism, instituted after the resurrection when Jesus said, "make disciples of all the nations, baptizing them in the name of the Father and of the Son and of the Holy Spirit." (Matt. 28:19) The other five so called sacraments: confirmation, confession, anointing of the sick, ordination of religious and matrimony, have no scriptural foundation. This is proven by the fact that, for example, the sacrament of confession wasn't officially recognized until 1215. What happened to believers before that year? Were they all destined for hell, just because they never had a chance to go to confession?

And, about the celibacy of priests, all I need to quote is God's own word. "It is not good for man to be alone." (Gen. 2:18)

Do I believe in purgatory? Of course not. It utterly amazes me how anyone can believe in such a place. It isn't mentioned anywhere in the Scriptures. Peter, their supposed first Pope, even said, "Christ suffered for sins once, the righteous for the unrighteous, that he might bring us to God." (1 Peter 3:18) Are we to suffer for our sins a second time? Isn't it written: "their sins and their iniquities will I remember no more?" (Heb. 10:17)

And to the Romanist's claim that their traditions are carriers of truth, equal to God's written word, I reply with Jesus' rebuke, "you have let go of the commands of God and are holding on to the traditions of men." (Mark 7:8)

Yes, traditions may be useful. But they have to be confirmed by Scripture.

The Roman understanding, for example, that we will be saved by faith and works is clearly contradicted by St. Paul's statement, "For it is by grace you have been saved, through faith—and this not from yourselves, it is the gift of God—not by works, so that no one can boast." (Eph. 2:8-9)

The one highly disputed Romanist practice for which the priest did not give an explanation, is the selling of indulgences. This is supposed to be a means for those still living on earth to help diminish the punishment of those being purified in purgatory. Martin Luther, one of the main reformers, saw right through the Church's scheme. In his time, around 1520, indulgences were sold for money. This money was to be used for the building of a new St. Peter's basilica in Rome. The priest who was licensed to raise this money, through the selling of indulgences, made a ridiculous claim. He guaranteed that these indulgences, when bought, would release a dead person from purgatory, no matter how wicked a life he or she had led. What humbug!

These are the things a church can teach when it's their "tradition."

Last but not least. The priest is right in saying that the bread and wine issue, their so called sacrament of the Eucharist, is the most questioned belief of his church. This bread, wafer, or cookie worship is an abomination. It boggles my mind to think how people with even a normal intellect can believe in such a doctrine.

Yes, at the last supper, when Jesus broke bread, he did say, "take and eat, this is my body." And, when he offered the cup to the disciples, he did say, "Drink from it, all of you. This is my blood of the new covenant which will be poured out for many, for the forgiveness of sins." (Matt. 26:26-28) But how can anyone possibly take these words of Jesus literally? Didn't Jesus also say, "I am the gate; whoever enters through me will be saved?" (John 10:9) Does that make Jesus a wooden gate with iron hinges?

If the priest wishes to hear any Protestant pastor preach on the verses 52-68 of the sixth chapter of the Gospel of John, he can call me. I'll gladly prepare a sermon about that. I'll simply compare that passage with the passage in which Jesus tells us that he is the vine and we are the branches. (John 15:5) I am sure he will agree, neither he, nor anyone else he knows, has ever looked for Jesus planted in some vineyard.

To top it all, by enacting Jesus' last supper, day after day in their celebration of Mass, they believe they are repeating the sacrifice of Jesus on the cross. Scripture very clearly says, "Jesus sacrificed Himself for our sins once and for all." (Heb. 7:27)

As you can read, Mr. Huete, my understandings of certain scriptures are different. And, as I see it, the bottom

line of the Eucharistic debate is this. If the members of this
church believe little wafers of bread, after consecration,
become the flesh of Jesus, you can ask yourself these two
questions: If this transformation does not take place, then
what are they worshipping? And, if this transformation
does take place and they eat it, then . . . aren't they
cannibals?

Sincerely, Pastor Gregg

"BINGO, DINGO!" I said, softly enough to ensure the lady with the hearing aid living below wouldn't hear me. "This fight is a done deal. Let's collect our winnings."

So I called Armand.

No answer. "Hmm," I said out loud. "Monday, 4.35 pm, where could he be?"

32

LIFE

"You cannibal," I hissed when looking through the half-open door into Armand's hospital room. Imagine! A Catholic priest was giving him the Eucharistic bread. Didn't pastor beat priest ten-nothing?

He had had a stroke around 3 p.m. that Monday. Joy, his PSW, had called the same night, informing us that he had also lost his speech and the use of his left arm. Jane and I wanted to go visit him right away, but he was in isolation. Friday—just the day Jane had a doctor's appointment—we were finally allowed to go and see him. So there I was, all alone with a new twist to the Armand saga.

*   *   *

While playing with my paper cup in the hospital cafeteria, I stewed. It now was clear. Despite all his big talk, this Armand was as locked up in a box as anybody—and a

Catholic box at that. On top of it all, I am stuck with this crazy letter Joy gave me. I'm *not* going to read it to whoever shows up this Sunday. I cannot possibly read to them about this far-fetched devil business when I don't even believe in a God. Hearing me talk about old clove-hoof, Jane will think her atheist husband has gone off the deep end. With a big sigh, I pulled the computer print-out from my back pocket and, for the third time, I read:

Dearest friends,

Unable to personally share my understanding of the antichrist on this last Sunday of our get-togethers, I hope Chris will read it to you.

I perceive our cosmos as an evolutionary system brought forth and guided by intelligence. I also believe its evolution depends on our human interconnected and interactive participation.

Physicists know that every sub-atomic particle has its anti-particle.

This cosmic law, when applied to the spiritual realm, could justify the belief that, if there is a Christ there also is an antichrist. And if the Christ is known as 'The Word,' then the antichrist could be called the anti-word. Trying to make us nullify the sacred laws of the cosmos would be right up such an individual's alley. Furthermore, if Christ is the personification of our collective righteousness, the antichrist will then, in due time, show up as the personification of our collective unrighteousness. After all, righteousness and unrighteousness have vied to be lord of human hearts 24/7 throughout human history. By entertaining righteous or unrighteous thoughts, speak righteous or unrighteous words, or do righteous or unrighteous deeds, we humans line up behind either one.

The Christ, I believe, has charge over hosts of angels. The antichrist rules over legions of demons. Angels will assist me in practicing righteousness. Demons gladly assist me in the practice of evil. With my free will, I decide whether the Christ, or the antichrist, is allowed to use my physical, mental, or spiritual powers to act out his inclinations. This explains how you, Gloria, at some moment after your mom's death, gave the spirit of hate access to your heart. When we humans allow ourselves to be thrown off kilter, to whatever degree by whatever source, we create an opening through which unrighteousness can force its way in.

To set you free, Gloria, I needed unwavering faith in my authority in and through Jesus, who is the Christ. The spiritual power to wield this authority, although generated through the blood shed by all righteous humans at the hands of the unrighteous, is embodied in the shed blood of Christ. Unrighteousness has no defence against it. That's why I covered us all with that power. We all hold a measure of unrighteousness in our heart. And evil always looks for a way to hook into that.

When you, Frankie and Gloria, asked Jesus into your heart, you asked for righteousness to become lord of your life. Instantly, the forces of the antichrist were mobilized against you. By stirring up doubts in your mind, these forces are now trying to regain the territory they lost.

Chris remarked once about the great number of religious wars. I believe only one war has been waged, is being waged, and will be waged. It is the spiritual war between righteousness and unrighteousness. Waged inside every human mind, it spills over into families, communities, ideologies, religions and nations.

So, that's the religion business; as confrontational as the decisive bout for a world boxing title. I bet, when Harry hears these satan-smarts, his blood-pressure will make the ring-bell clang.

Talking about the devil! I aggressively crumpled my paper cup. Hoping he hadn't seen me, I quickly turned my face. But . . . no such luck.

"Just the man I want to talk to," Harry said, while sitting down at my table. "Lucky coincidence! I'm here for a blood test. I meant to call you. I'm no longer interested in your friend's ideas. My pastor told me, there's nothing more dangerous than a man who separates himself from other people to make up his own theology."

"He won't be sharing them for a while. He had a stroke."

"I'm sorry to hear that. I hope he'll recuperate soon."

While I looked sideways at Harry, I began to feel some sympathy for the man. After all, I too had problems with Armand's ideas. Especially after what I'd just witnessed. Who knows? Maybe Harry's pastor was right. For Armand to try and tackle big theological issue like Jesus and the devil was presumptuous indeed. Leaning forward, I said, "If you have a minute, listen to this. It's a letter Armand wants me to read to whoever shows up this Sunday. You're not planning to be there; so, here is a part I'd like you to discuss with your pastor

> *Physical creation is brought forth in six time frames. This can be symbolized by the number six. The seventh time frame is indicated to be an open-ended time of rest. The antichrist, by using our bodies, minds, and spirits, abuses every aspect of this six-time-frame creation in three different ways. His unrighteousness has wrecked, is wrecking, and will continue to wreak havoc on earth, in the physical, mental, and spiritual realm until the power of the righteous has been broken. Three sixes, representing body, mind, and spirit, could therefore perfectly symbolize the antichrist. However, even though we humans are able to give him authority over all <u>we</u> have been given, he will never be allowed to enter the creator's rest. This rest, symbolized by the number seven, is for the Lord—our collective human righteousness only.*
>
> *Human unrighteousness manifests itself in our midst like a roaring lion. Yet, one day, it will be shown for what it really is. It is the jackass on whose back our collective righteousness, according to the Jewish prophet Zechariah, is triumphantly riding into eternity. And, jackass is right. For how much more ignorant can the unrighteous be than to persistently ignore history's*

proven catch-22. The more the righteous are persecuted, the more Christ-like they become.

"Enough," Harry shouted. "Who does he think he is? You should come to my church. Our pastor has a theology degree. He has been educated in how to interpret scripture. He has *real* answers."

He stood up, said goodbye, and left in his customary Harry huff.

Yes, who did Armand think he was? His closing words only seemed to confirm more big-time megalomania in the man.

How can I share the awareness I have of my human responsibility? How can I share my inkling of what unimaginable glory awaits the righteous? I believe the cosmos is their inheritance. When the righteous leave their body of flesh, they are given a body of light, just as was given to the resurrected Jesus. With this body of light they can be anywhere in the cosmos the very moment they think of being there. But the cosmos is sustained and permeated with the righteousness of the one who brought it forth. Therefore, created beings can only exist in its eternal now, for as far as they are judged righteous. And, for that, they depend on the infinite mercy of their creator.

As for me, I need much mercy. I have been unrighteous often.

My prayer is that you, Chris, Jane, Frankie, Gloria, and Harry will constantly strive with soul, mind and body, to attain to this righteousness. And, in doing so, rely without failing on your heavenly Father's mercy.

Armand.

Armand! Oh yes! While rehearsing what to say, I hurried back to his floor. I found him alone and blissfully at peace. He attempted a smile. The muscles of his mouth did not cooperate. He looked me in the eyes. No, I looked into his. Sky blue. What was it again that he had said about looking into the eyes of his future wife? 'It was as if, for one split second, I looked into another universe.' Split second was right. That's all it was. But, even though it was immeasurably short, it was undeniably real. Had I, through these two blue windows, looked into his spiritual dimension of purpose?

By extending his right arm, he seemed to be asking if he could give me a one-arm hug. I leaned forward, clumsily hugging him as well. A warm, fatherly love emanated from him. Uncomfortable with the emotions it stirred up, I let go and settled back by sitting on the side of his bed. His right hand reached for mine. I felt obliged to respond. After a while, still holding his hand with my right, I was somehow compelled from within to also put my left hand on top of his. Realizing neither one of us had spoken since I arrived, I grinned. He nodded and winked. Then, contently leaning back, he closed his eyes. Hardly noticeable at first, but quickly intensifying, an agreeable warmth, much warmer than from his hug, began flowing from his one hand into both of mine. It went up my arms, through my shoulders, filling my entire chest, before it settled overwhelmingly in my heart. In there, it felt as if some big chunk of plaque slowly started to dissolve. A peace like I had never known before made me close my eyes as well. Was he silently praying over me? Was I getting emotional? Or was my soul/self set free to express itself through my emotions. I tried letting go of his hand. I couldn't. Yet his hand was limp. He wasn't fighting it. I couldn't even open my eyes. What was this? Could Armand's hand possibly be channelling into my heart the same compassion a Pentecostal block-layer's hand had channelled into his?

"Your hour is up, sir," the nurse announced, rudely breaking into what, I thought, had only been a short moment of wonderful inner peace.

We opened our eyes simultaneously. He smiled. I returned the smile. It felt as if I smiled with my heart. He firmly squeezed my hand and winked again. I squeezed his hand even harder. Then I leaned forward and I hugged him like a son hugs a father he loves. The sides of our faces touched. I held him. He held me. Was my seventy-four-year-old heart crying a joyful cry?

"I'll be back tomorrow," I said after we tenderly disengaged. "And, oh yea, I will read the letter. We'll have them come to our apartment."

When I left the room, my step was light and my heart . . . whatever. I even smiled at the nurses and everybody else I passed in the hallway. How come I was so intensely aware of who and where I was? I seemed to be really with it. Was this what Armand meant by living in the *now*?

Saturday, March 24, 2012

At around 9 p.m. Armand had another stroke: fatal this time. Both his Detroit and Halifax family had visited him that Saturday afternoon. The daughter from Nicaragua had been too late.

Wednesday, March 28, 2012

The funeral was a low-key affair. Besides family, there were 15 members of Armand's church plus the choir, 20 acquaintances from our retirement community, Frankie, Gloria, Jane, and me. Harry was absent. Paul's colleague, the Muslim Armand had corresponded with, had brought five friends of Josh who had been on outings with Armand. And, when during the funeral Mass, my heart experienced a deep peaceful feeling similar to the one I had at his bedside, I just let it happen. If the solemnity of a ritual like this had spiritually enriched Armand, who was I to debunk it?

During the socializing, Gloria and Frankie told us their plan of moving out west together. Start a new life.

Not necessarily to tie a knot, but promising to, at least, help each other get off the ground. Frankie had a buyer for his business. He had already traded his "roaring lion," as Gloria had dubbed his chopper, for a truck. Gloria shared that she would keep the baby. If a boy, she'd name him Armand. If a girl: Armanda.

We also met the friend who had taken Armand to daily breakfast at his Father's house. This turned out to be daily Mass. But because they both loved singing, they would together, on Sundays, attend a certain Protestant church. By joining those who enter into their heavenly Father's presence through exuberant, heartfelt, hand-raising worship, they felt greatly enriched in their weekday, contemplative worship at Mass.

And Armand had been wrong. The man who killed Josh and David had indeed been a drunken bastard, a repeat offender driving without a license.

When I told Sandra about the recordings I had made of our social times with her dad, she invited us for Easter dinner. "Bring them," she said, "and we'll see what we'll do with them."

I suggested putting them in a book. But questioned the thought myself right away. True, this man had searched a lot and maybe spiritually, mentally and physically danced a lot. Still, like the rest of us, he too had lived in a box. And here he was, like we all will be one day, asleep forever in an ordinary six-sided wooden one.

33

DANCERS

Flashing his disarming smile, dead Armand lifts the lid of his coffin. He pokes me with his liquorice stick and holds up another letter. That's what I thought when Sandra handed me his clarinet case and an envelope. The clarinet he willed me. The envelope, with 'For Chris, if he asks,' written on it, had been on his table/desk. "You decide if you planned to ask for it," Sandra said.

It was a copy of a letter written by Armand, dated June 7, 1993.

Dear pastor Gregg and father John,

Since we met, ten years ago, I have pondered the questions of faith you both defended. Learning that early church fathers and reformers were equally at odds, I felt compelled to seek my own answers.

As a physicist, I know that the smallest particle of light, the photon, can be considered to be both a solid particle and an ever-moving vibration. By assuming that this phenomenon expresses a universal law, I asked myself the following question. Could it be that any cosmic and absolute truth must hold within itself the complementary duality of two absolute opposites? When I incorporated into this understanding the fact that the photon allows its observer to decide which of these two opposite attributes it will display, the insights I obtained were these:

Life, in order to be true and eternal, must be fathered in both the earthly *realm of water and the* divine *realm of the spirit,*

Jesus, in order to be the personification of absolute truth, must be both fully human *and fully* divine.

The Church, in order to be true Church, must be founded on both Petros, the insignificant human *skipping stone, and Petra, the unmovable rock, the* divinity *of Christ.*

Truth, in order to be a living truth, must be brought to life in man-made *traditions inspired by* divine *revelations.*

Faith, in order to be a living faith, must be expressed in an evolving church through human *works empowered by* divinely *given grace.*

Armed with these axioms, I have become comfortable in a specific denominational box. Here, while keeping my focus on the infinite cosmos, I experience an ever-growing awareness of the righteous love of its sustainer. I have come to know myself as His child: a child of His cosmos. Remaining open to any possible enrichment I may receive from other understandings, I now see the person of Jesus, in an amazing new light.

Could it be that He, who called himself THE Son of Man, is the personification of all righteous humans who have been, are, and will continue to be persecuted by the unrighteous? And could it be that, whenever the foolish, those who love evil, the ill-informed, and the mediocre, persecute or torture or murder the righteous of any persuasion, they are doing it to our collective human righteousness; they are doing it to Him? If this is so, could it then be possible that the great I AM, who brings forth all of existence, loves his workmanship so much that he made the Lord our righteousness, the Christ, step out of the eternal now into the dimension of time to manifest himself in the person of Jesus?

Taking these possibilities into account, could it then also be that the divine intelligence is patiently waiting for mankind to evolve to where universal wisdom, expressed in any Holy book, is appreciated by all who desire to live righteously? Could the holy book of the Sikhs, the Guru Granth Sahib, be expressing beautiful insights that could benefit us all? Could Buddhism be formulating some cosmic understandings that are helpful to all who strive to live right, think right, and act right? And, could it be that a mighty blessing awaits the human race when spiritual leaders of all persuasions would finally dare to say, "Wait! There are verses and statements in our holy book that do not encourage righteousness. Could these statements have found their way in because of the culture in which they were written?"

When St. Paul, in the Christian Bible, writes that women should not be allowed to speak in an assembly, was he inserting a cultural opinion of his day? And when the Holy Koran encourages people to lie in wait, to pounce on those who think differently, was that a war tactic at the time of writing? Isn't treating women as second class citizens or forcing fellow humans to believe a certain way the residue of a club-wielding Neanderthal mentality? Aren't such beliefs making a mockery of our equality as cosmic siblings and of our free will?

What can be wrong with humans realizing they have outgrown a childish or restricted way of thinking? Didn't Jesus, the founder of the Christian faith, challenge mankind by saying, "You have heard it said; 'an eye for an eye and a tooth for a tooth.' But I'm telling you, if you brother strikes you on the one cheek, you must turn the other"?

If complementary duality proves to be a cosmic law, wouldn't that imply that all mankind will greatly benefit when every home, every community, every institution—religious or secular—and every country implements laws that guarantee equality for men and women and religious freedom for all?

Muslims believe Jesus did not die on the cross. Christians believe he did. Why do we hate those who believe differently? Could our cosmic siblings in the

Islamic faith be right in that, 2000 years ago, <u>cosmic</u>
*righteousness was not annihilated? After all, how
can a handful of temporary worms on one tiny planet
do away with a cosmic truth? And could their cosmic
siblings in the Christian faith be right in that* <u>human</u>
*righteousness was, indeed, crucified in the person of
Jesus? Isn't the daily news on planet earth all about the
crucifixion of the righteous by the unrighteous? And
couldn't our cosmic siblings in the Jewish faith be right
in believing that, whoever kills one human is guilty of
killing all?*

    *Could the trunk of a tree reaching for the sky be a
fitting symbol for anyone's upright relationship with
the divine? And could a tree's outstretched branches
reaching all around be fitting symbols for anyone's
righteous relationships with other human beings? If
so, could the story of a righteous man nailed unto this
symbol be a sobering message to us all?*

    *With regards to the mother of the crucified, what can
be wrong with me loving her as much as her son does?
Isn't playing down Mary's role in the plan of salvation
equal to ignoring the heart-piercing pain endured by all
righteous mothers who helplessly witness the bullying,
persecution, torture, and/or murdering of an innocent
child? Mothers witnessing the crucifixion of innocence
and human dignity in children and daughters that
are mentally and physically abused and raped, should,
of course, be included herein. And could it be that the
crowd cheering on these crucifiers consists of those
husbands, fathers and sons who are paying to watch*

pornography on their electronic gadgets? And how can we ignore the unbearable pain endured by every mother who is forced to cradle a starving baby because of corporate crooks, dishonest politicians, religious fanatics, and/or those whose minds are bent on instigating and/or propagating the insanity of violence and war.

Ethnic wars? Holy wars? Religious horse-feathers, maybe? Aren't they crimes against humanity born out of spiritual ignorance? Isn't murdering a person because of his/her different belief system as ridiculous as burning a blossoming vineyard because it refuses to produce oranges?

Who knows? One day we may even come to see that the equation $E=mc^2$, which expresses a physical law, applies in the spiritual realm as well. E could be the energy, or the brightness, with which the righteous will shine on earth and into eternity. M could represent a person's mindset with regards to all cosmic siblings. If negative, no light will be available to encapsulate that soul/self after physical death. C could stand for mankind's collective righteousness; it's Christ-likeness. And this C, raised to the power of two, because it expresses itself in both the physical and spiritual realm, could then give a worthwhile value to anyone's, small, individual, compassionate thought. Who knows? This law could then even be used to prove the ridiculousness of all religious bickering.

"Highfalutin! I've said it before. I'll say it again." Shaking my head, I put the letter on the floor. While taking the blowpipe pieces of the clarinet to put them together, I noticed a note taped to the fingering chart. It read:

"Dear Chris; you played sax in high school. The tune, scribbled on the back, is from Beethoven's ninth. It's easy to Dixie with. Ask Jane to sing. She has a good voice. Have fun.

Love, Armand.
P.S. My magic formula when picking up litter: 'Father, forgive them, for they know not what they do.'"

When Jane walked in and heard me practice, her eyebrows went up. But after she had read the note, she was game. I played. She sang:

"God made man in his own image, gave him power to think and choose,
Made him lord of all creation, everything was his to use.
Ever singing march we onward, victors in the midst of strife,
Joyful music leads us sunward, in the triumph song of life."

We had never done anything like that before. But we had fun. Abruptly, Jane stopped. Sinking down on the sofa, she sighed, "He'd become like a father to me. I miss the man. I want to join a choir. I want to sing. I want to feel his love for life." She stood up and, with moist eyes, looked at me. Then, while heading for the kitchen, she added, "Why don't you try to make that big flute whistle like *he* could?" I swallowed a lump and, to hide my emotions, picked up Armand's epistle again.

If our personal, spiritual E in this equation turns out to depend on our dynamics of love with all cosmic siblings, we should be able to draw another clear conclusion. Any verse, law or command not enhancing this dynamic, regardless of what holy book it is written in, cannot possibly originate with the ultimate source of this E. Maybe true theology is the study of the dynamics of this love. Imagine a theology that will open our hearts, minds and eyes, thus enabling us to understand and embrace both our complex human spiritual multiplicity and our simple singularity.

With regards to indulgences, I agree with Gregg. To believe that the sins of the dead—who I believe are living in bodies made of photons—can be atoned for by acts of sacrifice of those living in bodies made of atoms, does not make sense. It is like believing that atoms, once entangled, even if they end up in different galaxies, are somehow still inter-dependent.

Last, but not least, the sacrament of communion.

In days of old, twelve loaves of bread embodied the presence of the twelve tribes of Israel. It was God's express desire to have this bread of their presence before Him for all generations. These twelve loaves became one under the new covenant made by Israel's anointed descendant. Could this bread, consecrated by Him at the last supper, now be the bread of the presence of our collective righteousness? This, personified in Jesus, would then truly be, in the Eucharist, before our God for all generations.

The photon, both particle and wave, lets me decide whether I wish to observe the one or the other. Could it be up to me to see either bread made by human *hands, or* divine *manna from heaven? After all, consecration is not about changing atomic structures. It is about inviting the divine to come, like the dewfall, to inhabit the void within these structures. And the majesty of this void is incomprehensible. If all empty spaces from all atoms that make up all human bodies were to be removed, all mankind would fit into the one large elevated host.*

What if I, when going forward to receive this manna, personally experience a stepping into the eternal now? What if I can picture myself reclining with the apostles, hearing Jesus say, "Take and eat, this is my body given up for you"? And what if I, when receiving this manna, can imagine myself standing at the foot of the cross as well as before the empty tomb? And, do I dare to confess that I, at times, experience communion for what I believe it is meant to be? Could it have been instituted by the embodiment of cosmic righteousness—the lover of my soul/self—so that I could be intimate with Him in the complementary duality of both His Spirit and His body? I used to go to church hoping to get something out of it. Now I go to bring my sacrifice of praise. I also go to unite myself with the righteous representative of all who, on account of their righteousness, suffer at the hands of the unrighteous.

I can easily imagine myself to be a photon dancing full of joy, like a child, in the seven-coloured spectrum of mankind's different religions. And when I do, I believe I can see righteous photons dancing everywhere?

Could finding an understanding that makes sense of all truly inspired verses be more enriching than finding a few verses to justify one understanding? And could the cosmos be the inheritance of all who, in every denomination, sect, culture, or creed, believe in and practice righteousness? Could we all be cosmic dancers in the eternal now of the one who fathered all, the 'I AM who AM'?

Sincerely / Armand Huete

"That messes up that fight," I said to Jane, as I walked into the kitchen.

"Remember, pastor creams priest? Well, dead Armand just jumped in the ring. Refereeing with his complementary duality whistle, he tries to make winners of us all."

34

THE REAL DEAL

WHILE DRIVING TO DETROIT, Jane and I tried to figure out why we were so much looking forward to joining Sandra and family for their Easter dinner. Having eagerly accepted Paul and Sandra's invitation, Jane thought it was because she couldn't remember ever having enjoyed a family festivity when growing up. With her dad being an alcoholic, any kind of celebration had always been filled with tension. Personally, I remember some wonderful dinners when my dad was still alive. But, after my stepfather moved in, those memories had soured.

Sandra welcomed us with open arms, hugging us like siblings. Paul shook my hand by holding it between both of his. Rachel treated me like a long lost uncle and apologized for her boyfriend's absence. He had the flu. Rob shook my hand quickly, but he acted in the same welcoming manner. And, amazingly enough, I felt at ease when tears welled up in my eyes in response to this loving hospitality from people we hardly knew. Imagine, even though they had spent most of that morning in church, while Jane and I were still very iffy about the Easter business, there wasn't a hint of judgment. Jerry or Sylvia never hugged us this warmly. Jerry kisses Jane on the cheek and slaps me on the back. I bet Jerry will crack up good when I tell him about the peace I experienced when Armand prayed over me.

Behind the family welcoming committee, stood an ebony, fragile, but feisty looking Nigerian woman named Jewel. Her English was poor. As a recent immigrant—Sandra explained—Jewel was having a tough time. When she had wandered into Sandra's church a few Sundays ago, Sandra had taken pity on her and invited her to this dinner. Now she was lavished with the same hospitable warmth as we were.

When I stepped into the wide open living room I could easily visualize the antics enjoyed here last Christmas in the way Armand had described them. Sandra and Rachel trying to walk like baby goats. Rob and Josh doing their leopard taming act followed by the whole family pouncing on legless Armand, teaching him how to walk on his hands. It felt as if, any minute, he would call from any chair, eager to give us his fatherly hug.

The day we brought Armand to Detroit for the funeral of Josh and his friend, we had stepped inside only briefly. That week-end we had tried to respect their privacy by keeping to ourselves. Although, the real reason for keeping our distance at that time had been my reluctance of getting involved with this family's religiosity.

In the adjoining dining-room, the table, covered with a white table cloth richly spilling over on all sides, looked as if set for a wedding banquet. Plates and side plates were a soft yellow-beige with a moss green blossom pattern and gold rim. Perfectly arranged silver cutlery lay beside each plate. To each plate's right stood a tall, transparent, gold-coloured wineglass. To each plate's left was a smaller side plate, partially covered with a bright yellow napkin imprinted with the words, "He has risen!"

Over the length of this inviting table, silver candle holders, with tall white candles, alternated with pairs of white Easter-lilies lying loose on the cloth. How come all this registered with me so clearly? Just as when I left Armand's hospital bed, this awareness of standing in the now was amazing. It was as if the love that embraced us at the door was here spread out before me in a tangible form. The joyful festive look brought back good memories. I saw my dad, mom, and sis, all happy as can be, ready to sit down for a birthday meal, which was one of our ways of celebrating family.

After we had all found our seats—behind each dinner plate was a small decorated card with our name—I noticed tears in Jane's eyes.

At Paul's prompting, each member of the family reached for the hand of the person seated next to them on either side. This made us all hold hands while Rachel prayed the blessing. Jane sniffled and, quickly, freed one hand to use the fancy yellow napkin to dab her eyes. Rachel's prayer was nothing profound. It was the way she said it. Expressing thankfulness, love, and faith, her prayer sounded as if she was talking to her own dad. Her words reminded me of Armand's prayer; the one I had overheard at the Hospital. What a difference with my stepfather's grand style and elaborate rhetoric.

The meal was something else. First we had squash soup with a hint of ginger. After that, Sandra, Rob, Rachel and Jewel brought in ham with pine-apple, sweet potatoes spiced with cinnamon, asparagus sprinkled with nutmeg, Belgium endive, coleslaw, Greek salad, bread, wine: you name it. And, in the center, Sandra put a fancy dish with spring-lamb in mint sauce.

Between eating, noisy talk, and laughing, each member of the family somehow found an opening to share a thought, short poem, or idea relating to the Easter story. This freely mixing of everyday talk with deeper thoughts was foreign to me. When young, the resurrection business had been beyond my scope. I simply believed what I was told. When old enough to understand it, I no longer believed a word. Now, feasting, laughing, and loving every minute of this celebration, I felt guilty. Here I was: tasting and seeing, as it were, the goodness of these people whose beliefs I had been debunking all my adult life. Armand was right when he said, 'Family celebrations are like diamonds sewn in the fabric of time.' And, what better way to celebrate family than with a festive meal?

For desert we settled in a big half circle in the living room. The fancy sweets we had brought from Armand's favourite Austrian bakery were a hit. And, while coffee and tea was still being poured, Rob started the sharing. He confessed how he, on his first Easter week-end home from university, had told Armand, he no longer believed the Bible-nonsense his parents had been feeding him. He had read how ridiculous it is to believe in a dead man coming back to life. And, he couldn't understand how papa, intelligent physicist as he was, could buy into these fairy tales. Papa sat him down and explained how the cosmos speaks to physicists in the language of simple numbers. These numbers reveal how the cosmos functions and how it obeys laws expressible in mathematical formulas.

With regards to the six-day-creation tale, papa had explained, the fairy-tale book certainly had the numbers right. Some thirty five hundred years after it was written, physicists have established that, indeed, there are six separate timeframes in the evolutionary process. It went from quarks to protons to nuclei to atoms to molecules to people. And, to rub in the number six, they also learned how in the first 600,000 years the cosmos was painted, consecutively, with six of the seven humanly visible colors. Starting with violet and ending with orange—today's color of the microwave background—all information for cosmic expansion is established. We humans are still being created in His image in time frame six. But He, in His eternal NOW, is present in all seven time frames. He fully IS in the duality of active involvement and peaceful rest.

"But most remarkable of all," Rob continued, radiating a bit of Armand's childlike enthusiasm. Papa gave him a number to silence all unbelievers. According to him, physicists try to constantly simplify their equations. They want simpler numbers to express ever greater concepts. The beauty of using a number to express a concept is that the value we give it increases as our understanding expands.

'Now imagine,' papa had said, 'we want to express in one simple number what the entire cosmos is all about in its relationship to mankind. First we take the number 100. This number has, from ancient times, been used to express all that we humans understand about the universe we live in. Next we take the number 53. It represents all the positive mass-energy the cosmos holds; ten kilograms raised to the power of *plus* 53. This total energy is constant. No matter how small the cosmos was, or how big it will be, this number doesn't change. But the amazing fact is that this positive mass-energy generates a negative gravitational energy which adds up to ten kilograms to the power of *minus* 53. And, as we all know, the negative cancels out the positive. This means the cosmos is, just as the fairy tale book says, born out of nothing. Now put the 100 and the 53 together and you have 153. This number, papa told him, was written in the fairy tale book 2000 years before physicists became aware of it.'

Jane shook her head. Jewel excused herself to go to the bathroom. Sandra got up to pour Paul more tea, and Paul helped himself to another treat. But Rob was not distracted. Now standing in the center of our half circle, he continued unperturbed.

"Papa suggested, I promise a free beer to the first of my classmates who could find this number mentioned in the book of fairy tales. He showed it to me. And after we read it together, he asked, 'What do you think, Rob? Could Jesus, by calling us 'children' and using the catch of 153 big fish as a metaphor, be expressing man's ability to catch on to all the laws of the cosmos, one at a time? Could he have hinted here that breakthrough understandings, like big fish, will end up in the nets of those whose minds are open and prepared?"

After Rob's serious fishy tale, I thought we needed to bring back the laughs. I pushed a button on the CD player and, through Paul's extravagant sound system, dead Armand stepped into our midst to tell his worm story. It wasn't long before we all either cried, laughed, or both. Even Jewell, judged by her laughing, seemed to have gotten the drift.

Then Jane suggested I follow it up by replaying our singing of, 'If I were a rich man.' It turned out Rachel knew the lyrics from a school performance she had been in. Right away taking the floor, singing along loud and clear with her papa, she inspired us all. And, just like that crazy Sunday morning in Armand's apartment, a mighty chorus rose up. We even drowned out Frankie's last *'Deedle-bubba-deedle-dum.'*

It was 1.50 a.m. when Jane and I finally bedded down on a blow-up mattress in the middle of the living room. We just laid there. Holding hands, allowing our minds to freely recall and cherish all we had experienced in the last, heart-warming, eight hours, we didn't say a word.

Wednesday, July 4, 2012

It was odd. Sitting on the bench on which Armand had first roped me in by his charm, I was bothered by a crumpled burger box and a flattened paper cup lying beside me in the grass. But, litter or no litter, it was Armand's day. The god-particle he, as a young man, had dreamed of finding, had been found. According to the newscaster that morning, physicists all over the world were ecstatic. To them, it was a news event equal to man's landing on the moon. Using the biggest atomic particle accelerator ever built, physicists had smashed two particles together and freed, for one billionth of a second, this long sought after 'boson,' as it was called. Responsible for giving mass to all elementary particles, this boson verified the existence of an invisible force field that stretches across the entire cosmos. Without this boson, which is the carrier of that force, electrons, protons and neutrons would not be able to stick together to make atoms. Atoms could not stick together to make molecules. And molecules would not be able to team up to make stars, planets, trees, buildings, or humans. Without this boson, nothing in the cosmos could have been created. At a cost of one dollar for every year of our cosmos' age, 13.8 billion, physicists had proven that their theory of how the cosmos works seems right.

A full moon, the moon Armand had taken us to for imaginary visits, was shining in a sunny sky. Milling around in my mind were Armand's words, songs and laughs, even his hugs. I also recalled the inner warmth, greater than I'd ever experienced, that had flowed from his hand into my heart while I sat on his hospital bed. I still see Jane's puzzled face when I walked in the door that afternoon with flowers. The maintenance guys have since been puzzled too. I now greet them with a smile and by first name. One hot day, I even brought them all an ice-cream.

But the big news, that 4th of July, 2012, was how scientists had ploughed billions into proving the existence of an invisible force field. This, while old geezer Armand had been shrugged off for quietly questioning, searching, and experiencing, without spending a dime, the reality of a spiritual dimension that's equally invisible. It somehow seems easy for people to flippantly name this crucial boson, without which nothing could have been made, the god-particle. But calling men and women, without whom nothing in our world could have been made, off-springs of God, or God's children, seems too far-fetched.

I eyed the moon again and smiled. Why not? If Armand could; so could I. And, after first making sure I was alone, I did it. Out loud I said, "Yes, higher power, or God, or whatever name you prefer, I'll make you a deal. Mind you, I'd love to call you father, papa even, but, to me, that still sounds pretty presumptuous. Anyway, here's the deal: If *I* forgive my stepfather for his misconceptions of you and his consequent rotten attitude towards me, will *you* forgive me for whatever I have done wrong in *my* life? And here's **the real deal.** If you want me to treat all other humans as my cosmic siblings, I need help. I can not possibly let go of my prejudices, my self-righteousness and my fears, **unless you**, possible God, **bless me** with a mega dose of your divine cosmic righteousness. Only when you fill my human heart with Your divine and righteous compassion, will I be able to make up, at times, for an ignorant one."

Nothing happened. Yet, I stood up, swallowed my pride and, without fear of someone behind the apartment windows watching and thinking, 'look; that stinkin browner picks up other people's litter,' I stooped.

As I dropped the litter into the bin, speaking Armand's magic formula was out of the question. But my mind replayed the words, 'Father, forgive them; for they do not know what they do.' Then, for whatever reason, my mind recalled Armand's strange complementary duality idea. Light has no meaning without darkness. Positive necessitates negative. Could it be that, if the omnipresent power I just made my deals with is an absolute truth, she, he or it needs to inhabit, simultaneously, even the most insignificant part of her, his or its handiwork? Furthermore, if this power is the heart of the whole of creation, shouldn't it be able to also inhabit every heart of each of its off-springs? Again I looked up at the moon. And, in an attempt to fathom Armand's understanding of the eternal now, I closed my eyes. Then . . . it slowly happened. Christmas, yes, even while my watch read July 4, 2012, 9:11 a.m., local Canada earth time, Christmas happened in my heart. The she, he or it distinctly embraced my innermost being, my soul/self as Armand called it, with 'fatherly' love. 'Imagine,' I thought, 'all along I've been His son. But today, Armand's great I AM has become my Father.'

Thank you, papa God!

To all

who

hunger and thirst

for

righteousness.

CONFESSION

With regards to Armand's hint, the one that irked me on Monday morning, March 19, 2012, I admit he was right. Jane and I now both know. Even his complementary duality is hitting home. When we celebrate our oneness as man and wife, we seem to experience the *mystery* of our intimacy. We now sense how we, for each other, simultaneously are the giver and the gift.

ACKNOWLEDGMENT

I am grateful to all the people, circumstances and inspirations that have helped me ponder and express, in this story, whatever I thought to be true. If any misconceptions or misunderstandings have found their way into this novel, I, the writer, take full responsibility.

Although events and dialogues are based on real life experiences, most locations and all characters are fictitious. Any resemblance to any person living or deceased is strictly coincidental.

POSSIBLE REFERENCES

The following references were picked from the many we gathered from the chaos on Armand's table/desk. For anyone trying to figure out how Armand could justify his out-of-the-box understandings, they may or may not be helpful.

His most dog-eared books were:

Hindu's Bhagavad Gita, translated by Graham M. Schweig. (BG)

Jewish Tanakh: Translation of the Holy Scriptures: Jewish Publication Society. (JT)

Christian community Bible: Clarentian Publications. (CB)

New International Version of the Holy Bible: Zondervan Publishers. (NIV)

Noble Qur'an translated by Abdalhaqq & Aisha Bewley: Bookwork Norwich (QU)

The following quotations are from the Jewish Tanakh, unless marked otherwise.
1Ch = 1 Chronicles, Da = Daniel, Dt = Deuteronomy, Ex = Exodus, Ez = Ezekiel, Ge = Genesis, Is = Isaiah, Je = Jeremiah, Jo = Joshua, Le = Leviticus, Nu = Numbers, Pr = Proverbs, Ps = Psalms, 1Sa =1 Samuel, Ze = Zechariah.

The following quotations are from the Christian Community Bible, unless marked otherwise.

Ac = Book of Acts, 1Co = 1 Corinthians, 2Co = 2 Corinthians, Ep = Ephesians, Ga = Galatians, He = Hebrews, Jo = John, 1Jn = First letter of John, 2Jn = second letter of John, Ja = James, Lk = Luke, Mk = Mark, Mt = Matthew, 1Pe = First letter of Peter, Ph = Philippians, Re = Revelations, Ro = Romans, 1Th = 1 Thessalonians, 2Th = 2 Thessalonians, 2Ti = 2 Timothy, Ws = Book of wisdom.

FRONT COVER
Ge 32:27 But he answered, "I will not let you go, <u>unless you</u> bless me."

CHAPTER 1
P 002 *Ez 3:15* I came to the exile community that dwelt in Tel Abib (Hill of Spring)

P 006 *Is 11:2-4* The Spirit of the Lord will rest upon him-a Spirit of wisdom and understanding, a Spirit of counsel and power, a Spirit of knowledge and fear of the Lord. 3. Not by appearances will he judge, nor by what is said must he decide, 4. but with justice he will judge the poor and with *righteousness* decide for the meek.

Re 1:4 from the seven Spirits of God which are before his throne.

Re 3:1 "Thus says he who holds the seven Spirits of God and the seven stars:

Re 4:5 Seven flaming torches burn before the throne; these are the seven Spirits of God

Re 5:6 with 7 horns and 7 eyes, which are the 7 Spirits of God sent out to all the earth.

P 007 *Lk 19:2* a man named Zaccheus was there. He was a tax collector and a wealthy man.

Buddhist's Eightfold path: right view, right thought, right action, right livelihood, right effort, right mindfulness, right concentration, right speech.

BG 18:78 "Where there is Krishna, the Supreme Lord of Yoga, where there is Partha, Holder of the Bow (Where Divinity and humanity are found together—with humanity armed and ready to fight wickedness)

There is fortune, triumphs, well-being, and lasting righteousness—that is my conclusion.

CHAPTER 2

P 018 *Re 5:6* I saw him with 7 horns and 7 eyes, the seven Spirits of God sent out to all the earth.

Ps 82:6 "You are gods," I said. "You are all sons (and daughters) of the Most High."

Jn 10:34 Is this not written in your law; I said, you are gods?

CHAPTER 3

P 022 *Ge 2:15* The LORD GOD took the man and placed him in the garden of Eden, to till and to tend

Ge 3:3 'You shall not eat of it or touch it, lest you die.'"

Ge 3: 24 He drove the man out, and stationed the cherubim and the fiery ever turning sword,

P 023 *Ge 3:19* by the sweat of your brow shall you get bread to eat.

P 026 *QU 50:16* We are nearer to him (man) than his jugular vein.

Ps 139:5 You hedge me before and behind; You lay Your hand upon me

P 027 *Jo 10:13* "Stand still, O sun, at Gibeon, O moon, in the valley of Aijalon!"

CHAPTER 4

P 034 *Ro 8:28* whom he has called according to his plan (purpose)

Mt 12:35 good person produces good things from his good store, an evil person evil from his evil store.

CHAPTER 5

P 045 *Jn 2:9* The steward tasted the water that had become wine,

P 046 *Mt 5:48* be righteous and perfect in the way your heavenly Father is righteous and perfect.

P 048 *Jn 1:3-4* Whatever has come to be, found life in him, life which for humans was also light.

CHAPTER 6

P 053 *Ps 22:3* But You are holy, enthroned upon the praises of Israel."

P 055 *QU 6:160* those who divide up their deen and form into sects, have nothing to do with them.

Dt. 6:4 Hear, O Israel! The LORD our God, the LORD is one."

Jn 17:21 May they all be one as you Father are in me and I am in you.

P 056 *Mt 7:6* Do not give what is holy to the dogs, or throw your pearls to the pigs.

P 057 *1Ch 21:13* Let me fall into the hands of the Lord, for his compassion is very great;

Mt 5:7 Fortunate are the merciful, for they shall find mercy.

Ps 82:8 Arise, O God, judge the earth, for all the nations are Your possession.

Ex 7:27 judge them according to their deserts. And they shall know that I am the LORD.

P 059 *Ge 32:27* But he answered, "I will not let you go, unless you bless me."

CHAPTER 7

P 062 *Ps 104:2* You are clothed in glory and majesty, wrapped in a robe of light;

Jn 8:12 Jesus spoke to them again, "I am the Light of the world;

QU 24:35 Allah is the light of the heavens and the earth

BG 11:17 A mass of light, shining everywhere, With the brilliance of the sun and blazing fires

P 064 *Is 11:6* The wolf shall dwell with the lamb, the leopard lie down with the kid;

CHAPTER 8

P 076 *Ex 33:11* The LORD would speak to Moses face to face, as one man speaks to another.

CHAPTER 9

P 088 *Lk 10:29-37* When he(Samaritan) came upon the man, he was moved with compassion.

Mt 25:31-45 whenever you did this to these who are my brothers and sisters, you did it to me.

Lk 13:34 to bring together your children, as a bird gathers her young under her wings

P 090 *Ps 82:6* "You are gods," I said. "You are all sons (and daughters) of the Most High."

Jn 10:34 Is this not written in your law; I said, you are gods?

Mt 25:34 Take possession of the kingdom prepared for you from the beginning of the world.

CHAPTER 10

P 094 *Ps 78:2* I will speak in parables, I will talk of mysteries, which our ancestors have told us.

Mt 13:35 Jesus taught all this to the crowd by means of parables.

QU 2:25 Allah is not ashamed to make an example of a gnat or of an even smaller thing.

Ex 12:37 The Israelites journeyed from Raamses to Succoth, about 600.000 men on foot,

P 095 *Ex 14:21* The LORD drove back the sea with a strong east wind all that night,

CHAPTER 11

P 102 *Lk 13:34* to bring together your children, as a bird gathers her young under her wings,

P 104 *Ps 42:1* Like a hind crying for water, my soul thirsts for God, the living God;

Ps 63:2 God, You are my God; I search for You, my soul thirsts and my body yearns for You

Ps 42:7 Deep calls to Deep as your cataracts thunder; waves and torrents have gone over me.

CHAPTER 12

P 114 *Ro 13:7* to whom taxes are due, pay taxes;

CHAPTER 14

P 133 *QU 3:30* Allah advises you to be aware of Him. Allah is Ever Gentle with His slaves.

P 134 *Ps 33:12* the people he has chosen to be his own

Ps 82:6 "You are gods," I said. "You are all sons (and daughters) of the Most High."

Jn 10:34 Is this not written in your law; I said, you are gods?

Ro 8:15 All those who walk in the Spirit of God are sons and daughters of God.

P 136 *QU 2:111* All who submit to Allah and are good-doers will find their reward with their Lord.

QU 3:19 deen (religion in the broadest sense) before Allah is Islam (submission to His will.)

Mt 20:28 Be like the Son of Man who has come to give his life to redeem many.

Ze 3:9 and I will remove that country's guilt in a single day

Mt 26:28 my (the) blood of the covenant, poured out for many for the forgiveness of sins.

Jn 1:29 John said, "There is the lamb of God who takes away the sin of the world."

Re 1:5 he who has washed away our sins with his own blood

P 137 *Ro 3:23* Because all have sinned and all fall short of the Glory of God.

Ro 7:23 but I notice in my body another law challenging the law of the spirit

1Jn 3:4 Anyone who commits sin acts as an enemy of the law of God

Lk 12:5 Fear the one who after killing you can throw you into hell. This one you must fear.

QU 3:191 So safeguard us from the punishment of the Fire.

P 139 *Ps 26:2* Probe me, O Lord, try me, test my heart and mind, my eyes are on your steadfast love.

Mt 22:37 love the Lord, your God, with all your heart, your soul and with all your mind.

Jn 14:23 and we will come to him and make a room in his home

Ja 1:27 blameless religion is helping orphans and widows and avoiding the world's corruption.

Is 1:18 Come let us reach an understanding, says the LORD

P 140 *Jn 3:5* No one can enter the kingdom of God without being born of water and Spirit

Re 12:10 Now has salvation come, For our brother's accuser has been cast out

CHAPTER 17

P 165 *BG 7:21* Human beings follow my path universally, O Partha

P 168 *QU 50:38* 'We created the heavens and the earth, and everything between them, in Six Days.'

QU 24:43 'Allah created every animal from water.'

Ge 1:1-31 creation story

P 169 *QU 22:047* 'A Day with your Lord is equivalent to a thousand years in the way you count.'

QU 7:022 If you do not forgive us and have mercy on us, we will be among the lost.'

QU 2:037 Then Adam received some words from his Lord and He turned towards him.

QU 4:157 They did not kill him and did not crucify him but it was made to seem so to them.

Ac 5:30 God raised Jesus whom you killed by hanging him on a wooden post.

Lk 23:46 Crying, "Father in your hands I command my spirit." he(Jesus) gave up his spirit.

Ph 2:8 He humbled himself by being obedient to death, death on the cross.

CHAPTER 18

P 176 *Jn 12:32* And when I am lifted up from the earth, I shall draw all to myself.

P 177 *Ge 3:1-4* Did God really say: You shall not eat of the fruit of the trees of the garden?

Ws 2:11 Let us set a trap for the righteous, for he annoys us and opposes our way of life.

P 178 *Mt 7:21* Not everyone who says to me: Lord! Lord! Will enter the kingdom, but only . . .

P 179 *Jn 6:63* It is the spirit that gives life; the flesh cannot help.

CHAPTER 20

P 199 *Jn 3:16* Yes, God so loved the world that he gave his only Son that whoever believes in him

Is 50:2 Is my arm, then, too short to rescue, Have I not the power to save?

Mt 20:28 Be like the Son of Man who has come, not to be served but to serve and to redeem

1Ti 2:6 Christ Jesus, himself human, who gave his life for the redemption of all.

CHAPTER 21

P 205 *Lk 10:22* no one knows the Father except the Son and he to whom He chooses to reveal him.

Jn 14:23 if anyone loves me, he'll keep my word, we will come to him and make a room . . .

P 209 *1Co 14:5* Would that all of you spoke in tongues!

P 210 *Ac 1:5* John baptized with water, but you will be baptized with the Holy Spirit

Ac 2:4 All were filled with the Holy Spirit and began to speak other languages,

Ac 8:15 They went down and prayed for them that they might receive the Holy Spirit,

Ac 19:6 Then Paul laid his hands on them + the Holy Spirit came down upon them;

CHAPTER 22

P 217 *Lk 17:21* See, the kingdom of God is among you.

P 218 *Jn 3:3* I say to you, "no one can see the kingdom of God unless he is born again from above."

CHAPTER 23

P 224 *2Co 6:15* What union can there be between one who believes and one who does not believe.

Mt 7:1 Do not judge and you will not be judged. As you judge others, so you will be judged.

P 226 *Dt. 12:23* for the blood is the life

Mk 1:34 Jesus healed many who had various diseases, and drove out many demons;

Mk 16:17 signs will accompany those who've believed; in my name they will cast out demons

P 227 *Mt 12:26* So if Satan drives out Satan, he is divided; how then can his reign stand?

Jn 14:6 He said, "I am the way, truth and life; no one comes to the Father but through me.

P 228 *1Pe 1:6-7* Thus will your faith be tested, like gold in a furnace.

P 230 *Mk 9:29* And he answered, "Only prayer can drive out this kind, nothing else."

Is 50:7 the Lord God will help me-therefore I feel no disgrace; I have set my face like flint,

CHAPTER 24

P 240 *2Co 5:17* For that same reason, the one who is in Christ is a new creature.

Ro 8:15 every time we cry, 'Abba! (this is Dad!) Father!

Ro 8:16 The Spirit assures our spirit that we are sons and daughters of God.

Ws 2:13 he (the righteous) has become a reproach to our way of thinking,

Jn 1:12 but all who received him (Jesus) he empowers to become children of God

Jn 3:3 I say to you, "no one can see the kingdom of God unless he is born again from above."

CHAPTER 25

P 244 *Ac 19:6* the Holy Spirit came upon them; and they began to speak in tongues and to prophecy

1Cor 14:22 prophecy is a sign for those who believe, not for those who refuse to believe.

1Cor. 14:39 So, my friends set your hearts on the gift of prophecy,

P 245 *Ac 1:5* John baptized with water, but you will be baptized with the Holy Spirit

Ac 2:4 All were filled with the Holy Spirit and began to speak other languages,

Ac 8:15 They went down and prayed for them that they might receive the Holy Spirit,

Ac 19:6 Then Paul laid his hands on them and the Holy Spirit came down upon them;

P 247 *2Ti. 3:16* All scripture is inspired by God and useful for teaching, refuting error, for correcting

P 248 *Mt 15:3* And you, why do you break God's command for the sake of your traditions?

2Th. 2:15 stand firm and hold to the traditions that we taught you by word or by letter.

P 250 *Jn 15:5* I am the vine you are the branches

CHAPTER 26

P 252 *Ro 8:14* All those who walk in the Spirit of God are sons and daughters of God.

Ro 8:15 not receive a spirit of slavery, but the Spirit that makes you sons and daughters,

Ro 8:16 we cry 'Abba! (Dad!) Father! The Spirit assures our spirit we are God's children.

P 253 *Ac 17:28* in him we live and move and have our being: for we too are his offspring.

Re 22:1 the river of life, clear as crystal, gushing from the throne of God + the Lamb.

P 257 *Lk 6:27* Love your enemies, do good to those who hate you. Bless those who curse you

P 259 *Ep 3:15* I kneel (before) the Father from whom every family in heaven and earth rec. its name.

CHAPTER 27

P 265 *Mk 10:18* Jesus answered, "Why do you call me good? No one is good but God alone.

P 267 *Ge 1:3* God said, "Let there be light"; and there was light.

Jn 1:2 The word was with God and the word was God; He was in the beginning with God.

Jn 1:3 All things were made through Him and without Him nothing came to be.

Jn 8:12 He said, "I am the light of the world."

Jn 1:14 And the Word was made flesh, He had His tent pitched among us,

Jn 8:58 And Jesus said, "Truly, I say to you, before Abraham was, I am."

Ex 3:14 God said to Moses, "Ehyeh-Asher-Ehyeh," or "I AM WHO AM."

Lk 17:21 Because the kingdom of God is within you. (NIV)

P 268 *Ge 3:14* And God said to Moses, "Ehyeh-Asher-Ehyeh." (I AM who AM)

Jn 14:6 Jesus said, "I am the way, the truth and the life.

P 269 See chapter # 3 page 30 regarding particles.

Re 1:8 I am the Alpha and the Omega, He who is, was and who is to come: Master of the universe.

Re 1:17 He said, Do not be afraid, It is I, the First and the Last.

Re 21:6 He said; "It's already done! I am the Alpha and the Omega, the Beginning and the End.

Re 22:13 I am the Alpha and the Omega, the First and the Last, the Beginning and the End.

CHAPTER 28

P 273 *Dt 30:15* See, I set before you this day life and prosperity, death and adversity

P 275 *Ex 20:13* You shall not murder

Mk 10:19 You know the commandments; Do not kill,

P 277 *Jn 19:11* therefore the one who handed me over to you is more guilty."

P 279 *Ge 4:10* He said, "Hark, your brother's blood cries out to Me from the ground!

P 280 *Lk 1:46–47* My soul proclaims the greatness of the Lord, my spirit exults in God my saviour!

CHAPTER 29

P 282 *Mt 16:18-19* I say to you: You are Peter(or Rock) and on this rock I will build my church;

Is 22:22 I will place the keys of David's palace on his shoulders, what he locks none may . . .

P 283 *Ac 2:14* Peter stood up and, with a loud voice, addressed them, "Fellow Jews and all foreigners

Ac 3:6 what I (Peter) have I give to you (a cripple): In the name of Jesus, the Messiah, walk!"

Ac 4:8 Then Peter, filled with the Holy Spirit, spoke up, "Leaders of the people! Elders!

Ac 10:28 God has made it clear to me, no one should call any person common or unclean;

P 284 *2Th 2:15* hold to the traditions that we taught you by word (of mouth) or by letter.

1Co 13:2 faith great enough to move mountains, but had no love, I would be nothing.

Ja 2:26 So, just as the body is dead without its spirit, so faith without deeds is also dead.

Jn 20:22 he said to them, for those whose sins you forgive, they are forgiven;

Lk 5:24 Now you shall know that the Son of Man has authority on earth to forgive sins."

Mt. 6:15 If you do not forgive others, your Father (in heaven) will not forgive you either.

Mt 5:24 leave your gift in front of the altar, go and make peace with (your brother first)

Mt.22:32 God said: am I not the God of Abraham, Isaac and Jacob? He is God, of the living

P 285 *Jn 19:25* Then he said to the disciple,(while referring to Mary) "There is your mother."

Lk 1:42 Elizabeth, filled with Holy spirit said, You are most blessed among women and . . .

Re 12:1 clothed with the sun, the moon under her feet and a crown of twelve stars on he head.

P 286 *1Co 3:13* The fire will test the work of everyone.

He 12:29 Our God is indeed a consuming fire.

Mt 26:27 "'Drink this all of you, for this is my blood, the blood of the Covenant,

Mt 26:28 the blood of the covenant, which is poured out for many for the forgiveness of sins.

P 287 *Ac 20:7* On the first day of the week we were together for the breaking of the bread.

1Co 11:29 examine yourself before eating of the bread and drinking of the cup

CHAPTER 30

P 293 1*Sa 26:23* the Lord will requite every man for his right conduct and loyalty (righteousness)

Mt 5:10 Fortunate those who are persecuted for the cause of justice, theirs is the kingdom

Is 33:22 For the Lord shall be our judge, (NIV)

Jn 12:47-50 for I have come, not to condemn the world, but to save the world.

Lk 19:10 The Son of Man has come to seek and to save the lost.

Mt 9:13 Go and find out what this means: What I want is mercy, not sacrifice

Ro 11:32 So God has submitted all to disobedience, in order to show his mercy to all.

1Pe 1:3-7 Let us praise God, the Father of our Lord Jesus Christ, for his great mercy

Jn 1:29 John said, "There is the lamb of God, who takes away the sin of the world.

1Jn 2:2 He is the sacrificial victim for our sins and the sins of the whole world.

Ph 2:7-8 in his appearance found as a man. He humbled himself by being obedient to death.

1Pe 3:18 Remember how Christ died, once and for all, for our sins.

P 294 *Jn 1:1-14* He was in the beginning with God.

Da 7:13 like a human being came with the clouds of heaven; He reached the Ancient of Days.

Mt 16:13 Jesus asked his disciples, "What do people say of the Son of Man?

Mt 24:30 Then the sign of the Son of Man will appear in heaven . . .

Mt 26:64 you will see the Son of Man seated at the right hand of the Most Powerful God

P 295 *Jer. 23:6* The Lord Our Righteousness (NIV)

Mt 3:17 a voice from heaven was heard, "This is my Son, the Beloved; he is my chosen One."

Ps 2:7 the Lord said to me, "You are my son, I have fathered you this day.

Ro 1:4 Son of God endowed with Power, upon rising from the dead through the Holy Spirit.

Jn 3:35 For the Father loves the Son and has entrusted everything into his hands.

Jn 6:51-68 I am the living bread which has come from heaven

Jn 8:12 "I am the light of the world; the one who follows me will not walk in darkness

Jn 11:25 I am the resurrection; whoever believes in me, though he die, shall live.

Jn 14:6 I am the way, the truth and the life;

Re 1:8 I am the Alpha and the Omega, he who is, was and is to come: Master of the universe.

Jn 16:12 I still have many things to tell you, but you cannot bear them now

P 296 *Jn 14:6* I am the way, the truth and the life; no one comes to the Father but through me.

Re 19:8 Fine linen, bright and clean, stands for the(righteous deeds) of the holy ones.

Jn 17:5 Father give me in your presence the Glory I had with you before the world began.

Ep 1:10 under him God wanted to unite, in fullness of time, everything in heaven + on earth.

Lk 3:38-4:1 Son of Seth, son of Adam, son of God, Jesus full of the Holy Spirit

P 297 *1Co 15:22* All die for being Adam's, and in Christ all will receive life

1Co 15:45 Adam, was given natural life; the last Adam has become spirit that gives life.

Ro 5:17 those who receive the gift of true righteousness through one person, Jesus Christ.

He 2:6-8 What is man that you should be mindful of him, You gave him dominion . . .

He 12:23 There is God, Judge of all, with the spirits of the (righteous) brought to perfection

Mt 3:17 "This is my Son, the Beloved; he is my Chosen One,"

Mt.7:21 Not everyone who says to me: Lord! Lord! will enter the kingdom of heaven.

Mt 13:43 Then the just (righteous) will shine like the sun in the kingdom of their Father,

Mt 22:42 If David, inspired by God, calls the Messiah Lord, how can he be his son?

Lk 14:14 you will be repaid at the Resurrection of the (righteous)

QU 74:56 He (Allah) is the Lord of Righteousness and of Forgiveness (*Abdullah Yusuf Ali*)

Je 23:5 I will raise up to David a righteous branch. The Lord Our Righteousness. (*NIV*)

P 298 *Jn 10:16* I have other sheep who are not of this fold.

Jn 17:5 Now, Father, give me in your presence the same Glory I had before the world began.

Mt 5:10 Fortunate are those who are persecuted for the cause of Justice (righteousness)

Ph 1:21 For me to live is Christ, and even death is profitable for me.

Ph 2:5 Let what was seen in Christ Jesus be seen in you

Ph 2:7-8 the nature of a servant made in human likeness, in appearance found as a man

P 299 *Mt. 5:6* Fortunate are those who hunger and thirst for justice (righteousness), . . .

Mk 16:15 go out to the whole world and proclaim the Good News to all

Jn 1:12 but all who received him he empowers to become children of God.

Jn 3:3 I say to you, no one can see the kingdom of God unless he is born again from above."

Jn 3:16 God so loved the world, he gave his only Son.

P 300 *Ph 4:19* And my God will meet all your needs according to his riches in Christ Jesus.*(NIV)*

Ep 3:16 I pray that out of his glorious riches he may strengthen you with power

Ph 3:7 I now consider all as garbage, if instead I may gain Christ. May I be found in Him

Lk 12:21 how it will be with anyone who stores up for himself but is not rich toward God

CHAPTER 31

P 305 *Mt. 16:18* You are Peter(or rock) and on this rock I will build my church.

Mt 16:19 I give you the keys of the kingdom of heaven

Mt. 18:18 whatever you unbind on earth, heaven will keep unbound.

Mt 23:9 do not call anyone on earth Father, you have one Father, and he is in heaven. (NIV)

Mt 6:14 If you forgive others their wrongs, your Father in heaven will also forgive yours.

P 306 *Jn 2:4* Jesus replied, "Woman, your thoughts are not mine! My hour has not yet come.

Jn 19:26 Jesus said to the Mother, "Woman here is your son."

1Ti 2:5 there is one God, there is one mediator between God and humankind, Christ Jesus

P 307 *Lk 22:19* broke the bread and gave it to them saying, "This is my body which is given for you.

Mt 28:19 Go, therefore, and make disciples from all nations. Baptize them . . .

Ge 2:18 The Lord God said, "It is not good for man to be alone;"

1Pe 3:18 Remember how Christ died, once and for all, for our sins.

He 10:17 Their sins and evil deeds I will remember no more

P 308 *Mk 7:8* You even put aside the commandment of God to hold fast to human tradition.

Ep 2:8-9 By the grace of God you have been saved through faith. It is God's gift.

P 309 *Mt 26:26* Jesus took bread, said a blessing, broke it, and said Take and eat; this is my body."

Jn 10:7 Jesus said, "Truly, I say to you, I am the gate of the sheep.

Jn 6:51 I am the living bread which has come down from heaven, whoever eats of this bread will live

Jn 15:5 I'm the vine, you are the branches

He 7:27 He offered himself in sacrifice once and for all.

Jn 6:51 I am the living bread which has come from heaven; whoever eats of this bread will live

P 310 *Jn 6:53* if you do not eat the flesh of the Son of Man and drink his blood, you have no life

CHAPTER 32

P 312 *1Jn 2:18* You were told that an antichrist would come;

P 313 *Ps 91:11* For he will order his angels to guard you wherever you go

He 1:14 spirits (angels) are only servants, God sends them to help those who shall be saved.

2Co 11:14 It is not surprising; if Satan disguises himself as an angel of light,

Mt 9:34 they said, "He drives away demons with the help of the prince of demons."

Lk 4:41 Demons were driven out, howling as they departed from their victims

1Ti 4:1 some will abandon the faith and follow deceitful spirits and things taught by demons.

P 315 *Ge 2:2* and He (God) ceased on the seventh day from all the work that he had done.

Da 12:7 when the breaking of the power of the holy people comes to an end,

Re 13:18 calculate the number of the beast, for it is man's number. His number is 666

Ge 2:2 on the seventh day he (God) rested from all his work. (NIV)

Ps 95:11 I declared on oath in my anger, "They shall never enter my rest."(NIV)

He 3:18 To whom did God swear that they would not enter into his rest?

He 4:3 We are now to enter this rest because we believed, as it was said (in Ps 95:11)

Ep 6:12 Our battle is against the rulers and authorities and dark powers governing this world.

QU 5:91 Shaytan wants to stir up enmity and hatred between you by means of wine and gambling.

1Pe 5:8 the devil prowls about like a roaring lion seeking someone to devour.

Ze 9:9 your king is coming to you. He is victorious, triumphant, humble, riding on an ass.

Jn 12:14 Jesus found a donkey and sat upon it, as Scripture says; (in Ze 9:9)

1Co 1:27 Yet God has chosen what the world considers foolish, to shame the wise

P 316 *Re 7:14* came out the great persecution; made their clothes white in the blood of the lamb

Ph 2:1 If you have any encouragement from being united with Christ, (NIV)

2Co 5:21 in him we be the righteousness of God (NIV)

1Co 2:9 No eye has seen, no ear heard, no mind conceived what God has prepared (NIV).

<u>CHAPTER 33</u>

P 322 *Jn 3:5* No one can enter the kingdom of God without being born of water and the Spirit.

Jn5:18 but (Jesus) also made himself equal with God, calling him his own Father.

Ph 2:6 Though being divine in nature, he did not claim in fact equality with God

Jn 10:34 Is it not written in your law: I said: you are gods?

Jn 1:12 all who received him he empowers to become children of God

Mt 16:18 I say to you: You are Peter (or Rock) and on this rock I will build my church;

2Th 2:15 hold to the traditions that we taught you by word or by letter.

Ja 2:24 So you see a person is acknowledged by works and not by faith alone.

1Co 13:2 if I had faith great enough to move mountains, but had no love, I would be nothing.

P 323 *Mt 5:10* Fortunate are those who are persecuted for the cause of (righteousness).

1Sa 26:23 The Lord rewards every man for his righteousness and faithfulness (NIV)

Mt 20:28 Be like the Son of Man who has come, not to be served but to serve and . . .

Je 23:6 This is the name by which he will be called, The Lord our Righteousness (NIV)

Jn 3:16 God so loved the world that he gave his only Son that whoever believes in him . . .

P 324 *1Ti 2:12* I allow no woman to teach or to have authority over men. Let them be quiet.

QU 9:5 slay pagans wherever you find them, seize them, lie in wait for them (Ab. Yusuf Ali)

Ex 21:24 eye for an eye, tooth for tooth, hand for hand, foot for foot, burn for burn

Mt 5:38 I tell you, do not oppose evil with evil; if some slaps you on the right cheek, offer the other.

P 325 *QU 4:156* They did not kill him and they did not crucify him but it was made to seem to them.

Ac 5:30 (He) raised Jesus from the dead-whom you had killed by hanging him on a tree.

Ga 3:13 Christ redeemed us by becoming a curse for us, there's a curse on anyone hanged on a tree

2Ti 2:12 if we endure with him, we shall reign with him. If we deny him, he will also deny us.

1Pe 3:18 Christ died for sins once for all, the righteous for the unrighteous, to bring you to God (NIV)

Dt 6:5 love the Lord your God with all your heart and with all your soul and with all your might.

Mt 22:39 "there is another one very similar to it: You shall love your neighbour as yourself."

1Jn 4:7 My dear friends, let us love one another, for love comes from God.

Ge 4:9 "Where is your brother (Able)?" And (Cain) said, "I do not know. Am I my brother's keeper?"

Mt 22:32 He is God, not of the dead but of the living.

Jn 19:27 Then he said to the disciple, "There is your mother."

Lk 2:35 the thoughts of many hearts will be revealed and a sword will pierce your own soul too

P 326 *Mt 13:43* Then the righteous will shine like the sun in the kingdom of their Father. (NIV)

Ps 37:6 He will make your righteousness shine like the dawn. (NIV)

Pr 15:29 The Lord is far from the wicked but he hears the prayer of a righteous man.

Is 5:16 and the holy God will show himself holy by his righteousness (NIV)

Is 26:9 when Your judgments are wrought on earth, the inhabitants of the world learn righteousness.

Ro 3:10 As it is written: there's no one righteous, not even one; no one who understands. (NIV)

1Pe 3:12 For the eyes of the Lord are on the righteous and his ears are attentive to their prayer (NIV)

Re 19:8 Fine linen was given her to wear, fine linen stands for the righteous acts of the saints. (NIV)

P 328 *1Co 15:29* Tell me: what are these people doing who are baptized on behalf of the dead?

1Co 3:13 If your work will withstand the fire, you will be rewarded.

Ex 25:30 Put the bread of the Presence on this table to be before me for all times. (NIV)

Nu 4:7 Over the table of the Presence they are to spread a blue cloth (NIV)

Mk 8:6 Taking the 7 loaves and giving thanks, he (Jesus) broke them and (had them distributed)

Jn 6:31 as scripture says: they were given bread from heaven to eat.

P 329 *Mt. 26:26* Jesus took bread, gave thanks, broke it and said, "Take and eat this is my body

Ex 16:15 Moses said to them, "That is the bread which the Lord has given you to eat."

Ex 16:31 The house of Israel named it manna; it was like coriander seed, white and tasting like wafers.

Re 2:17 The spirit says to the churches: To the victor I will give the hidden manna.

1Co 11:23 This is the tradition of the Lord that I received and that I in my turn have handed to you;

Lk 10:21 Jesus, filled with joy of the Holy Spirit said, "I praise you, Father, Lord of heaven and earth,

Lk 10:21 you have hidden these things from the wise and the learned and revealed them to the little ones.

P 330 *1Sa 26:23* The Lord rewards every man for his righteousness and faithfulness. (NIV)

1Pe 3:12 For the eyes of the Lord are on the righteous and his ears are attentive to their prayer. (NIV)

Jn 5:28-29 Those who have done good shall rise to live, who've done evil will rise to be condemned.

Lk 14:14 you will be repaid at the resurrection of the righteous. (NIV)

Ro 12:1 offer your bodies as living sacrifices, holy and pleasing to God, for this is your spiritual worship.

Is 56:3 Let no foreigner say, "Surely Yahweh will exclude me from his people." (CB)

Ac 10:34 God doesn't show partiality, He listens to everyone who fears God and does good.

Mt 18:3 unless you change and become like little children, you can't enter the kingdom

1Jn 3:2 Beloved we are God's children and what we shall be has not yet been shown.

Mt 5:6 Blessed are those who hunger and thirst for righteousness, for they will be filled. (NIV)

2Pe 3:13 looking forward to a new heaven and a new earth, the home of righteousness (NIV)

Ge 15:6 Abraham believed the Lord and He credited it to him as righteousness. (NIV)

1Pe 2:9 For he called you from your darkness to his own wonderful light.

Jn 1:9 For the light was coming into the world, the true light that enlightens everyone.

1Jn 1:5 God is light in there is no darkness in him.

1Th 5:5 All of you are citizens of the light and the day; we do not belong to night and darkness.

Da 12:3 Those who lead the many into righteousness will be like the stars forever and ever.

Jn 8:58 And Jesus said, "Truly, I say to you, before Abraham was, I am."

Ex 3:14 God said to Moses, "Ehyeh-Asher-Ehyeh," or "I AM WHO AM."

CHAPTER 34

<u>P 334</u> *Ps 34:9* Taste and see how good the LORD is;

<u>P 337</u> *Jn 21:11* It (the net) was full of big fish—one hundred and fifty three—

<u>P 340</u> *Lk 6:31* Do to others as you would have others do to you.

Jn 14:23 and my Father will love him; and we will come and make a room in his home.

Ge 4:9 Am I my brother's keeper?

<u>P 341</u> *Ps 82:6* I had taken you for divine beings, sons of the Most high, all of you.

Jn 10:34 Jesus replied, "Is this not written in your law: I said: you are gods?

Ga 4:7 no longer a slave but a son or daughter, and yours is the inheritance by God's grace.

Ps 2:7 the Lord said to me, "You are My son, I have fathered you this day.

Ps 89:27 He shall say to Me, You are my father, my God, the rock of my deliverance.

2Sa 7:14 I will be a Father to him, and he shall be a son to Me.

Jn 14:20 On that day you will know that I am in my Father and you in me, and I in you.

Ps 2:7 He said to me, "You are my son; today I have become your Father. (NIV)

ACKNOWLEDGEMENTS

Ph 4:8 Finally brothers and sisters, fill your minds with whatever is true, noble, etc. (NIV)

BACK COVER

Ge 22:18 All the nations of the earth shall bless themselves by your descendants,

Ps 2:1-10 Why do nations assemble, and peoples plot (utter) vain things;

Jn 17:21 May they all be one as you Father are in me and I am in you.

WORD INDEX

die 34, 83, 157, 169-70, 173, 195,
    286, 324, 347, 357-8
digital 72, 268
dimension 15, 34-5, 38-40, 43-4,
    105-9, 113, 157, 187, 192, 237,
    255, 258, 270, 279, 295, 298, 317,
    323, 340
dinghy 70, 84
dinner 42, 47-8, 91, 127-9, 163-4,
    172, 320, 331-3
disciples 286, 307, 309, 357, 359
divine 129-30, 134-5, 137, 139,
    174-5, 178-9, 181, 292, 296,
    322-3, 325, 329, 340, 361, 365
divinely 48, 322
division 245
dixieland 104
DNA 294
Doused 236, 240
dream 5, 10, 41, 84, 109, 134, 158,
    259
drug 44, 108, 145, 195, 216, 218, 225,
    242
drugs 196, 212
drunk 112-14, 120
drunken 113, 116, 235, 320
dual 62, 72
duality 62-3, 69, 74, 97, 125, 188-9,
    237-8, 240, 252-3, 265, 293,
    303-4, 322, 324, 330, 341
Dumb 17, 92, 108, 131, 149-50, 153,
    173, 209, 219, 302
dynamics 328

E

E=mc2 326
eagle 40, 58

earth v, vii, 15, 26-8, 31-2, 35, 64, 67,
    76, 89, 106, 121, 128, 133, 136,
    158, 166, 168, 170, 176, 182-3,
    185, 188-9, 196, 205-6, 211, 226,
    233, 243, 247, 252, 260, 271, 273,
    279-80, 285, 289, 293, 297-9,
    305, 308, 315, 325-6, 341, 346-8,
    350-1, 354-5, 358-9, 363-5
earthling 252
earthly 131, 183, 229, 252, 305, 322
Easter 320, 331-5
eclipse 67
edelweiss 201
edifying 274
effortless 254
Egypt 76, 92, 94
Eightfold path 7, 346
Eindhoven 268
elders 193, 355
elect 60
electromagnetic 17
elevator 2-3, 5
email 13, 162, 164-5, 167, 170, 173-4
emanated 11, 65, 317
embodiment 218, 296
emotionalism 209, 221, 224
encapsulate 326
encounters 5, 10, 15, 20-1, 31, 106,
    112, 244
enlightenment 61
Enrich 38, 48, 239
enriched 38, 239, 319-20
enrichment 240, 323
entangled 103, 234, 328
entanglement 166-7, 279
envelope 50, 218-19, 321
eternal 44, 58, 137, 139, 176, 181,
    183, 187, 189-90, 229, 242, 258,

232, 255, 258, 268, 273, 277, 296,
313, 318, 324, 337
friends 47, 184, 196, 203-4, 244, 272,
312, 319, 353, 362
fuddle-duddle 197
Full 56-7, 105, 114-15, 194, 204, 213,
229, 244, 251, 285, 330, 339, 358,
365
funeral 50, 111-12, 117, 121, 130,
138, 141-3, 146, 162, 174, 234,
319, 332

G

galaxy vi, 18, 128, 132, 183, 294
game vi-vii, 6, 91, 101, 172, 219, 243,
256, 327
gang 86, 88, 196
gate 15, 22, 94, 198, 309, 360
geezer 39, 270, 339
genocide 278, 280
genocides 110, 278-9
genuine 144, 166, 246, 266
geyser 143
gift 45, 49, 219, 242, 245, 275, 280,
308, 343, 355, 358, 360, 362
Giver 343
gladiator 152
Gloria 224-5, 227-8, 230-2, 238,
242, 256, 262, 271-8, 280-2, 291,
297-8, 300-2, 313, 316, 319-20
glorified 176
God 1, 6, 8-11, 14-18, 20-30, 32-7,
39-40, 46-8, 50, 52-63, 69, 73-7,
80, 83-4, 86, 90-2, 94, 96, 98-9,
101-3, 105, 107-8, 115, 118-23,
125-6, 128, 130, 133-6, 141,
143-6, 148, 150, 154, 166-7, 170,

176, 182-3, 185, 187-8, 190, 192,
194, 198, 203-10, 217, 219, 221,
228-9, 232, 234-40, 242-4, 247-8,
252, 257, 265, 267-8, 283-4, 286,
293-4, 296, 304-8, 312, 327-9,
338, 340-1, 346-65
god/man 182-3, 187-8, 190, 203,
234-5, 238
god-particle 9, 338, 340
goose 202, 238-9
Gospel 191, 203-4, 207, 220, 244,
282, 287, 303, 305, 309
gospel-singing 203
Gothic 142
grace 5, 228, 245, 257, 285, 308, 322,
360, 365
grandeur 68, 107, 126, 142, 253, 259,
297, 299
grandmothers 273
grave 307
greed 240, 283
green 1, 5, 17, 22, 25, 28-9, 49, 111,
127, 184, 333
greeters 194
grief 115, 117
groceries 20, 211
grumpy 178-9
guests 45, 220
guidance 58, 238
gullibles 206
Guru-Granth-Sahib 323
gurus 206

H

Hallelujah 176, 232, 261
hammering 144
hand-clapping 203, 206

I

J

N

Y

Z